De-Pathologizing Resistance

In a time of renewed interest in insurrectionary movements, urban protest, and anti-austerity indignation, the idea of resistance is regaining its relevance in social theory. *De-Pathologizing Resistance* re-examines resistance as a concept that can aid social analysis, highlighting the dangers of pathologizing resistance as illogical and abnormal, or exoticising it in romanticised but patronising terms. Taking a de-pathologizing and de-exoticising perspective, this book brings together insights from older and newer studies, the intellectual biographies of its contributing authors, and case studies of resistance in diverse settings, such as Egypt, Greece, Israel, and Mexico. From feminist studies to plaza occupations and anti-systemic uprisings, there is an emerging need to connect the analysis of contemporary protest movements under a broader theoretical re-examination. The idea of resistance—with all of its contradictions and its dynamism—provides such a challenging opportunity. This book was originally published as a special issue of *History and Anthropology*.

Dimitrios Theodossopoulos is a Reader in Social Anthropology at the University of Kent, Canterbury, UK. He has conducted research in Greece and Panama, and published extensively on topics that examine processes of resistance, exoticisation, indigeneity, authenticity, and the politics of cultural representation and protest. His latest research project examines the social consequences of the financial crisis.

De-Pathologizing Resistance

Anthropological interventions

Edited by
Dimitrios Theodossopoulos

Routledge
Taylor & Francis Group

LONDON AND NEW YORK

First published 2015 by Routledge

2 Park Square, Milton Park, Abingdon, Oxon OX14 4RN
711 Third Avenue, New York, NY 10017, USA

Routledge is an imprint of the Taylor & Francis Group, an informa business

First issued in paperback 2017

British Library Cataloguing in Publication Data
A catalogue record for this book is available from the British Library

ISBN 13: 978-1-138-93024-7 (hbk)
ISBN 13: 978-1-138-09475-8 (pbk)

Typeset in Minion
by RefineCatch Limited, Bungay, Suffolk

Publisher's Note
The publisher accepts responsibility for any inconsistencies that may have
arisen during the conversion of this book from journal articles to book chapters,
namely the possible inclusion of journal terminology.

Disclaimer
Every effort has been made to contact copyright holders for their permission to
reprint material in this book. The publishers would be grateful to hear from any
copyright holder who is not here acknowledged and will undertake to rectify
any errors or omissions in future editions of this book.

Contents

Citation Information   vii
Notes on Contributors   ix

1. On De-Pathologizing Resistance   1
   Dimitrios Theodossopoulos

2. The Ethnography of Resistance Then and Now: On Thickness and
   Activist Engagement in the Twenty-First Century   17
   Jacqueline Urla and Justin Helepololei

3. Upending Infrastructure: *Tamarod*, Resistance, and Agency after the
   January 25th Revolution in Egypt   38
   Julia Elyachar

4. Resistance and the City   58
   Dan Rabinowitz

5. The Ambivalence of Anti-Austerity Indignation in Greece: Resistance,
   Hegemony and Complicity   74
   Dimitrios Theodossopoulos

6. Indigenous Autonomy, Delinquent States, and the Limits of Resistance   93
   John Gledhill

7. Too Soon for Post-Feminism: The Ongoing Life of Patriarchy in
   Neoliberal America   116
   Sherry B. Ortner

Index   137

Citation Information

The chapters in this book were originally published in *History and Anthropology*, volume 25, issue 4 (October 2014). When citing this material, please use the original page numbering for each article, as follows:

Chapter 1
On De-Pathologizing Resistance
Dimitrios Theodossopoulos
History and Anthropology, volume 25, issue 4 (October 2014) pp. 415–430

Chapter 2
The Ethnography of Resistance Then and Now: On Thickness and Activist Engagement in the Twenty-First Century
Jacqueline Urla and Justin Helepololei
History and Anthropology, volume 25, issue 4 (October 2014) pp. 431–451

Chapter 3
Upending Infrastructure: Tamarod, *Resistance, and Agency after the January 25th Revolution in Egypt*
Julia Elyachar
History and Anthropology, volume 25, issue 4 (October 2014) pp. 452–471

Chapter 4
Resistance and the City
Dan Rabinowitz
History and Anthropology, volume 25, issue 4 (October 2014) pp. 472–487

Chapter 5
The Ambivalence of Anti-Austerity Indignation in Greece: Resistance, Hegemony and Complicity
Dimitrios Theodossopoulos
History and Anthropology, volume 25, issue 4 (October 2014) pp. 488–506

Chapter 6

Indigenous Autonomy, Delinquent States, and the Limits of Resistance
John Gledhill
History and Anthropology, volume 25, issue 4 (October 2014) pp. 507–529

Chapter 7

Too Soon for Post-Feminism: The Ongoing Life of Patriarchy in Neoliberal America
Sherry B. Ortner
History and Anthropology, volume 25, issue 4 (October 2014) pp. 530–549

For any permission-related enquiries please visit:
http://www.tandfonline.com/page/help/permissions

Notes on Contributors

Julia Elyachar is Associate Professor of Anthropology and Director of the Center for Global Peace and Conflict Studies at the University of California, Irvine, CA, USA. Her research revolves around a set of problems at the intersection of political economy, social theory, Middle Eastern studies, and anthropology. Her first book, *Markets of Dispossession: NGOS, Economic Development, and the State in Cairo*, was awarded the Sharon Stephens first book prize by the American Ethnological Society in 2007.

John Gledhill is Emeritus Professor of Social Anthropology at the University of Manchester, UK. He is a specialist on Latin America and his research interests are in political, economic and historical anthropology. His latest book is *The New Wars Against the Poor: Social Justice and Securitization in Latin America*.

Justin Helepololei is a Graduate Student in the Department of Anthropology at the University of Massachusetts, Amherst, MA, USA. His current research explores the expansion of treatment and re-entry programs in US jails.

Sherry B. Ortner is Distinguished Professor of Anthropology at the University of California, Los Angeles, California, USA. Her most recent book is *Not Hollywood: Independent Film at the Twilight of the American Dream*.

Dan Rabinowitz is Professor in the Department of Sociology and Anthropology at Tel Aviv University, Israel, and Head of the Porter School of Environmental Studies. He wrote the first comprehensive book in Hebrew about global warming and a groundbreaking book about the Cross-Israel Highway. From 1997 to 2000 he served as Chair of the Israeli Anthropological Association.

Dimitrios Theodossopoulos is a Reader in Social Anthropology at the University of Kent, Canterbury, UK. He has conducted research in Greece and Panama, and published extensively on topics that examine processes of resistance, exoticisation, indigeneity, authenticity, and the politics of cultural representation and protest. His latest research project examines the social consequences of the financial crisis.

Jacqueline Urla is Associate Professor and Director of the Modern European Studies Program in the Department of Anthropology at the University of Massachusetts, Amherst, MA, USA. She has undertaken long term ethnographic research on the Basque language revival movement, examining such issues as language standardization, youth community media projects, music, and the political uses of language censuses.

Introduction

On De-Pathologizing Resistance

Dimitrios Theodossopoulos

This introductory essay draws attention to two processes, the pathologization and exoticization of resistance. Working independently or in parallel, these two processes silence resistance by depoliticizing it as illogical or idealizing it in out-worldly terms. In both cases, resistance is caricatured as abnormal or exotic and distanced from current political priorities. I argue that analytical de-pathologization and de-exoticization of resistance can (a) provide valuable insights on the silencing of resistance and (b) help us understand the relationship between hegemony and resistance in terms that stretch beyond the moderately pathologizing view of political inaction as apathy or "false consciousness". In my analysis, I also engage with James Scott's seminal view of resistance, which, despite its de-pathologizing orientation, fails to capture the dialectical relationship of resistance and hegemony. I suggest that attention to the pathologizing and exoticizing workings of power may reveal the complexity and compromising ambivalence of resistance and contribute to the broader field of resistance studies, conceived as renewed interest in insurrectionary movements, rebellion, and protest.

The concept of resistance was not that long ago a great source of inspiration for anthropology. More recently, however, anthropological interest has shifted to a variety of related topics: urban protest, insurrectionary movements, anti-austerity mobilization, and the increasing discontent with hegemonic economic policies. These topics are undoubtedly timely and have captured the imagination of a new generation of researchers. Their popularity highlights an emerging need to reunite anthropological discussion about resistance in a more encompassing conversation. In this introductory essay, I take a small step in this direction by outlining the relevance of two conceptual tools that can encourage such a unified conversation: the notions of de-pathologizing and de-exoticizing resistance.

The *de-exoticization* of resistance invites an approach to the study of resistance that aims to expose the denigrating or idealizing caricaturing of the resisting experience. If exoticization idealizes resistance as taking place in another (liminal) space and time, the de-exoticizing perspective repositions the analysis of resistance within social life. Similarly, the *de-pathologization* of resistance attempts to redress our view of resistance by exposing the pathologizing interpretations of politicians, institutions, ideological frameworks—the various "pathologizers" of the resisting experience. To the degree that the pathologizing gaze strives to de-normalize resistance by (re)presenting it as less-than-rational or worthy of preoccupation, the de-pathologing perspective attempts to refocus attention on the cultural embeddedness and situated meaningfulness of resistance.

Those who have reason to be threatened by the challenge posed by resistance, and the possibility of change this challenge engenders, are tempted to engage—and often do—in the practice of undermining resistance, de-rationalizing it as illogical (a social abnormality), representative of disorder, or the result of impulsive behaviour. This pathologizing process is sometimes complemented by an idealizing attitude, which is nonetheless condescending: it endorses the exoticization of resistance in sensational, yet patronizing and caricaturing terms. These two tendencies towards resistance—which pathologize and exoticize—intersect with each other in various permutations to re-represent resistance as a matter out of place. Even previously established movements, such as the feminist project of dismantling patriarchy, as Ortner illustrates in her contribution to this special issue, can be sidelined in terms of an idealizing (but exoticizing) tendency to see resistance as representative of an "other" (static) time of previous mobilization.

In anthropology, a number of critical anthropological interventions have contributed to the refinement of "resistance" as an analytical concept, which resulted in a more nuanced treatment of its complexity and local meaningfulness (see among many, Abu-Lughod 1990; Keesing 1992; Gledhill 1994; Ortner 1995). Despite intermittent complaints that the concept of resistance has been overused and over-generalized (see Brown 1996), successive waves of theoretical engagement and review have resulted in enhancing its relevance for anthropology and social analysis more generally (see for example, Miller, Rowlands, and Tilley 1989; Reed-Danahay 1993; Gutmann 1993; Kaplan and Kelly 1994; Fox and Starn 1997; Moore 1998; Fletcher 2001; Seymour 2006; Urla and Helepololei 2014). In fact, in some fields, for example in anthropological work written about Latin America, the idea of resistance has remained a "hot" and stimulating topic since the 1970s. Gledhill's (2012) recent volume, *New Approaches to Resistance in Brazil and Mexico*, provides a good example of the centrality of the concept in questioning power and understanding social change.

In other areas of anthropological engagement, a majority of recent analyses approach resistance-related topics through the lens of alternative themes: occupation (Hickel 2012; Juris 2012; Juris and Razsa 2012; Razsa and Kurnik 2012), social movements (Edelman 2001; Nash 2005), metropolitan protest (Rabinowitz 2014), anti-austerity protest (Theodossopoulos 2013, 2014), the "Arab Spring"/anti-authoritarian revolution (Elyachar and Winegar 2012; Werbner and Spellman-Poots 2014), militant investigation/activist scholarship (Shukaitis and Graeber 2007; Hale 2008; Graeber 2009; Urla and Helepololei 2014), and more generally, a critique of neoliberalism (for example, Gledhill 2004; Harvey 2007; Ortner 2011; Elyachar 2012; Muehlebach 2012).

I argue that it is time to consider reuniting academic discussion about the above-mentioned topics under the broader field of resistance studies. Such an inclusive perspective will allow the "related topics" to benefit from four decades of theoretical fine-tuning that have resulted in conceptualizing the relationship between domination and resistance beyond binary terms (see also, Gledhill 1994, 2012; Ortner 1995). The older analyses from the 1990s, as Urla and Helepololei's (2014) demonstrates, can provide a valuable framework for addressing contemporary challenges related to the study of occupation movements, anti-neoliberal protest, and activist research. In turn, and as Gledhill (2012, 3) suggests, the broader field of resistance studies will benefit from enlarging its perspective to include "contentious politics", the collective, non-institutional challenges to power that also include social movements (Tarrow 1996, 874).

In a similar manner, academic analysis will benefit from expanding our view of resistance to embrace the countless local understandings of the resisting experience. The exact label of each particular movement is of lesser importance. Labelling and categorizing resistance can contribute to its essentialization as a limited and self-contained problem that can be potentially repaired or patched up (Shukaitis and Graeber 2007, 32). Thus, instead of imprisoning our analysis in narrow definitions of an explosive, always transforming experience—such as resistance—we will do much better if we focus our critical attention on the interplay of resistance with the workings of power, and the distortions and compromises that arise out of this interplay. The de-pathologizing and de-exoticizing perspective I outline in the following sections provide an antidote to such distortions.

Exoticizing Resistance

The spectre of exoticization sets some of the most challenging obstacles to the study of resistance; these are hard to overcome, as they relate to more than one exoticized view: one that denigrates resistance, another that idealizes it, and many others that denigrate and idealize resistance simultaneously. Many of these exoticizing predispositions are often deeply entrenched in the imagination of resistance as stemming from a world exterior to power. They may refer to indigenous leaders protesting for land claims, or working-class union leaders striking for pay-rise, nevertheless such views, in their exoticizing capacity, reduce complexity to caricature, and social change to performative imagery. The resisting subjects are either explicitly denigrated—as "primitive", violent and "uncivilised"—or idealized, but patronizingly degraded—as noble (but savage), bigger than life (yet somewhat unrealistic), idealistic (although naive), daring (but nonetheless temporary); or often, more than one permutation of the above.

In both its denigrating and idealizing capacity, the exoticization of resistance is patronizing. It reflects upon the established order—and supposedly, its reversal—from a vantage point of relative safety: usually a comfortable position not directly threatened by the type of resistance in question. Thus, even when the exoticized gaze contemplates social change, it accentuates the liminal character of resistance, idealizing while parochial-izing the exotic-naïve, the exotic-pure-and-uncompromising, the exotic-heroic (but out of this world). Caricaturing of this sort encourages the silencing of resistance and its indirect dismissal as temporary, romantic, and inconsequential.

The simplification engendered by exoticizing resistance usually starts by providing a name for it. Labelling resistance—for example, "Occupy Everywhere", "Indignant Citizens Movement", "the Zapatistas Movement"—opens the door for its stereotypical reduction, the essentialization of the sub-categories of resistance into static images of homogenous, undifferentiated resisting subjects. Such frozen images of the resistance of Others—with a label—inspire the imagination of resistance from afar: the safe distance of the exoticizing gaze. Sanitized (and idealized) images of resistance enacted elsewhere, serve as decontextualized examples to support our arguments: the anonymous indignant protestor beaten by police outside the Greek parliament or the anonymous Kayapo leader recording his oppressor with a video camera.

This process of placing resistance at a convenient distance (in physical or social space) remind us of how colonial powers essentialized indigenous ethnic groups (and their resistance)—freezing them in time as naturalized unchanging categories (see Monteiro 2012); a distortion propagated, with less sinister intentions, by old fashioned anthropology (Fabian 1983). In a similarly exoticizing manner, "Occupy London", Taksim Square, or Plaza del Sol become undifferentiated moments, muted and frozen, tribalized, but firmly placed (as exotic liminal exceptions) within an established framework of power imbalances. In this respect, the exoticized idealization or derision of resistance naturalize existing inequalities as solid and unchanging blocks that obstruct or excite resistance, hence discouraging the questioning of inequality itself, and its social parameters.

There is a further problem with the exoticization of resistance: the binary logic it often perpetuates, dividing the word into dominators/power-holders set against dominated/powerless victims. The resulting oppositions exaggerate the differences between elites and disenfranchised groups, and even worse, encourage a homogenous treatment of the polarized categories. Such a homogenizing view detracts analytic attention from the ambivalence experienced by resisting social actors (Ortner 1995, 187) and the grey area of interests that divide (or partially unite) them. In real life, subalterns may resist some things, while accept other things, or even dominate other subalterns (Gledhill 1994, 89). In fact, it is often the articulation of not radically separated interests (or political positions) that determines the future of a protest, encouraging complicity or adaptation to pre-existing and available structures of power or inequality.

Another binary is provided by Scott's (1990) Goffmanesque dichotomy between "off-stage" (hidden, indirect) and "on-stage" (public, engaging with power) resistance. In this model, the hidden transcripts of the disempowered emerge within autonomous subaltern spaces that appear to be uncontaminated by power (Gledhill 1994). This very dichotomy—power vs. a world untouched by power—exoticizes subaltern discourse by isolating it in contexts of secretive opposition, what Gledhill describes as "muttered defiance behind the backs of the dominant" (2012, 6). As several anthropologists have noticed, this view perpetuates the homogenization of the resisting subjects and their internal politics (Gledhill 1994, 2012; Ortner 1995; Moore 1998; Fletcher 2001). In real life, it is hard to find subaltern spaces completely uncolonized by power, while in resisting domination, subalterns also (partly) reproduce the categorical structures of domination (Keesing 1992).

So far I have identified several analytical obstacles that emerge as a result of the exoticization of resistance. Yet, I would like to end this discussion on an optimistic note. There is some scope to rescue the idealization of resistance from its caricaturing propensities, and identify a spark of inspiration within idealization. Kapferer (2013) has recently attempted to refigure the anthropological use of the exotic, focusing on the moment of the exotic recognition: "the exotic as a challenge to understanding", the discovery of new possibilities "at the edge of knowledge" (Kapferer 2013). The problem, for Kapferer, is not the exotic per se, but the dualisms it propagates. From this point of view, the recognition of the resistance of Others, however, exoticizing this may be, can serve as a moment of inspiration—a recognition of the possibility of change—encouraging rifts with established power. The resistance of Others, however, simplified or idealized, can be "contagiously" inspiring across national borders or political regimes. The Arab spring and the anti-austerity resistance movements (in 2011–2013) are good recent examples of this type of inspirational contagion.

Pathologizing Resistance

There is a further danger lurking in the accentuation of liminality and eccentricity of resistance: this is its naturalization as "uncivilized" or impulsive behaviour, presented as irrational or representative of disorder. This denigrating view (and its countless nuances) encourage a perception of resistance as a "pathology", a problem for society, or a negation of social order and its established values. For those who take the first step in describing resistance as less-than-rational, it is only a matter of time before they assume that it also represents a type of "social abnormality", a malfunction that needs to be remedied. In consequence, the implicit or explicit pathologization of resistance is intimately connected with its official or unofficial silencing, under the pretext that resistance is atypical, illogical, and unreasonable.

When applied to social processes, pathologization—the tendency to treat a condition as psychologically abnormal—usually aims at de-legitimizing the social process in question: its dismissal as either detrimental or unreasonable, or even unhealthy and potentially destructive. In the previous section, I discussed how idealization or denigration—two faces of exoticization—contribute to the silencing of resistance: by distancing resistance from ourselves as something enacted in another (exotic, liminal, or isolated) social space or time, it is possible to ignore resistance altogether, or downgrade it as a lesser priority. We see a similar process at work when resistance is pathologized as abnormality. Pathologization works hand in hand with idealization and denigration to render resistance insignificant, yet it shakes our faith in resistance even further.

Pathologized resistance represents a deviation from reason, when "the reasonable"—broadly conceived—stands for the established order. This form of stigmatization capitalises upon the visible expression of emotion in resistance, translating the passion of those who dare to protest as lack of judgement or common sense. Violence, even if this is exercised to suppress resistance, can be similarly used to highlight its precarious nature, cultivating further the image of pathology; the violent and hot-tempered protesters remain stigmatized as violent and hot-tempered even when they evidently fall victim to brutal suppression. "They must have been crazy to challenge the police at the first place!" argue those who see resistance as an anomaly.

The stress on what is presented as defective logic relies on selective de-contextualization. Pathologizing narratives rely on isolating the complexity of resistance from its representation. The emotional, anti-structural elements of resistance are separated from their situational logic, usually by shifting attention to those aspects of resistance that appear—from the outside—to be sensational, over-zealous, and perhaps somewhat "irrational". The resulting view of resistance as the product of sub-rational minds, hides from view its contextual specificities—which may be too complex and not directly translatable to outsiders—superimposing sensationalism (resistance seen in performative terms) on meaning (resistance substantiated by culturally embedded logic). Stripped of justification, resistance may then be decoded as abnormal behaviour, unconscionable conduct, yet another rebellion that looks structurally similar to so many others—an eye-grabbing two-minute video clip in the news.

As we have seen so far, the pathologization of resistance relies heavily on reducing complexity to essentialist stereotypes. Helepololei, who has conducted fieldwork among squatters in Barcelona, provide us with a good example of this homogenizing process (Urla and Helepololei 2014). The police and state intelligence agencies depicted the resisting subjects as rebels without a cause—having no "rational" economic theory or political agenda—thus, being "unreasonable" political actors unable to negotiate. Rationalisations of this type close the door to political dialogue, justifying the suppression of resistance under the "pretexts of security and counter-terrorism" (Urla and Helepololei 2014). Similarly, Rabinowitz in his contribution to this special issue illuminates how the established authorities in Israel succeeded in "de-legitimizing" the urban protest movement as violent and dangerous for public security. The protagonists of the 2011 social justice demonstrations in Tel-Aviv were stopped from protesting in 2012 through a well-orchestrated hegemonic attempt to issue a warning against and violently suppress occupation-related activities. The authorities rationalized their regime of suppression in securitization terms: they appealed on the grounds of public safety, contested the purpose of resistance (as unnecessary or unreasonable), and essentialized the protesters—as if mass protest represented a homogenous ideological project or an undeserving underclass (Rabinowitz 2014).

Thus, pathologization confines the explosive meaningfulness of resistance to a static mould, a template that fits all possible forms of resistance to a singular and taken for granted frame of meaning. Such a reductionist treatment of resistance is not surprising if we consider that the threat of resistance—for those who see it as threatening—emerges from the questioning of established conventions or truths. Without a doubt, narratives of resistance often emerge when established interpretations of political and social life fail to explain visible injustices. Consequently, and as far as the resisting mind upsets the *status quo* by challenging certainty, pathologizing explanations of resistance attempt to re-establish confidence in one or other official explanation. To the degree that resistance provides innovative interpretations of events and relationships—supported by alternative exegeses of justice and injustice in the world—those who see resistance as "illogical" respond by reiterating their preferred official reading of causality, usually a rationalization of the status quo.

The analytical proclivity of pathologizing resistance as conspiratorial is a case in point. As with conspiracy theory (Marcus 1999; Sanders and West 2003), the discourse that supports resistance is built upon culturally meaningful values; its underlying logic is often hidden within what may be seen from outside as contradiction. Commentators who pathologize conspiracy—including academics (Hofstadter 1965; Pipes 1996)—choose to stress the inconsistencies in conspiratorial thinking, "the curious leap in imagination" that such narratives entail (Hofstadter 1965, 37). Nonetheless, resisting local actors on the peripheries of power may entertain conspiracy-prone ideas with a much more political intention in mind, such as, for example, to expose power and shed light on its abuses (Brown and Theodossopoulos 2000). They may search for meaning in underlying patterns in history (the lessons from the past), interpreting the present in terms of recurring themes in the workings of power (Sutton 1998).

Anthropology has shown that such alternative readings of history and political causality, far from being worthy of pseudo-psychological treatment, deserve recognition as culturally embedded "sense making practices" (Sutton 2003; see also, Sanders and West 2003; Kirtsoglou 2006; Kirtsoglou and Theodossopoulos 2010). The pathologizing treatment of conspiracy as irrational and paranoid shows how pervasive the de-legitimization of anti-hegemonic logic as illogical can be; especially under the reign of neoliberal "hyper-rationalization" (Comaroff and Comaroff 2001, 44). "Conspiracy theories start their trajectory just like other theories, and only later do they become (labelled as) conspiracy theories" (Pelkmans and Machold 2011, 74). It is this process of labelling that represents what I call here pathologization. When conspiracy is unquestionably equated with paranoia, resistance may also be discharged, in turn, as conspiratorial, along the lines of very similar pathologizing naturalisations.

Hegemony Yes, "False" Consciousness No

One of the greatest challenges in the study of resistance is to explain why its initial momentum so often fades away. Certainly there are various structural implications that explain the decline of many resistance and protest movements: the exhaustion of the protesters, their limited knowledge of hegemony's bureaucracy, the fragmentation of the resisting group, or the co-optation of protesting leaderships. Even more often, resistance falters due to lack of available resources, as in most cases, those who resist have less means at their disposal than those resisted. Such evident imbalances encourage us to put in perspective Abu-Lughod's insightful reversal of Foucault's' axiom—"where there is resistance, there is power" (1990, 42). Resistance may engender new forms of power, yet the power of resistance, apart from being corruptive or occasionally divisive, is very often framed in terms of the very categories resisted. This last observation invites attention to the issue of consciousness.

Those who resist resistance have good reasons to target its logic and cultural meaningfulness. Often this take the form of relentless undermining, de-legitimizing, or, to follow the analysis presented so far, "pathologizing": the systematic dismissal of resistance as illogical, wicked, and immoral—a threat to security or civil order, a product of inchoate or dangerous minds, and an act of unlawful rebellion and terrorism. Over and over again, the justification for ascribing illegal status to resistance relies on its previous systematic pathologization. Undoubtedly, the undermining of the moral or ideological basis of resistance can shed some light on why resistance so often declines with time, or fails to achieve its original purpose.

Several generations of Marxist thinkers have engaged with this problem, and a related question: to what degree do the disenfranchised internalize the pathologizing interpretations of their dominators? The orthodox Marxist position attempts to expose this process, by presenting it as a paradox: the disempowered act against their obvious interests in a self-defeating manner; they are prevented from having a clear view of their exploitation due to their "false" political consciousness, the product of ideological mystification. Although ideological mystification often relies on and contributes to the pathologization of resistance, the use of the adjective "false" in classic Marxist constructions essentializes subaltern consciousness, reducing political awareness to either a pathologized or non-pathologized alternative.

Later Marxists views, such as for example the Gramscian perspective, escaped the problems of this narrow conception of political consciousness by developing the notion of hegemony. If hegemony, in strict Marxist terms, creates ideology, for Gramsci, it constructs a broader domain of cultural meaningfulness that includes material, economic, and social relations. This broader view of how hegemony propagates itself, even within the premises of those who oppose it, provides a very compelling explanation of the elusive endurance of dominant ideological and political trends, such as, for example, capitalism-disguised-as-neoliberalism. Yet, for the purposes of this discussion, I would like to turn my attention to a theorist of resistance who has criticized the idea of false consciousness.

In his influential work on indirect resistance, Scott (1985, 1990) critically engages with the hegemony-and-mystification thesis as this is represented by, what he calls, the "thick" and "thin" versions of false consciousness. The "thick" versions of false consciousness, he argues, attribute "consent" in the misguided acquiescence of the dominated (who are persuaded by dominant ideology to accept the values that sustain their exploitation), while the "thin" versions interpret compliance as "resignation" (based on the imposed conviction that the dominant order is inescapable or natural) (Scott 1990,

72). In contrast to the premises of most Marxist points of view, Scott has stressed the subaltern awareness of domination, including the clear view subalterns have of their dominators and their capacity to visualize a hypothetical reversal of their situation.

Indirectly, and through his objections to the notion of false consciousness, Scott has contributed to the de-pathologization of indirect resistance. He brought to light the non-dramatic dimensions of resistance, the tactics of subversion in day-to-day life. The meaning and purposefulness of such everyday tactics inspires a reconsideration of the distinction between pre-political and political consciousness (Gledhill 2012, 8). In particular, Scott's emphasis on the ability of the disenfranchised to subvert certain aspects of their exploitation draws attention to subaltern agency. We might be prepared to accept that dispossessed groups are not that much mystified as to enjoy or passively accept their predicament. Their small daily acts of insubordination —"weapons of the weak" in Scott's terms—demonstrate a certain degree of awareness of the order of domination: subalterns undermine it, although temporarily and covertly, because they understand its subtle workings. Thus, the off-stage discourse of subordinate groups—"the hidden transcript", according to Scott—is not simply true or false (Tilley 1991, 597), but deserves analysis on its own right and its own terms.

These considerations invite us to see in some de-pathologizing light, the notion of "false consciousness" itself. There is nothing fundamentally irrational in the inaction or complicity of the dominated. The attribution of "false consciousness" in classic Marxist analysis dismisses alternative, culturally embedded but non-resisting logics as pathological—illogical, apathetic, and self-defeating—a practice of de-legitimization that resembles conservative neoliberal rationalizations. Although Scott does not make this point explicitly, his persistent opposition to the falsification of subaltern consciousness provides useful insights for the reconsideration of the "false consciousness" thesis, or preferably, its revision in more politically correct terms.

At the same time, however, and in the context of the same topic of debate, Scott (1985, 1990) has made a fundamental mistake, which lies at the heart of his classic analysis of resistance. His separation between hidden and public transcripts hides from view the degree to which such discourses are "intimately intertwined" (Roseberry 1994, 361). Subaltern resistance is not autonomous from the wider cultural and politico-economic relationships that make it meaningful and morally justifiable at the first place (Gledhill 1994, 2012). "There is never a single, unitary, subordinate" (Ortner 1995, 175), or a completely autonomous subaltern subject (Keesing 1992). Even hegemony itself is not static and fixed, but adapts to its ideological opposition—as the top-down pathologization of resistance consistently demonstrates.

Gramsci's insightful perspective can help us contextualize this problem. His view of hegemony is often misread—conflated with culture (Kurtz 1996) or a non-anthropological understanding of culture (Crehan 2002), or simplified as a finished, static ideological project (Rosebery 1994)—while in fact it was originally conceived as a dynamic process that involves tension and negotiation between diverse social forces. Rabinowitz, in this special issue, succinctly compares Gramsci and Scott. While Gramsci's perspective can help us understand that "hegemonies are built on people's inclination to suspend the critique of power", as Rabinowitz (2014) stresses, "Scott's analysis leaves little room for such consent"; the dominated and disenfranchised appear to be "consistently aware of the injustices that shape their lives". It is in this respect that Scott over-rationalizes the subaltern as consistently rational (see Gledhill 2012). Such a generalizing approach, argues Rabinowitz (2014), "essentialises agents of domination as well as their victims".

Thus, although we may feel compelled to praise Scott for de-pathologizing subaltern agency, it is not hard to see that his emphasis on the rationality of the resisting —representing a consistent and uninterrupted vision of the order of domination— equates agency with narrow calculation, or what Sahlins (1978) would critically describe as "practical reason". "Scott presents the subaltern", clarifies Gledhill, "as a deeply knowing, non-mystified elaborator of rich cultural practices of disguised resistance inhibited from more overt action only by a shrewd assessment of its impracticality" (2012, 9). Conceived in such calculative terms, indirect resistance is constrained by its practical functionality, isolated within hidden transcripts muttered under one's breath and is thus expediently pathologized (by dominators) as conspiratorial.

Analyses of resistance that focus too much on the calculative rationality of resisting actors may hide from view the simple fact that discourses of resistance communicate with—and sometimes form in juxtaposition to—previous discourses that represent, more or less explicitly, a dominant view of the world. Urla and Helepololei (2014) underline the contribution of Foucault in reminding us that the logic of resistance takes shape within established systems of knowledge. Situated actors may sincerely attempt to challenge hegemony, yet their success is often impeded by broader historical interpretations—for example, nationalism—that are made available by the hegemonic regime in question. In the empirical case study I provide in this special issue, I present a good example of the limits of anti-hegemonic discourse. An increasing number of citizens afflicted by austerity in Greece turn against the calculative logic of the economic establishment, challenging in their everyday commentary Germany's hegemony in the European Union, and the role of more powerful nations in the world order. The resulting anti-hegemonic critique, however, is often tainted by xenophobic or nationalist overtones and recycles previous hegemonic-cum-nationalist and cryptocolonial narratives (cf. Herzfeld 2007, 2011).

As a result, indirect resistance, despite challenging power, is not, in most cases, completely isolated from pre-existing hegemonic ideological influences, which, in turn, shape how local actors interpret causality when they attempt to explain their current predicament. In this respect, Scott, despite his perceptive de-pathologization of indirect resistance, fails to get across what Gramsci conveys so well, a relational and processual view of subalterity. Neither static nor isolated, the categories of domination as accepted by subalterns—and the categories of domination as adapted to subaltern opposition—are shaped dialectically in unpredictable but (locally) meaningful configurations. The process of resistance, Keesing aptly observes, "is a highly complex dialectical one in which the categorical structures of domination may be negated or inverted—hence doubly subverted—as well as reproduced in opposition" (1992, 238).

Resisting as a Way of Life

When resistance marks a great rift of structural inequality—as it repeatedly does—small and great victories may appear ephemeral or as bearing little consequence to the everyday life of disempowered but resisting subjects. This is one of the greatest limitations of resistance; it may address inequality, but often has little effect in reducing the structural violence that inequality has engendered. Resistance may be successful in generating change, yet change may be limited in scope: the result of compromise or merely a change of roles—frequently, the replacement of one elite by another. In such cases, those who resist may find themselves in the position of resisting for long periods of time or resisting again and again in successive bursts of uprising, provoked by similar abuses of power by the very same elites. For some groups, resistance may become a way of life.

Even more predictably, when inequality is deeply entrenched in the fabric of a particular nation or society, the history of a group's resistance may seem as if it repeats itself. Gledhill (2014) presents us with a case of protracted resistance in Mexico. The Nahua inhabitants of Ostula have defended the integrity of their community for generations against all sorts of outsiders: non-indigenous elites (desiring Ostulan lands and resources), and more recently, criminal organizations (operating with impunity in its territory). The resilience of the Ostulans represents an ethos of resisting against the odds—a culture of resistance—a permanent feature of social life. Their periodic victories do not eradicate structural or physical violence; thus there is no foreseeable end to their struggles. Resistance here substitutes government inaction and the failure of institutions that uphold social justice.

Very often, the reasons that may lead to resistance at the first place are never resolved, and the resisting subjects realize, as Elyachar (2014) shows, that "the tail-event of the impossible and unimaginable has become the stuff of everyday life". More often than not the frustration of those who resist, but cannot see how their struggle has improved their everyday lives, remains unnoticed. There are very few avenues that allow outsiders access to the self-interrogation of resistance, with the exception of a rare ethnography or a penetrating novel. Capturing this sense of exhaustion, desperation, and more importantly, self-interrogation enables us to see deeper into the process of resistance and the contradictions that emerge in day-to-day life after resistance. "Why did we make the revolution?" ask Elyachar's Egyptian respondents two years after the 2011 revolution, "salaries are low, and prices are higher … what is going to happen?" (Elyachar 2014).

Impermanent and yet incomplete, resistance as experienced in the everyday remains one of the greatest challenges for social analysis—a big ethnographic hole that pre-1995 ethnographies, for the most part, failed to fill (Ortner 1995). Various questions remain unanswered: How do local actors deal with the unfinished status of resistance? How easy or difficult is it to switch from the modality of resistance to the mundane concerns of the everyday? How incompleteness—the unending and protracted nature of most resistance movements—shapes the identities of resisting subjects? It may be difficult, undoubtedly, to answer these questions, yet the questions themselves—which stem from anthropological engagement, including the articles in this special issue—demonstrate that the social experience of resistance is not taken for granted anymore in social analysis.

Conclusion

However incomplete, resistance is a necessary ingredient of change in social life: a series of dialogues among many parties (Howe 1998, 6), small constituents of a never-ending process. The people with whom anthropologists share their lives during fieldwork say that resistance is what they do in their everyday struggles (Gledhill 2012, 1–2; 2014). We may choose to create categories to refer to these struggles and create new typologies and sub-fields of study, such as the various resistance-related topics I referred to in the introduction—revolutionary demonstration, urban protest, insurrectionary move-ment, anti-austerity mobilization, and anti-globalization. Yet, I doubt if the analytical fragmentation of the multiple experiences of resistance will facilitate analysis. Adding "a name on the directions of tomorrow's revolutionary fervour", Shukaitis and Graeber argue, can be "the first step in institutionalizing it, in fixing it" (Shukaitis and Graeber 2007, 32).

An awareness of this danger—the essentializing de-politicization of resistance—encouraged me to focus on its exoticization and pathologization, two processes that distantiate the resisting experience from its actual context, to Otherize subaltern struggle as a matter out of place (and time) or delegitimize discontent as impulsive, illo-gical, or representative of disorder. The view of resistance as fixed in space and time—sensationalized in idealistic terms or naturalized as unconscionable conduct—is stripped of its political referents. Positioning oneself at a distance to decode social inter-action as a remote object of study may perhaps undermine our capacity to appreciate the interplay of social practice (Juris 2007, 165). A more engaged type of research, as Urla and Helepololei argue in this special issue, can complement Ortner's (1995) pre-vious call for a thicker ethnographic perspective in resistance, and help us understand the constituent power of those bursts of resisting action that reshape social life (Shu-kaitis and Graeber 2007).

Earlier perspectives in the study of resistance have redirected attention on the pur-posefulness of non-dramatic resisting actions. The work of Scott (1985, 1990) has made a great impact in this respect, reconceptualizing indirect resistance beyond the moder-ately pathologizing concept of "false" consciousness. Nevertheless, Scott's emphasis on the tactics of the disenfranchised has isolated indirect resistance from the pervasive influence of hegemony, perpetuating the analytical separation of subaltern discourse from its broader ideological and political nexus. In other words, Scott exoticized resist-ance as taking place in a world exterior to power, and several anthropologists have aptly criticized him for that (Starn 1992; Gutmann 1993; Gledhill 1994, 2012; Gal 1995; Moore 1998; Fletcher 2001).

Therefore, instead of isolating resistance in hidden transcripts of uncontaminated subaltern consciousness—exoticizing the resisting actor as an uncompromising icon (a caricature)—social analysis would benefit from focusing on the local meaningfulness of resistance in "culturally intimate" contexts (Herzfeld 1997); a meaningfulness that emerges from creativity, struggle, and compromise in social experience. Classic anthropological accounts have taken important steps towards this direction, explaining the cultural embeddedness of resistance within local meaningful contexts, parts of broader regimes of power (see among many, Comaroff 1985; Stoler 1985; Herzfeld 1985; Ong 1987; Comaroff and Comaroff 1991; Howe 1998). Such nuanced accounts have captured the ambivalence of resistance (Ortner 1995), its metaphoric richness (Keesing 1992), and implications with power (Abu-Lughod 1990, Foucault). As with other all-embracing concepts—including some that resisting actors oppose, such as globalization for example (Theodossopoulos 2010)—resistance is empowered by its semantic ambiguity, which embraces so many types of local discontent.

Successful analytical constructs are often flexible enough to benefit from imprecision. The imprecision of the notion "hegemony"—as that of resistance—"has made it good to think with" and inspires, rather than constrains, analysis (Comaroff and Comaroff 1991, 19). In their interrelationship, hegemony and resistance are subject to continuous transformation. Thus, a processual view of hegemony (Williams 1977) will, in turn, inspire a processual view of resistance, realized dialectically as a response to hegemony. In this respect, the pathologization and exoticization of resistance, which may take the form of either "scientific rationalism" (Bourdieu 1998) or idealizing sensationalism, can be seen as an unending processes, continuously adapting to confront (and silence) defiant and transformative challenges.

As a remedy to the resulting de-rationalization of resistance, we may choose to adopt a de-pathologizing perspective to guide us in our studies of engagement with power. Such engagements may include a variety of timely topics: urban protest, occupation movements, anti-totalitarian rebellion, anti-globalization, and anti-neoliberalism. And indeed, I see no better time to put forward a call for the resurgence of resistance studies—de-pathologized, de-exoticized, and conceived as a broader field—than our current moment of engaging with power; perceived not as "alochronic" (Fabian 1983) projection, limminal, exotic, de-rationalized caricature of abnormality, but re-contextualized in the here and now of social experience.

Acknowledgements

Earlier versions of this essay were presented at the seminar of the Anthropology department at the University of Manchester and the Think Tank seminar at the University of Kent. I am grateful to all colleagues for the constructive criticisms and comments.

References

Abu-Lughod, Lila. 1990. "The Romance of Resistance: Tracing Transformations of Power Through Bedouin Women." *American Ethnologist* 17 (1): 41–55.
Bourdieu, Pierre. 1998. *Firing Back: Against the Tyranny of the Market 2*. London: Verso.
Brown, Michael F. 1996. "On Resisting Resistance." *American Anthropologist* 98 (4): 729–735.
Brown, Keith, and Dimitrios Theodossopoulos. 2000. "The Performance of Anxiety: Greek Narratives of the War at Kossovo." *Anthropology Today* 16 (1): 3–8.

Comaroff, Jean. 1985. *Body of Power Spirit and Resistance: The Culture and History of a South African People*. Chicago, IL: University of Chicago Press.

Comaroff, Jean, and John Comaroff. 1991. *Of Revelation and Revolution: Christianity, Colonialism, and Consciousness in South Africa*. Chicago, IL: The University of Chicago Press.

Comaroff, Jean, and John Comaroff. 2001. "Millennial Capitalism: First Thoughts on a Second Coming." In *Millennial Capitalism and the Culture of Neoliberalism*, edited by J. Comaroff and J. L. Comaroff, 1–56. Durham, NC: Duke University Press.

Crehan, Kate. 2002. *Gramsci, Culture and Anthropology*. London: Pluto.

Edelman, Marc. 2001. "Social Movements: Changing Paradigms and Forms of Politics." *Annual Review of Anthropology* 30: 285–317.

Elyachar, Julia. 2012. "Before (and After) Neoliberalism: Tacit Knowledge, Secrets of the Trade, and the Public Sector in Egypt." *Cultural Anthropology* 27 (1): 76–96.

Elyachar, Julia. 2014. "Upending Infrastructure: Tamarod, Resistance, and Agency after the January 25th Revolution in Egypt." *History and Anthropology*. doi:10.1080/02757206.2014.930460

Elyachar, Julia, and Jessica Winegar (eds). 2012. "Revolution and Counter-Revolution in Egypt a Year after January 25th." *Fieldsights—Hot Spots, Cultural Anthropology Online*. http://www.culanth.org/fieldsights/208-revolution-and-counter-revolution-in-egypt-a-year-after-january-25th

Fabian, Johannes. 1983. *Time and the Other: How Anthropology Makes its Object*. New York: Columbia University Press.

Fletcher, Robert. 2001. "What Are We Fighting For? Rethinking Resistance in a Pewenche Community in Chile." *The Journal of Peasant Studies* 28 (3): 37–66.

Fox, Richard G., and Orin Starn (eds). 1997. *Between Resistance and Revolution: Cultural Politics and Social Protest*. New Brunswick, NJ: Rutgers University Press.

Gal, Susan. 1995. "Language and the 'Arts of Resistance'." *Cultural Anthropology* 10 (3): 407–424.

Gledhill, John. 1994. *Power and its Disguises: Anthropological Perspectives on Politics*. London: Pluto Press.

Gledhill, John. 2004. "Neoliberalism." In *A Companion to the Anthropology of Politics*, edited by David Nugent and Joan Vincent, 332–348. Oxford: Blackwell Publishing.

Gledhill, John. 2012. "Introduction: A Case for Rethinking Resistance." In *New Approaches to Resistance in Brazil and Mexico*, edited by John Gledhill, 1–20. Durham, NC: Duke University Press.

Graeber, David. 2009. *Direct Action: An Ethnography*. Edinburgh: AK press.

Gledhill, John. 2014. "Indigenous Autonomy, Delinquent States, and the Limits of Resistance." *History and Anthropology*. doi:10.1080/02757206.2014.917087

Gutmann, Matthew C. 1993. "Rituals of Resistance: A Critique of the Theory of Everyday Forms of Resistance." *Latin American Perspectives* 20 (2): 74–92.

Hale, Charles R. (ed.) 2008. *Engaging Contradictions: Theory, Politics, and Methods of Activist Scholarship*. Berkeley, CA: University of California Press.

Harvey, David. 2007. *A Brief History of Neoliberalism*. Oxford: Oxford University Press.

Herzfeld, Michael. 1985. *The Poetics of Manhood: Contest and Identity in a Cretan Mountain Village*. Princeton, NJ: Princeton University Press.

Herzfeld, Michael. 1997. *Cultural Intimacy: Social Poetics in the Nation State*. New York: Routledge.

Herzfeld, Michael. 2007. "Small-Mindedness Writ Large: On the Migrations and Manners of Prejudice." *Journal of Ethnic and Migration Studies* 33 (2): 255–274.

Herzfeld, Michael. 2011. "Crisis Attack: Impromptu Ethnography in the Greek Maelstrom." *Anthropology Today* 27 (5): 22–26.

Hickel, Jason. 2012. "Liberalism and the Politics of Occupy Wall Street." *Anthropology of this Century*, no. 4 (no page numbers). http://aotcpress.com/articles/liberalism-politics-occupy-wall-street/

Hofstadter, Richard. 1965. *The Paranoid Style in American Politics, and Other Essays*. Cambridge, MA: Harvard University Press.

Howe, James. 1998. *A People Who Would Not Kneel: Panama, the United States and the San Blas Kuna.* Washington, DC: Smithsonian Institution Press.

Juris, Jeffrey. 2007. "Practicing Militant Ethnography with the Movement for Global Resistance in Barcelona." In *Constituent Imagination: Militant Investigations, Collective Theorization*, edited by S. Shukaitis and D. Graeber, 11–34. Edinburgh: AK Press.

Juris, Jeffrey. 2012. "Reflections on #Occupy Everywhere: Social Media, Public Space, and Emerging Logics of Aggregation." *American Ethnologist* 39 (2): 259–279.

Juris, Jeffrey, and Maple Razsa (eds). 2012. "Occupy, Anthropology, and the 2011 Global Uprisings." *Fieldsights—Hot Spots, Cultural Anthropology Online.* http://culanth.org/fieldsights/63-occupy-anthropology-and-the-2011-global-uprisings

Kapferer, Bruce. 2013. "How Anthropologists Think: Configurations of the Exotic." *Journal of the Royal Anthropological Institute* 19 (4): 813–836.

Kaplan, Martha, and John D. Kelly. 1994. "Rethinking Resistance: Dialogics of 'Disaffection' in Colonial Fiji." *American Ethnologist* 21 (1): 123–151.

Keesing, Roger M. 1992. *Custom and Confrontation: The Kwaio Struggle for Cultural Autonomy.* Chicago, IL: University of Chicago Press.

Kirtsoglou, E. 2006. "Unspeakable Crimes: Athenian Greek Perceptions of Local and International Terrorism." In *Terror and Violence; Imagination and the Unimaginable*, edited by A. Strathern, P. Stewart, and N. Whitehead, 61–88. London: Pluto.

Kirtsoglou, Elisabeth, and Dimitrios Theodossopoulos. 2010. "The Poetics of Anti-Americanism in Greece: Rhetoric, Agency and Local Meaning." *Social Analysis* 54 (1): 106–124.

Kurtz, Donald V. 1996. "Hegemony and Anthropology." *Critique of Anthropology* 16 (2): 103–135.

Marcus, George E., ed. 1999. "Introduction to the Volume: The Paranoid Style Now." In *Paranoia within Reason: A Casebook on Conspiracy as Explanation*, edited by G. E. Marcus, 1–11. Chicago, IL: Chicago University Press.

Miller, Daniel, Michael Rowlands, and Christopher Tilley, eds. 1989. *Domination and Resistance.* London: Unwin Hyman.

Monteiro, John. 2012. "Rethinking Amerindian Resistance and Persistence in Colonial Portuguese America." In *New Approaches to Resistance in Brazil and Mexico*, edited by John Gledhill, 25–43. Durham, NC: Duke University Press.

Moore, Donald. 1998. "Subaltern Struggles and the Politics of Place: Remapping Resistance in Zimbabwe's Highlands." *Cultural Anthropology* 12 (3): 344–381.

Muehlebach, Andrea. 2012. *The Moral Neoliberal: Welfare and Citizenship in Italy.* Chicago, IL: University of Chicago Press.

Nash, June. 2005. "Introduction: Social Movements and Global processes." In *Social Movements: An Anthropology Reader*, edited by June Nash, 1–26. Oxford: Blackwell.

Ong, Aihwa. 1987. *Spirits of Resistance and Capitalist Discipline: Factory Women in Malaysia.* New York: University of New York Press.

Ortner, Sherry B. 1995. "Resistance and the Problem of Ethnographic Refusal." *Comparative Studies in Society and History* 37 (1): 173–93.

Ortner, Sherry. 2011. "On Neoliberalism." *Anthropology of this Century*, no. 1 (no page numbers). http://aotcpress.com/articles/neoliberalism/

Pelkmans, Mathijs, and Rhys Machold. 2011. "Conspiracy Theories and Their Truth Trajectories." *Focaal*, no. 59: 66–80.

Pipes, D. 1996. *The Hidden Hand: Middle East Fears of Conspiracy.* New York: St. Martin's Griffin.

Rabinowitz, Dan. 2014. "Resistance and the City." *History and Anthropology.* doi:10.1080/02757206.2014.930457

Razsa, Maple, and Andrej Kurnik. 2012. "The Occupy Movement in Žižek's Hometown: Direct Democracy and a Politics of Becoming." *American Ethnologist* 39 (2): 238–258.

Reed-Danahay, Deborah. 1993. "Talking About Resistance: Ethnography and Theory in Rural France." *Anthropological Quarterly* 66 (4): 221–229.

Roseberry, William. 1994. "Hegemony and the Language of Contention." In *Everyday Forms of State Formation: Revolution and the Negotiation of Rule in Modern Mexico*, edited by Gilbert M. Joseph and Daniel Nugent, 355–365. London: Duke University Press.

Sahlins, Marshall. 1978. *Culture and Practical Reason*. Chicago, IL: University of Chicago Press.

Sanders, Todd, and Harry G. West. 2003. "Power Revealed and Concealed in the New World Order." In *Transparency and Conspiracy: Ethnographies of Suspicion in the New World Order*, edited by H. G. West and T. Sanders, 1–37. Durham, NC: Duke University Press.

Scott, James C. 1985. *Weapons of the Weak: Everyday Forms of Peasant Resistance*. New Haven, CT: Yale University Press.

Scott, James C. 1990. *Domination and the Arts of Resistance: Hidden Transcripts*. New Haven, CT: Yale University Press.

Seymour, Susan. 2006. "Resistance." *Anthropological Theory* 6 (3): 303–321.

Shukaitis, Stevphen, and David Graeber. 2007. "Introduction." In *Constituent Imagination: Militant Investigations, Collective Theorization*, edited by S. Shukaitis and D. Graeber, 11–34. Edinburgh: AK Press.

Starn, Orin. 1992. "'I Dreamed of Foxes and Hawks': Reflections on Peasant Protest, New Social Movements, and the Rondas Campesinas of Northern Peru." In *The Making of Social Movements in Latin America: Identity, Strategy and Democracy*, 89–111. Boulder, CO: Westview Press.

Stoler, Ann L. 1985. *Capitalism and Confrontation in Sumatra's Plantation History, 1870–1979*. New Haven, CT: Yale University Press.

Sutton, D. 1998. *Memories Cast in Stone: The Relevance of the Past in Everyday Life*. Oxford: Berg.

Sutton, David. 2003. "Poked by the 'Foreign Finger' in Greece: Conspiracy Theory or the Hermeneutics of Suspicion?" In *The Usable Past: Greek Metahistories*, edited by K. S. Brown and Y. Hamilakis, 191–210. Lanham, MD: Lexington Books.

Tarrow, Sidney. 1996. "Social Movements in Contentious Politics: A Review Article." *American Political Science Review* 90 (4): 874–883.

Theodossopoulos, Dimitrios. 2010. "Introduction: United in Discontent." In *United in Discontent: Local Responses to Cosmopolitanism and Globalization*, edited by D. Theodossopoulos and E. Kirtsoglou, 1–19. Oxford: Berghahn.

Theodossopoulos, Dimitrios. 2013. "Infuriated With the Infuriated? Blaming Tactics and Discontent About the Greek Financial Crisis." *Current Anthropology* 54 (2): 200–221.

Theodossopoulos, Dimitrios. 2014. "The Poetics of Indignation in Greece: Anti-Austerity Protest and Accountability." In *The Political Aesthetics of Global Protest: Beyond the Arab Spring*, edited by Pnina Werbner, Kathryn Spellman-Poots, and Martin Webb, 368–388. Edinburgh: Edinburgh University Press.

Tilley, Charles. 1991. "Domination, Resistance, Compliance… Discourse." *Sociological Forum* 6 (3): 593–602.

Urla, Jacqueline, and Justin Helepololei. 2014. "The Ethnography of Resistance Then and Now: On Thickness and Activist Engagement in the Twenty-First Century." *History and Anthropology*. doi:10.1080/02757206.2014.930456

Werbner, Martin Webb, and Kathryn Spellman-Poots (eds). 2014. *The Political Aesthetics of Global Protest: Beyond the Arab Spring*. Edinburgh: Edinburgh University Press.

Williams, Raymond. 1977. *Marxism and Literature*. Oxford: Oxford University Press.

The Ethnography of Resistance Then and Now: On Thickness and Activist Engagement in the Twenty-First Century

Jacqueline Urla & Justin Helepololei

This article seeks to convey some of the theoretical frameworks and commitments that characterize how anthropologists have approached the ethnography of resistance. Using our individual biographies as a point of departure, we describe and contrast the intellectual influences that shaped our ethnographic engagements as well as the unanticipated dilemmas we each faced with regard to writing, thick description, and accountability to research participants and their struggles. Our narratives reveal a continued interest in ethnographic thickness while at the same time pointing to new challenges that emerge from the growing interest in engaged or activist research paradigms. Our experiences show that studying actors engaged in political struggle calls for rethinking the pedagogy and practice of ethnography. We conclude by considering steps we can take within our institutions to support such reflexivity and engagement in ethnographic work.

For a generation of anthropologists, the publication of James Scott's *Weapons of the Weak* in 1985 is closely identified with the emergence of resistance as an analytical and ethnographic object of study. This now classic study of "everyday" forms of peasant rebellion, targeted principally as an intervention into peasant studies, became the catalyst for a much broader conversation about the nature of power, domination, hegemony, and routine backstage forms of evasion and subterfuge that occur in the absence of organized revolution or formal protest. The current wave of popular protests that captured worldwide attention with the "Arab Spring" of 2011 and the subsequent chain of occupy movements together with the preceding global resistance movement that culminated in the World Social Forum have put the issue of resistance at front and centre once again. The nature of the object under study has shifted to be sure. If the 1980s was a time of concern with resistance with a small "r", what is now garnering attention and stimulating conferences and special journal issues in anthropology and elsewhere are the newer tactics of self-conscious political mobilizing.[1] Today's anthropologists (and many other scholars) find themselves in a moment of acute questioning about the forms and goals of the emergent modalities of protest we are witnessing, their potential for transformative change, and what our role can or should be in their study.

Resistance, and therefore, the ethnography of resistance, continues to be as galvanizing an issue as ever. In this essay we collaborate as anthropologists of these two aforementioned generations (the 1980s and the contemporary moment) to describe and contrast our experiences with the ethnography of resistance. "Take One" recounts the experience of Urla; "Take Two", that of Helepololei. We characterize our specific intellectual contexts and trajectories, the theoretical frameworks that influenced us, as well as our ethnographic experiences. Our goal is to paint a portrait of different generational perspectives by identifying key texts, assumptions, and debates that shaped (and continue to shape) our work, as well as different kinds of challenges we have faced. We find that some of the challenges that arise today for the ethnography of resistance come out of the growing interest in engaged or activist research paradigms. We take up the way such paradigms instantiate more reflexivity about research methods, writing, and relationships with subjects in projects of social struggle. We conclude by considering steps we can take within our institutions to create meaningful support for this kind of ethnographic work.

The Ethnography of Resistance: Take One

Resistance was without doubt a core concept for anthropologists who, like myself, went to graduate school in the 1980s. In my entering cohort at UC Berkeley, there were quite a few of us interested in reinventing political anthropology and looking for new kinds of fieldsites and methods for studying power and social change outside the classical format of rural villages and traditional societies. The moment was turbulent; the internal criticisms within the discipline ran deep regarding its theoretical models as well as its historical and conceptual ties to colonialism. The collection of essays in *Reinventing Anthropology* (Hymes 1972) can be seen as the forerunner to a subsequent decade of reassessments of the discipline and its methods. Among the most salient were *Europe and the People Without History* by Wolf (1982), *Anthropology as Cultural Critique* by Marcus and Fischer (1986), *Writing Culture* by Clifford and Marcus (1986) and *Decolonizing Anthropology* by Harrison (1991). To this, we have to also add the profound impact of the emergence of feminist anthropology, which not only contributed insights into gender inequality (see Leacock 1978; Reiter 1975; Rosaldo and Lamphere 1974) but was also a vibrant arena for theorizing power, resistance, and ethnographic methods more generally.

In this climate of intellectual ferment, the description and theorization of "everyday" forms of resistance took root, provoked as much by work being produced outside as inside anthropology: the work of Marxist sociologists in the Birmingham School tradition of cultural studies on urban working class youth, or the innovative work on oppositional practices by French historical sociologist de Certeau (1980). Together, this work offered anthropologists new conceptual tools, made Gramsci required reading in a way he had not been before, and chipped away at the rigid opposition drawn between the materialist and symbolic/interpretive paradigms that had anthropology in a stranglehold at the time.

A conundrum for analysts early on in these discussions was the issue of defining resistance. By what criteria were acts to be considered challenges to structures of power? This was a particularly complex problem when it came to precisely the kinds of quotidian actions premised on anonymity, dissimulation, and deniability. To what extent do the perspectives of actors matter in defining an action as resistance? How do we infer intentions? Scott recognized the problematic nature of translating the idiom and actions of peasants who might see themselves as just trying to survive into the analytical vocabulary of social scientists.[2] He opted to define resistance as actions by subordinate classes that aim to mitigate or deny the material and symbolic claims the dominant classes made upon them (Scott 1986, 22–31). In so doing, his analysis defined resistance by its target, whether explicitly articulated or not, and endowed actions otherwise regarded as petty forms of criminality, laziness, or deceit with social structural significance in the longue durée of class antagonism.

The question of intentionality remains with us, however, as a perennial problem in the study of resistance and speaks to the broader issue of how to theorize the dynamics of ideological domination, and the ambiguities of consensus, hegemony, and consciousness.[3] Foucauldian analytics of power, knowledge, and subjectivity were simultaneously making headway in anthropology during this decade, most especially at Berkeley where Foucault was in residency at various points. These radically different framings posed a second key challenge to the study of resistance. Abu Lughod's (1990) essay, "The Romance of Resistance", was one of the earliest attempts in anthropology to identify the significance that such a perspective posed for the upsurge of interest in everyday forms of resistance. In liberal political theory, power and resistance are conceptualized as antitheses of each other; power has been conventionally understood primarily as repressive and resistance as *emancipation*—that is, as action that seeks fundamentally to shed power.[4] When resistance is conceptualized in such a fashion, the role of the analyst is frequently assumed to be that of determining the extent to which acts of resistance meaningfully challenge the structures of domination: are they "really" resistant? Foucault (1980, 1982) advanced both a different notion of power and a different analytical stance towards its study. Without denying systems of repression and exploitation, his work drew attention to a "productive" notion of power that operates through discourses and practices that construct subjects as objects of knowledge, classification, and discipline. He sought to show, for example, that the actors in gay, women's, and other liberation movements are not in a position of exteriority to the legal, medical, and sociological discourses of knowledge about them; rather, the logics of their resistance take shape within these. Foucault advised approaching oppositional discourses and tactics not as expressions of a free will, but as diagnostics of power, "chemical catalysts" capable of telling us something about the overarching discourses, relations of power, and the terrain of subjectivities in which subordinated actors are enmeshed and make sense of their lives (Abu Lughod 1990, 42).

Abu Lughod's essay lucidly traced and exemplified the value of an analytical shift away from what she called a kind of romanticized paradigm focused on assessing the status of resistance and the consciousness of resistors, towards examining sites of struggle as windows into the workings of power. In the paradigm she advocated, *how* questions predominate: how is resistance expressed? Why does it take this shape and especially what does that tell us about forms of disciplinary control, modernization, and other discursive regimes? Ong's (1987) ethnography, *Spirits of Resistance*, a study of outbreaks of spirit possession among young Malaysian factory women, was an early and brilliant synthesis of how Foucauldian analytics could be combined with feminist and political economic questions. Her ethnography, like the more Gramscian-inspired ethnography of Willis (1981) or Hill (1985), showed how contradictions and embeddedness in larger discourses are the stuff of most acts of defiance.

The Pursuit of Thickness

If intentionality or consciousness was one analytical conundrum in the study of resistance, and the dichotomous view of resistance and power another, a third was the issue of ethnographic thickness, a term Sherry Ortner uses in "Resistance and the Problem of Ethnographic Refusal", a sweeping assessment and critique of the burgeoning body of research on resistance that characterized the second half of the 1980s and into the 1990s (Ortner 1995). James Scott had been quite explicit in arguing for the value of ethnographic methods in the study of quotidian resistance. Curiously then, ethnography, argued Ortner, was exactly what was most lacking in the subsequent surge of scholarship on resistance. Ethnography, she reminds us, is not just a qualitative method of data gathering, it is also a mode of analysis committed to richly detailed, textured, and contextualized understandings of our subjects' life worlds and cultural practices. Playing on Geertz's (1973) concept of "thick description", she calls upon scholars to deliver greater ethnographic "thickness" and spends the better part of the essay spelling out what makes for a thick description of resistance and why it is valuable. Too much of the literature on resistance exhibits, as she puts it, a *thinning* of culture and a *sanitizing* of politics, resulting in an overly unified and homogenous portrait of resistance and resistors that belies their complex dynamics. Thick descriptions, in contrast, are those that explore the internal politics and tensions of subaltern groups, the heterogeneity of perspectives, as well as asymmetries and hierarchies that characterize their social groupings. Thick descriptions should inquire into the cultural grounding of resistant

practices, the forms and symbols they deploy paying attention not only to social structure, but also to the agency of specific actors.[5] And finally they should provide, argues
Ortner, a much more nuanced and dynamic understanding of consciousness, exploring
the ambiguities and ambivalences that surround resistance, and describing how the
intentions and perspectives of actors evolve through praxis.

The concreteness with which Ortner detailed the epistemological entailments of a
thick ethnography has been helpful in clarifying what this method could bring to the
understanding of resistance. All three of these analytical issues—the aspiration of thickness, the debates on hegemony, and Foucauldian conceptualizations of power—deeply
shaped my own ethnographic research on minority language activism in the Basque
country (Urla 2012a). Here, however, I want to consider some challenges that I
wrestled with in the course of my research and writing about the language movement
for which the aforementioned debates left me unprepared.

The scholarship of my time helped me to think in a complex way about resistance,
subjectivity, and subaltern consciousness, but not how to think about the political
dimensions of the resulting analyses, how these would circulate and potentially
impact the subjects and activism about which I wrote. These kinds of concerns were
curiously absent from debates on the study of resistance, but they were percolating elsewhere: not only in the heightened reflexivity about ethnographic authority and the
politics of knowledge instigated by the writing culture debates, but also coming from
within feminist ethnography, where I found penetrating critiques of the power
dynamics, goals, and betrayals of conventional forms of ethnographic practice and
writing (for example, Abu Lughod 1993; Enslin 1994; Stacey 1988). Feminists were
ahead of the curve in bringing together analytical questions about power and resistance
with questions about research praxis and accountability.

At various points, language activists I worked with in the Basque Country expressed
an interest in what I might have to say about their movement. I had the luxury to be
able to read, theorize, and write, they said, while their exhausting rhythm of work left
them little time to reflect or write about their activities. But the disconnect was acute
between my analysis of the logics of their resistance strategies and their interest in practical theories of language revival. Locating a common ground was not easy. I would
often feel that my observations were either extraordinarily obvious to them or too
abstract. My writing was talking to other audiences and I was often possessed by an
uncomfortable sense that I was betraying their hopes and confidence in my work.

I do not think most anthropologists of my generation necessarily expected to be in
conversation with their subjects about their academic writing. The disconnect was
taken for granted. But when we are writing about activism, we can find ourselves entering a highly politicized and public field of discourse that can be complex to negotiate
and increase the stakes of writing choices. In my case, I had been observing the increasing vilification of Basque nationalism over the course of my fieldwork. In the 1990s, a
new wave of political murders by Euskadi ta Askatasuna (ETA) together with a political
shift to the right by the Spanish government created a hostile environment for Basque-
identified social movements and non-violent civil disobedience. Leading criminal court
justice Balthasar Garzón had initiated numerous indictments on the thesis that ETA

effectively controlled a vast infrastructure of activist organizations in civil society. This brought about massive surveillance, unprecedented arrests, and mass trials of activists as well as the pre-emptive closing of the only Basque-language newspaper. The grass-roots Basque language movement became the object of intense criticism from right wing intellectuals who in well-funded publications were equating language revival with totalitarianism, quasi-racist ethnic exclusion, and even terrorism. The ease with which Garzón's thesis became the position of the mainstream media and the criminalization of an entire swathe of civil society it set in motion was breathtaking.

Neither political violence nor state terror was the subject of my research. This had become almost an incantation of mine because of the tendency of the violence issue to subsume all other discussions of politics. In addition, language activists were themselves keen to build a positive, community-based approach to language revival dissociated from the contentious issue of political violence. But the boundary became increasingly hard to maintain as the new anti-terrorist measures began to directly condition the language movement and people with whom I worked. One of my friends and collaborators fell victim to the wave of arrests. A non-profit organization for which she had worked coordinating civil disobedience workshops for activist youth was accused of being part of ETA's shadow infrastructure. I remember vividly her telling me of the account of her arrest, with hooded anti-terrorist police squad breaking down her door in the middle of the night, and then the months that she had to commute to Madrid every week for the long drawn-out trial where she and 51 other defendants sat accused behind bulletproof glass. I can still recall the shock wave that went through my body when the sentence of nine years came down and her neighbours and friends posted a YouTube video of the police taking her to jail.[6] The conceptual firewall I had drawn between political violence and language activism crumbled in these events. I felt compelled to step out of my more abstract theoretical arguments in order to bear witness to the violations of civil rights that were taking place and yet were so under-reported. I felt it urgent to understand and to write about how the logics of anti-terrorism could put language revitalization at risk.

Events presented me with morally and politically loaded questions about what I should be writing and how. As Sluka (2000) and Scheper-Hughes (1995) have both argued, we anthropologists have close contact and ethnographic understandings of social struggles that can place us in a unique position to provide the perspectives of actors who do not get airtime in mainstream media outlets.[7] This is equally relevant to the ethnography of marginalized populations and the poor as it is for the ethnography of political dissent. Conveying the perspectives of people who are not favoured in mainstream public opinion, deemed socially deviant, or terrorist comes with undeniable risks of being misconstrued, accusations of bias, or worse.[8] Reflexivity about these writing choices was absent in the ethnography of resistance of my generation that was more focused on analytical questions of power and agency than it was on the practice and politics of ethnography itself.

Quite apart from whether or not my long-time research collaborators were interested in my writing, I nevertheless tried to imagine any one of them reading over my shoulder. Although daunting and sometimes paralysing, in the end I think it made for better scholarship, thick description, and a less hegemonic way of writing. It pushed me to try to write accessibly and to be acutely aware of potential "othering" in my writing voice. I am not sure I succeeded, but imagining a Basque activist audience made me more concerned than I otherwise might have been about showing that the activists I studied were themselves engaged in a process of continual reassessment and debate about their intentions and strategies. Keeping activists in mind as a potential audience pushed me to explain in a more nuanced way the forces shaping their actions. In the study of resistance movements we often encounter examples of co-optation and contradiction. For example, one part of my research looks at the appropriation of corporate managerial techniques by language activists in the design of minority language planning (Urla 2012b). I could have pointed to this as an example of activists succumbing to neoliberal logics, but this struck me as both too simplistic and too much like writing from the ivory tower. The co-optation thesis often relies on superficial similarities and does not tell us what we really want to know, which is how and why activists choose their strategies. We have to give some history and context to these choices, think through the appeal they hold for actors in the confines and opportunities of their social location, and also examine how they actually put these choices into practice. The tougher analytical task, as I saw it, was to puzzle through the origins, advantages, and shortcomings of these political strategies in a way that might be insightful for activists and their aims.

The dilemmas I have recounted in my own efforts to do ethnography of resistance centre mostly on writing, voice, and audience. The relationship of scholarly writing to activism was not a salient part of the largely theoretical debates that emerged in the 1980s around the nature of power and resistance. We are in a different moment now. The last 15 years have seen a much more explicit and sustained discussion in anthropology about scholars' engagement with public issues, with activists, and with social movements that is linked to a broad and deep reassessment about our ethical responsibilities towards the communities we study and the social problems of our times. The emergence of "public anthropology" is a sign of this. Our publications and conferences show more discussion and experimentation with questions of voice and writing leading, among other things, to a greater acceptance of genre blurring, personal narrative, and appreciation for work that transgresses the confines of conventional social scientific writing. The critique of power relations between the researcher and the researched that had been pioneered by feminist, indigenous, and scholars of colour has gained wider currency. The research practices of two decades ago are no longer normative and many students are keenly interested in alternatives. Job listings increasingly ask for scholars with records of "community engagement". Once relatively marginal, Participatory Action Research and Community-based Research have become much more widely known and legitimate methodologies. Anthropology and the social sciences more generally have undergone a "morally engaged turn" that is manifest in reflexivity about research practice, a concern to communicate with a larger public around critical social problems, and an interest in finding ways to be of benefit to our subjects of study (Hemment 2007; Lyon-Callo and Hyatt 2003; Tedlock 2005). All of this has created a new set of expectations and context for anthropology as a whole, and for the ethnography of resistance in particular. In this next section, Hele-pololei, a graduate student in cultural anthropology who both studies and participates in a variety of movements, describes the authors and experiences that have influenced his approach as well as some of the challenges he has faced in his encounters with the ethnography of resistance in the twenty-first century.

(Activist)#Ethnography of Resistance: Take Two

My path to anthropology and the ethnography of resistance has been propelled and shaped by a commitment to working towards social justice. It was in trying to figure out how to better organize towards social change that I came to see ethnography as a means for simultaneously studying and supporting projects in progressive social change. While scholars' earlier questions about the definition of resistance and how to best document it remained just as pressing (and just as difficult to address), for myself and an increasing number of students, a more complex understanding and thick description of resistance were not, in itself, sufficient as a research outcome. I and others were coming to the ethnography of resistance with a desire to make this thick ethnography useful for the struggles we were studying.

The radical questioning of the positivist paradigm accomplished by critical theory, the post-modern, and morally engaged turn of earlier generations has meant that for many of us a dispassionate value-free intellectual interest can no longer be assumed as a scholar's default position. Partisan participation that blurs the line between scholar and activist is no longer taboo (King 2007). By the time I started studying anthropology, militant ethnography had become a recognized, if not uncomplicated, stance (Juris 2007, 2008). As an undergraduate at Arizona State University, I had my first foray into this kind of ethnography doing a study of student mobilization with the campus chapter of MEChA, the Chican@ Student Movement of Aztlán. I emerged from that experience hopeful that research could be useful to activists as well as of the possibility of enacting anti-hierarchical relations with my activist collab-orators. I was not only as interested as previous generations in social theory, but also drawn to participatory methods and more explicit forms of knowledge mobilization for communities or groups in struggle.

At the time, I was heartened to find a community of scholars with similar commit-ments. Work was burgeoning on social movements (Nash 2005), but two edited volumes in particular stood out for me at the time. *Constituent Imagination* (Shukaitis, Graeber, and Biddle 2007) was a straight-on challenge to a social science that produces, as the editors say, "knowledge about" others. In its place, they provide case studies of "militant research" that take as their point of departure "the understandings, experi-ences, and relations generated through organizing as both a method of political action and as a form of knowledge" (Shukaitis, Graeber, and Biddle 2007, 9). The volume opened my eyes to how individuals and collectives outside the university are using ethnographic methodologies. It was exciting to me to find essays by non-academics, such as BRE (writing autoethnographically against the criminalization of homelessness), *Colectivo Situaciones*, and the CrimethInc Ex-Workers' Collective, whose analyses are derived from—and for—particular struggles. Although the editors were highly critical of academic knowledge production and sceptical of whether in fact the university could ever be a site for producing truly radical critique, they did not entirely reject the potential for academics to leverage their positions towards emancipatory social change.

In the assemblage of approaches and authors, I found Ieff Juris' contribution "Practicing Militant Ethnography with the Movement for Global Resistance in Barcelona" particularly encouraging in its defence of ethnographic inquiry centred on activists' questions. He shows how direct participation in the movement can contribute not only to the communities with which we work, but also to the discipline of anthropology in challenging some of our own assumptions and practices. Juris goes beyond Scheper-Hughes' earlier call for a militant anthropology in which the ethnographer is a morally engaged witness and partner in struggle. Beyond solidarity, he argues for modelling our ethnographic practice on the praxis of activists. For the militant ethnographer, Juris writes:

> ... the issue is not so much the kind of knowledge produced, which is always practically engaged and collaborative, but rather, how is it presented, for which audience, and where is it distributed? These questions go to the very heart of the alternative network-based cultural logics and political forms that more radical anti-corporate globalization activists are generating and putting into practice. Addressing them doesn't just respond to the issue of ethical responsibility toward one's informants, colleagues and friends, it also sheds light on the nature of contemporary movements themselves. (2007, 172)

Research that emerges from and for particular struggles challenges academics to think beyond the politics of knowledge production to addresses the potential and necessity of its mobilization. Anthropologists have increasingly taken on this charge by distributing their work not only through the traditional media of books, talks, and academic journals, but also through "copyleft", open-access publications, frequent op-ed pieces, blogs, and interviews.[9] Attention to what happens with the products of ethnographic research after fieldwork—often provoked by research communities' expectations of reciprocity—is not just a means of giving back, but rather a deliberate strategy for creating a more inclusive and expanded horizon of readership and dialogue among research peers.

A second important influence on me was the volume *Engaging Contradictions* (Hale 2008). Here the contributors make a case for how radically democratic and transformative research praxis can still emerge from within the university. As an undergraduate contemplating the merits of an academic career path, reading this collection was a pivotal moment for me. Not only were these established scholars making their intellectual homes in the complicated and compromised position of activist research, but they also valued the ethical minefield of personal involvement as an object of study in itself. As the title suggests, the volume as a whole seeks to recognize and explore the difficulties that straddling research and activism can entail. It also, however, points to the advantages. Deeper insights can be gained through collaborative research in a way that serves the interests of both better scholarship and social change. George Lipsitz, for example, writes that activists often demonstrate "tactical brilliance" and sophisticated insights into social problems. In the process of struggle, they "develop new ways of knowing as well as new ways of being. They discover nontraditional archives and generate nontraditional imaginaries as constitutive parts of mobilization for resources, rights, and recognition" (Lipsitz 2008, 117). Working with activists as partners in producing rich and engaged ethnography is something I wanted to work towards.

Fieldwork Dilemmas: When "Informants" Resist Thick Description

In the last three years I have been conducting research in Barcelona alongside anti-authoritarian squatter collectives, called "okupas" (a modification of the Spanish word for occupation). From the start I was motivated by an affinity with their fight against urban speculation and state repression. However, finding a way to make my academic position useful to squatters, in the ways described by scholars such as Hale and Juris, has been a less straightforward task than I had previously experienced. For example, while the okupas I met welcomed "participant observation"—allowing me to live in several established okupas and even join a group working to open a new one—my attempts to solicit formal interviews from residents were frequently rejected and met with scepticism and even hostility. The "failure" of particular ethnographic methods, in this case the interview, offers a starting point for understanding potential limits for activist research. In the following I want to describe how actions of the state on the one hand, and okupa political values on the other, constrained my attempts at activist ethnography.

When I began fieldwork in the spring of 2012, programmes of economic austerity in Spain and throughout Southern Europe were being fought in the streets. Public demonstrations had been growing in strength since the general strike on 29 March 2012 against labour reform and were gaining momentum with the one-year anniversary of the 15 May plaza occupations of the *indignados* fast approaching. In preparation for a European Central Bank meeting held from 3 May to 5 May, several thousand police officers from various regional and national agencies were brought into the city. Squatted social centres became the targets of intensified observation and harassment in the campaign to pacify the city. Justifying the expense of increasing security forces, Spain's Minister of the Department of the Interior, Jorge Fernández Díaz, declared the police surge necessary for maintaining public safety, both during and after the meeting, insisting before the press that: "Barcelona cannot be the *antisistema* capital of Europe" (Baquero 2012). This statement was one of many characterizations of protestors as "antisistema"—or anti-system—a pejorative suggesting that protesters lack clear political economic critiques or reasonable demands. They protest simply to protest. Against such attempts to depict demonstrations as mindless reaction, I imagined a thick description of activist praxis, one that seriously engaged their motivations and concerns, and could help to counter the reductive message of the Spanish state. And while this might have been true, it became apparent that I was not alone in wanting to describe the activities of activists.

During this same period, a master's thesis written by Piqué i Batallé (2009), a coordinator of the Catalan regional police, the *Mossos d'Esquadra*, was found and made public. In it, Piqué i Batallé outlined a strategy for suppressing "antisistema" dissent. Subtitled "Sherwood Syndrome", the thesis makes the case for controlling radical activists, characterized as modern-day "Robin Hoods", by shutting down the spaces from which they operate. The thesis describes in great detail not only the physical locations of various okupas, but also their ideological tendencies and connections with other regional and international organizations. For squatters I knew, this amount of detail only confirmed suspicions that the *Mossos* had long used undercover officers to infiltrate activist spaces. The confirmation that police were indeed employing ethnography-like strategies made activists even more wary of trusting an outside researcher, especially when it came to recording interviews and asking to take pictures. In the crowded field of ethnographers, journalists, and cops, detailed description by an embedded observer was the last thing some people wanted.

Understanding the process by which activists are made into security threats and how they are policed is critical for understanding how resistance takes place and what tactics and framing are possible. These processes also shape the kinds of opportunities open for anthropologists hoping to conduct research in support of resistance efforts (Weldes 1999, 12). Spying and the suspension of civil rights have become routine practice in the war on terror—a war without fixed battlefields (Goldstein 2010). The now almost constant invocation of a state of "insecurity" authorizes unprecedented forms of covert and overt surveillance that bleed into the world of activist protest, their homes, workplaces, and online activities (Holbraad and Pedersen 2013, 8). During my time in Barcelona, police were often suspected of, and on several occasions discovered, adopting the aesthetic appearance and practice of activists. In some cases undercover police were recorded provoking conflicts such that uniformed police could justify a violent dispersal of otherwise non-violent protests.

Squatting collectives in Barcelona, like anti-authoritarian and anarchists activists elsewhere, have responded by working to remain as inscrutable to authority as possible, protecting their own and each other's identities through practices of "security culture" by working only among networks of trusted individuals, carefully limiting discussions with outsiders, as well as insiders, especially via cell phone, email, or social networking (Kroijer 2013).[10] The control of information was not only seen as a security issue, but it also stemmed from much broader critiques okupas had of authority and representation.

Three key principles guiding okupa modes of activism put serious roadblocks in the way of my attempt to interview activists: first, the embracing of anonymity as a political strategy; second, a broad critique of representation; and lastly, a do-it-yourself ethic connected to horizontal and egalitarian forms of organizing. These values inform a practice that resists authority from multiple angles: as exercised by state institutions and would-be movement leaders, as well as outside journalists and researchers hoping to imprint their own authorship on diverse and diffuse communities of squatters. Even during moments of heightened repression, okupas chose not to engage with journalists. Rather than seeking larger audiences by appealing through channels of mass media in the ways many activist organizations use press releases, okupas relied on their own media—whether print, online, radio, or even a pirate television station—insisting on direct control over the means and message. As part of the larger political project of refusing representation by others, okupas utilize these alternative means as a way of getting their ideas out directly, refusing even internal forms of representation in the form of movement leaders or spokespeople. These commitments share strong affinities with the practice and philosophy of direct communication of the free radio movement that originated in the Italian autonomous left and started to gain significant following in Spain in the 1980s (Guattari 1981; Radio Bronka 2013; Urla 1995). The reluctance to take on the role of spokesperson and to seek out recognition has extended to research-ers as well as journalists. Fernández Gómez, a historian writing an account of squatting in Catalonia, reports a number of refusals in his attempts to record life stories: one respondent gave "an absolute no", convinced his words would be manipulated; another declined, insisting that the researcher "would not make a living off him" (Fernández Gómez 2010, 14). In her essay "Refusing the Subject", Visweswaran (1994) describes a similar situation of a prominent Indian nationalist's refusal to be interviewed by her. Visweswaran argues that the rejection has to be understood as a broader refusal of a certain kind of subject-hood, a kind of individual protagonism that for this activist contradicted the Gandhian ethic of "work as its own reward" by which she lived (1994, 66). Attention to the conjuncture of historical processes that either encourage or discourage individuals to become subjects, argues Visweswaran, is a necessary feature in the practice of feminist ethnography. But it is equally relevant to the ethnography of resistance, inviting us to recognize the refusal of the subject by activists, not only as a methodological impediment but also as a means of gaining insight into the politics of representation specific to certain contexts.

Central to the politics of squatting (and other direct action practices) is a do-it-your-self ethic that discourages a reliance on leaders. Hoping for expert interviews with experienced squatters, I was instead given manuals produced by "Oficinas de Okupa-ción" (Offices of Occupation) and encouraged to meet with other newcomers also looking to open a squat. The collectives that organized these "offices" gave weekly advice sessions, but they required that those asking for information already be involved in an active squatting project. In other words, individuals were encouraged to act on their own, to learn by doing. This insistence on autonomy and self-management (or *autogestión*) carried into the consensus-based assemblies used to organize most okupas. While these values were held in common by many participants in different col-lectives, the decisions and priorities that emerged from each assembly diverged greatly. Okupas varied in their legal status and the activities they organized—from boxing workshops to language classes—as well as in the degree to which they collaborated with other activists. Okupas cited this diversity in experience as yet another reason for refusing to speak on behalf of or as an authority on "okupas".

These experiences suggest that a thick description of resistance stands to benefit from incorporating reflection on the contingencies that shape our agency as ethnographers and the research encounter—especially when it takes the form of resistance *to* ethno-graphy itself. Graeber's (2009) definitively thick ethnographic study of direct action is a good model of such reflexivity. Informed by years of participation as an activist within the same circles he writes about, Graeber explains that his motivations to become an ethnographer were to provide a deeper understanding of practices like consensus-based decision-making as well as to document the violent tactics of police repression that are often hidden in mainstream reporting. Graeber's attunement to the movement's ethics and anxieties prompts him to account for his ethnographic decisions, discussing participants' concerns about confidentiality and reflecting on his own positionality as a university professor, an activist insider, and a reluctant representative. Likewise, reflecting on the obstacles I encountered in okupa fieldwork ended up helping me to better appreciate the values that shape okupa political agency, knowledge production, and mobilization. If at first I saw the rejection of interviews to be primarily a function of the intensified surveillance to which okupas were subject—a condition that made it difficult for an ethnographer to gain trust—reflection on these refusals has subsequently led me to better grasp the clash between the kind of expertise and political subject-hood interviews presume and the forms of sharing knowledge and political collectivity I was trying to study.

Paths of Thick Resistance

The juxtaposition of our trajectories reflects the shifting intellectual landscape of anthropology and aspirations that are brought to the ethnography of resistance. One way to think about our two "takes" on the ethnography of resistance is through the distinction Hale (2006) draws between cultural critique and activist anthropology. Urla's work is aligned with the premises of cultural critique, while Helepololei exemplifies a growing interest among social movement scholars to enact a more activist research practice.

As formulated by Hale, cultural critique and activist anthropology share a common interest in exposing mechanisms of inequality and contributing to progressive social change. Cultural critique tries to do this through scholarly analysis: through theoretical innovation and ever more sophisticated and complex understandings of social and cultural life. Ortner's rationale for thicker descriptions of resistance fits neatly within this paradigm, and indeed cultural critique seems an apt description of how many ethnographers of resistance continue to understand the contribution of their work. Cultural critique reflects an interest on the part of researchers to use the tools of anthropological research to shed light on naturalized logics of capitalism, gender inequality, or other dynamics of power in ways that can be useful for public debate and challenge. For Hale it was important to differentiate the stance of cultural critique from that of activist anthropology in which ethnographers

> affirm a political alignment with an organized group of people in struggle and allow dialogue with them to shape each phase of the process, from conception of the research topic to data collection to verification and dissemination of the results. (2006, 97)

Activist anthropology implies not a different object of study, but a different stance towards research participants and a questioning of "the material relations of anthropological knowledge production" that was absent in cultural critique (Hale 2006, 101).

Hale's point is not to claim that all research should (or even could) be activist. He argued, rather, that we must understand more fully the particular kinds of tensions and challenges generated by this approach. We need to understand the complexities of a form of knowledge production that is simultaneously concerned with productively helping groups with the political practicalities of their struggle.

In her recent review of publically engaged anthropology, Osterweil (2013) supports this endeavour but finds flaws with aspects of Hale's initial formulation. She takes to task the contrast he makes between intellectually oriented academic work (that is, cultural critique) and activist research. This contrast replicates a long-standing, and in her opinion, false opposition between theory and action. Hale's examples of the dilemmas activist researchers face, she argues, set up a contrast between scholars who are interested in analytic complexity on the one hand, and activists who gravitate towards less sophisticated but politically expedient analyses and concepts on the other. Osterweil then draws on her own research with the Italian alter-globalization movement to demonstrate that political activism does not necessarily imply a suspension of analytic sophistication or an aversion to experimentation and uncertainty. Critical reflection, analysis, and deconstruction are taking place in social movements, argues Osterweil, and it should be our task to recognize it, collaborate in this, and, very importantly, find ways of spelling out the implications of this critical epistemological work.

We find Osterweil's destabilization of the opposition between critique and activism useful. Her appeal for an expansive understanding of the forms political engagement can take is compelling. For example, the networked and mobile forms of recent activism prompt questions about the boundaries of the activist "community" and what that means for accountability. In many respects her intervention valorizing the political potential of what she calls epistemic work by scholars and social movements only reinforces what Hale called for and what our own fieldwork dilemmas underscored: the need to rethink how we teach, design, and carry out ethnography. It makes apparent the need for spaces where we could examine personal encounters and complications that so often remain in the periphery of our current pedagogy or publications.

Conclusion

Through the exposé of our personal trajectories in the ethnography of resistance, we have sketched some of the intellectual inheritances, motivations, and dilemmas that have informed our approaches in the 1980s and today. In lieu of a review of the literature, a gaze from nowhere, we have offered brief "takes" on our individual engagements with the study of resistance at specific historical junctures. This has allowed us to reflect on some of the shifts in the field through contextualized accounts that keep foregrounded the situated nature of all knowledge practices and the kinds of challenges we face in doing ethnography. Because both of us have been studying organized activism, the dilemmas that we encountered have a great deal to do with the implications of working with people in political struggles. We each sought to pursue analytical and descriptive thickness and we both have wrestled with how our work positively or negative impacted the political struggles we were studying. Urla felt her theoretical training left her unprepared for choices having to do with writing and accountability, while Helepololei, coming out of an overtly activist methodology, found that the security scape and okupa do-it-yourself kind of politics made it difficult to actualize some aspects of his approach. No doubt other dilemmas might surface in different kinds of ethnographic projects.

Many of the issues that we have raised in this paper having to do with research praxis, writing, audience, competing loyalties, and gaining trust were the point of departure for organizing a workshop, "Challenges in the Ethnography of Activism", held at the University of Massachusetts Amherst in the spring of 2013. Participants were eager to share details on the different forms engagement can take during as well as after fieldwork, our own processes of negotiating research goals, dilemmas, failures as well as solutions. We were acutely aware of how the structure of the academy that requires finished work and demonstrating mastery gives us so few opportunities to share our fieldwork experiences and anxieties.

What we have not addressed so far, and yet was a central issue in these workshop discussions, is the issue of how we can build support for engaged research within the University. In short, how can we be activists within our places of work for this kind of research? We had the good fortune of having with us some established anthropologists with substantial trajectories as ethnographers of activism as well as experience in attempting to teach classes and build academic programmes amenable to activist research. We wanted to create a space of dialogue about the kinds of obstacles institutions of higher learning currently place in the way of teaching and practising engaged ethnography, and to brainstorm about how these could be overcome. We discuss three—Institutional Review Boards (IRBs), merit and promotion criteria, and time to degree constraints—and then present the brief outlines of a project through which we hope solutions can emerge.

Anthropologists have frequently commented on the difficulty of reconciling ethnographic methods with IRB.[11] This problem has become more apparent as the regulatory role of IRB in academic research has grown and the review has become more involved. It is challenging to make a methodology like ethnography that gathers much of its information informally through participant observation, and relies on a fair amount of serendipity and the blurring of research and daily life, fit into a standardized IRB protocol. The latter expects an unambiguous demarcation of roles and research activities, as well as a clear beginning and end to the "research project" that flies in the face of the multifaceted and protracted relations fieldworkers have with their communities of study. This task is exponentially more difficult for researchers using participatory or collaborative methodologies. There is a stark disconnect between the praxis, ethics, and goals of activist research and the hierarchical and do-no-harm ethical framework that informs standard IRB protocol. It is not that the latter is too stringent. We would argue, in fact, that existing conventional protocols are vastly inadequate for the kind of consultation, negotiations, and accountability that activist researchers regard as essential to an ethical practice of research. High on the agenda for an activist and publically engaged ethnography of resistance is the need to develop protocols that are appropriate to its needs and methods. We could try to follow the example of the University of Chicago and persuade our Universities to limit the scope of IRB review,[12] but in the absence of that, it seems that our best way to proceed is to educate IRB committees and provide them with alternate evaluation criteria.

Practising an activist ethnography of resistance can also run afoul of the current criteria used by the academy to evaluate scholarly productivity. As Lassiter (2008) and indeed many other scholars who advocate collaborative methods warn, it takes time to build the level of trust and negotiate the mutually acceptable methods that engaged scholars need and want for their research. Additionally, the "products" of engaged projects can be quite varied: from websites, to white papers, workshops to downloadable handbooks, community radio to popular theatre. To the extent that peer-reviewed articles continue to be the gold standard for assigning merit, making promotions, and granting tenure, engaged scholars will be at a serious disadvantage, doing double duty trying to keep their jobs and produce work that is meaningful to the community organizations and struggles with which they work. We have to push back against the insidious tendency of the academy to classify engagement and its output as "service"—by far the lesser of the three categories (research, teaching, and service) by which scholars are evaluated. In short, engaged research is not currently compatible with an increasingly audit-oriented academy pushing for more efficiency, shorter time to degree, and quantifiable impact in a narrow range of scholarly publications.[13]

It is all the more curious that the concept of engagement seems to have captivated universities. The word has gone viral. On our campus and others, we are witness to the creation of new offices for "community engagement", courses in civic engagement, new (usually small) sources of funding, and a proliferating discourse that seemingly wants to encourage this as a goal. But are we all talking about the same thing? Engaged research can refer to a wide gamut of practices from public interest anthropology that seeks to influence policy and public opinion at one end of the spectrum to anarchist-inspired forms of militant ethnography that are located outside the academy. Nor can we ignore growing state and corporate employment of ethnographers and ethnographic methods that can range from private sector use of participant observation for product and research design to the counterinsurgency applications we described earlier (see Albro, Marcus, and McNamara 2012). How do we situate our goals with this array of forms of "applied" anthropology?

The current enthusiasm for engagement may offer us some opportunities for advancing activist ethnography of resistance, but misunderstandings and frustrations can arise from the different meanings that "engaged" research can have for administration versus the activist ethnographer. The meaning of "public anthropology" is equally vexed (Lassiter 2008). We take to heart Rylko-Bauer, Singer, and vanWilligen's (2006) critique of the academic tendency to sort ourselves into tribes and assign divisive labels. What we need is not more labels, but contexts that will give us opportunities to explore how an ethnography of resistance can fit into the different kinds of goals that currently come under this label of engaged research.

The Laboratory for Transformative Practice in Anthropology is an initiative that moves in that direction.[14] Still in its infancy, we can do no more here than to convey its vision as a kind of manifesto in the hopes that it will grow, be copied, and be improved upon. The Laboratory is imagined as both a physical and a virtual site of exchange, dialogue, and collaboration for faculty and graduate students interested in pursuing activist and engaged research broadly conceived. Spearheaded by junior faculty who are working with indigenous and racialized communities, the Laboratory departs from the awareness that the different nature and scope of activist and engaged research and knowledge production require imagining forms of support that do not currently exist. Dialogue and mutual mentoring are envisioned as key methods for sharing information on how to navigate the complications engendered by the multiple commitments engaged scholars face. The Laboratory is intended as a site of sharing work in progress and fostering collaboration in research, advising, and teaching. In this sense, it intentionally seeks to counter the "relentlessly individualizing" nature of work, reward, and recognition of academia in favour of the more collective nature of activist work (Lipsitz 2008). New interactive and broadcasting technology, such as online Spreecasts, can expand the network of participants and disseminate the conversations, tools, or working papers produced to more directly support activist research. The Laboratory seeks to make the Universities where we work more hospitable to activist scholars. Thus in its first year, members seek to assemble ethical protocols and appropriate merit criteria that activist scholars very much need. At the same time, the Lab is committed to knowledge mobilization, one of the primary goals of an activist research paradigm: exploring ways that the design and outcomes of research can be useful for the subjects and struggles with which we work.[15]

As the term Laboratory is meant to suggest, the idea behind this initiative is to create a space of experimentation, where answers are not known in advance, where uncertainty, trials, and failures are explored, not covered over. Focused specifically on activist research—which might or might not be about resistance—we note that The Laboratory for Transformative Practice in Anthropology dovetails in interesting ways with similar calls being made to re-examine the teaching and conceptualization of ethnographic practice in other domains of anthropology focused on science and technology, reason, and the contemporary (Faubion and Marcus 2009; Holmes and Marcus 2008; Rabinow et al. 2008). We seem to be in a tectonic shift on various fronts when it comes to ethnography. While we may not all have the same agendas, we nevertheless look to these other experiments in re-conceptualizing ethnography and its pedagogy, as well as social movements themselves, as allied endeavours in new methods and forms of knowledge production. The Laboratory for Transformative Practice hopes to be a means of supporting alternate approaches to the ethnography of resistance. It is not a call for a new handbook so much as it is an attempt to open a space for questioning and for conjoining experimentation in the purpose and nature of ethnographic practice today with the equally expansive and ongoing question about what constitutes engagement. "Caminando preguntamos"—walking we ask questions—say the Zapatistas (Casas-Cortés, Osterweil, and Powell 2008), a motto that can serve us well as a way of imagining the project of the engaged ethnographer. We believe that such an open-ended "collaboratory"[16] project can enable a more dynamic, thicker, and publicly engaged ethnography of resistance.

Acknowledgements

The authors thank Jane Anderson and Julie Hemment, co-organizers of the workshop "Challenges in the Ethnography of Activism", 12 April 2013, as well as all the participants and our invited guests, Arturo Escobar, Charles Hale, and Jeff Juris. This paper has benefitted greatly from conversations during and after the workshop. We also thank the National Science Foundation, OISE-0968575, "Cultural Heritage in European Societies and Spaces", for funding of Helepololei's fieldwork.

Notes

[1]   See, for example, the journal *Cultural Anthropology*'s online "Hot Spots" edition on "Occupy, Anthropology and the 2011 Global Uprisings", http://www.culanth.org/?q=node/641.

[2]   Jonsson (2012) makes a provocative critique along these lines arguing that Scott's (2009) analysis of peasant resistance against the state marginalizes the self-understandings of peasants.

[3]   For a highly useful analytical framework for the study of hegemony, see Comaroff and Comaroff (1991).

[4]   For an especially lucid analysis of liberal political theory and the way it shapes thinking on both freedom and resistance, see Mahmood (2005).

[5]   See Ortner (1997) for a more elaborated discussion of thick cultural analysis and its relevance to the study of political agency.

[6]   See "Epilogue" (Urla 2012a) for a fuller account of these events.

[7]   Tsing (2005) has made a similar argument. Lamphere's (2003) call for anthropologists to become savvier in dealing with the media is especially relevant in this regard.

[8]   Joseba Zulaika's experience in writing about political violence in the Basque country is a good example of the risks that can arise. See Zulaika and Douglass (1996) and Zulaika (1995).

[9]   For some examples of projects attempting to circulate ethnographic research to larger audiences, see The Open Anthropology Cooperative (http://openanthcoop.ning.com/) (accessed July 21, 2013), the open-access journal *Hau* (http://www.haujournal.org/index.php/hau/index), and the popular blog: Savage Minds (http://backupminds.wordpress.com/).

[10] Stine Krøijer in Holbraad and Pederson (2013) shows how even in planning meetings, activists at the Copenhagen Climate Summit used techniques for decision-making that decoupled individuals from action proposals to produce a constant state of desired "indeterminacy" that not only insulated protesters from possible criminal charges, but also created an open space for fluid ideologies and tactics.

[11] See, for example, the collection of essays in the AE Forum: IRB's: Bureaucratic Regulation and Academic Freedom, *American Ethnologist* 33 (4), November 2006.

[12] See Shweder (2006) for an informative account of the University of Chicago effort to exercise the legal right of universities to restrict the reach of IRB.

[13] For an activist ethnographic approach to the neoliberalization of the university, see Shear and Zontine (2010).

[14] The initiative was made possible by a Mellon Foundation Mutual Mentoring Grant (2013–2014), University of Massachusetts Amherst.

[15] As described in the proposal "Laboratory for Transformative Practice in Anthropology" by Jane Anderson, Sonya Atalay, Jackie Urla, and Whitney Battle-Baptiste.

[16] We borrow the term collaboratory from the Anthropology of the Contemporary Research Collaboratory (ARC) at UC Berkeley. See Collier (2007). Founded on a critique of the "individual project model" that informs most anthropological inquiry, the ARC is focused on fostering collaboration among researchers following a design studio process.

References

Abu Lughod, Lila. 1990. "The Romance of Resistance: Tracing Transformations of Power Through Bedouin Women." *American Ethnologist* 17 (1): 41–55. doi:10.1525/ae.1990.17.1.02a00030.

Abu Lughod, Lila. 1993. *Writing Women's Worlds: Bedouin Stories.* Berkeley, CA: University of California Press.

Albro, Robert, George Marcus, and Laura A. McNamara, eds. 2012. *Anthropologists in the Securityscape: Ethics, Practice, and Professional Identity.* Walnut Creek, CA: Left Coast Press.

Baquero, Antonio. 2012. "7.000 policías blindarán la cita del BCE en Barcelona." *El Periódico,* April 20.

Casas-Cortés, María Isabel, Michal Osterweil, and Dana E. Powell. 2008. "Blurring Boundaries: Recognizing Knowledge-Practices in the Study of Social Movements." *Anthropological Quarterly* 81 (1): 17–58. doi:10.1353/anq.2008.0006.

de Certeau, Michel. 1980. "On the Oppositional Practices of Everyday Life." *Social Text* 3 (1): 3–43. http://www.jstor.org/stable/466341.

Clifford, James, and George E. Marcus, eds. 1986. *Writing Culture: The Poetics and Politics of Ethnography.* Berkeley, CA: University of California Press.

Collier, Steven J. 2007. "The Collaboratory Form in Contemporary Anthropology." www.anthropos-lab.net

Comaroff, Jean, and John Comaroff. 1991. *Of Revelation and Revolution: Christianity, Colonialism and Consciousness in South Africa.* Vol. 1. Chicago, IL: University of Chicago Press.

Enslin, Elizabeth. 1994. "Beyond Writing: Feminist Practice and the Limitations of Ethnography." *Cultural Anthropology* 9 (4): 537–568. doi:10.1525/can.1994.9.4.02a00040.

Faubion, James D., and George E. Marcus, eds. 2009. *Fieldwork is Not What it Used to Be: Learning Anthropology's Method in a Time of Transition.* Ithaca, NY: Cornell University Press.

Fernández Gómez, Francisco de Paula. 2010. *Okupació a Catalunya: 1984–2009.* Manresa: Edicions Anomia.

Foucault, Michel. 1980. *The History of Sexuality. Volume 1: An Introduction.* Translated by Robert Hurley. New York: Vintage Books.

Foucault, Michel. 1982. "Afterword: The Subject and Power." In *Michel Foucault: Beyond Structuralism and Hermeneutics,* edited by Paul Rabinow and Hubert Dreyfus, 208–226. Chicago, IL: University of Chicago Press.

Geertz, Clifford. 1973. "Thick Description: Toward an Interpretive Theory of Culture." Chap. 1 in *The Interpretation of Cultures,* 3–30. New York: Basic Books.

Goldstein, Daniel. 2010. "Toward a Critical Anthropology of Security." *Cultural Anthropology* 51 (4): 487–517. doi:10.1086/655393.

Graeber, David. 2009. *Direct Action: An Ethnography.* Oakland, CA: AK Press.

Guattari, Felix. 1981. "Las Radios Libres Populares." In *De Las Ondas Rojas a Las Radios Libres,* edited by Lluís Bassets, 231–236. Barcelona: Editorial Gustavo Gili.

Hale, Charles R. 2006. "Activist Research v. Cultural Critique: Indigenous Land Rights and the Contradictions of Politically Engaged Anthropology." *Cultural Anthropology* 21 (1): 96–120. doi:10.1525/can.2006.21.1.96.

Hale, Charles R., ed. 2008. *Engaging Contradictions: Theory, Politics, and Methods of Activist Scholarship.* Berkeley, CA: University of California Press.

Harrison, Faye Venetia. 1991. *Decolonizing Anthropology: Moving Further Toward an Anthropology for Liberation.* Washington, DC: Association of Black Anthropologists.

Hemment, Julie. 2007. "Public Anthropology and the Paradoxes of Participation: Participatory Action Research and Critical Ethnography in Provincial Russia." *Human Organization* 66 (3): 301–314.

Hill, Jane H. 1985. "The Grammar of Consciousness and the Consciousness of Grammar." *American Ethnologist* 12 (4): 725–737. doi:10.1525/ae.1985.12.4.02a00080.

Holbraad, Martin, and Morten Axel Pedersen. 2013. *Times of Security; Ethnographies of Fear, Protest and the Future.* Hoboken, NJ: Taylor and Francis.

Holmes, Douglas R., and George E. Marcus. 2008. "Collaboration Today and the Re-Imagination of the Classic Scene of Fieldwork Encounter." *Collaborative Anthropologies* 1: 81–101. doi:10.1353/cla.0.0003.

Hymes, Dell H. 1972. *Reinventing Anthropology*. New York: Pantheon Books.

Jonsson, Hjorleifur. 2012. "Paths to Freedom: Political Prospecting in the Ethnographic Record." *Critique of Anthropology* 32 (2): 158–172. doi:10.1177/0308275X12437980.

Juris, Jeffrey S. 2007. "Practicing Militant Ethnography with the Movement for Global Resistance in Barcelona." In *Constituent Imagination: Militant Investigations, Collective Theorization*, edited by Stevphen Shukaitis, David Graeber, and Erika Biddle, 164–178. Oakland, CA: AK Press.

Juris, Jeffrey S. 2008. *Networking Futures: The Movements Against Corporate Globalization*. Durham, NC: Duke University Press.

King, Mary S. 2007. "Emergent Socialities, Networks of Biodiversity and Anti-Globalization." Doctoral diss., University of Massachusetts Amherst.

Kroijer, Stine. 2013. "Security is a Collective Body: Intersecting Times of Security in the Copenhagen Climate Summit." In *Times of Security: Ethnographies of Fear, Protest and the Future*, edited by Martin Holbraad and Morten Axel Pedersen, 33–56. Hoboken, NJ: Taylor and Francis.

Lamphere, Louise. 2003. "The Perils and Prospects for an Engaged Anthropology: A View from the United States." *Social Anthropology* 11 (2): 153–168. doi:10.1111/j.1469-8676.2003.tb00166.x.

Lassiter, Luke Eric. 2008. "Moving Past Public Anthropology and Doing Collaborative Research." *NAPA Bulletin* 29: 70–86. doi:10.1111/j.1556-4797.2008.00006.x.

Leacock, Eleanor. 1978. "Women's Status in Egalitarian Society: Implications for Social Evolution." *Current Anthropology* 19 (2): 247–275. http://www.jstor.org/stable/2741993.

Lipsitz, George. 2008. "Breaking the Chains and Steering the Ship: How Activism Can Help Change Teaching and Scholarship." In *Engaging Contradictions*, edited by Charles Hale, 88–114. Berkeley, CA: University of California Press.

Lyon-Callo, Vincent, and Susan Brin Hyatt. 2003. "Anthropology and Political Engagement." *Urban Anthroplogy* 32 (2): 133–146.

Mahmood, Saba. 2005. *Politics of Piety: The Islamic Revival and the Feminist Subject*. Princeton, NJ: Princeton University Press.

Marcus, George E., and Michael M. J. Fischer. 1986. *Anthropology as Cultural Critique: An Experimental Moment in the Human Sciences*. Chicago, IL: University of Chicago Press.

Nash, June C., ed. 2005. *Social Movements: An Anthropological Reader*. Malden, MA: Blackwell.

Ong, Aihwa. 1987. *Spirits of Resistance and Capitalist Discipline: Factory Women in Malaysia*. Albany: SUNY Press.

Ortner, Sherry. 1995. "Resistance and the Problem of Ethnographic Refusal." *Comparative Studies in Society and History* 37 (1): 173–193. doi:10.1017/S0010417500019587.

Ortner, Sherry. 1997. "Thick Resistance: Death and the Cultural Construction of Agency in Himalayan Mountaineering." *Representations* 59 (1): 135–162. doi:10.2307/2928818.

Osterweil, Michal. 2013. "Rethinking Public Anthropology Through Epistemic Politics and Theoretical Practice." *Cultural Anthropology* 28 (4): 598–620. doi:10.1111/cuan.12029.

Piqué i Batallé, David. 2009. *El fenomen okupa/antisistema circumscrit al districte de Gràcia (Barcelona), com a factor de risc per a la convivència i potencial focus de percepció d'inseguretat. Polítiques públiques de seguretat aplicables per evitar que esdevingui un problema d'ordre públic o delinqüencial i conseqüentment de solució únicament policial: La Síndrome de Sherwood* [The Okupa/Anti-system Phenomenon Limited to the Gràcia District (Barcelona), as a Risk Factor to Co-existence and Potential Source of Perceptions of Insecurity. Applicable Public Security Policies to Avoid the Development of a Problem of Public Order or Delinquency and Consequently the Only Political Solution: Sherwood Syndrome]. Masters thesis, Open University of Catalonia.

Rabinow, Paul, George E. Marcus, James D. Faubion, and Tobias Rees. 2008. *Designs for an Anthropology of the Contemporary*. Durham, NC: Duke University Press.

Radio Bronka. 2013. *25 Años de Bronka: El Libro de Una Radio, Tres Diales y Mil Cabreos*. Barcelona: Self-edited.

Reiter, Rayna R., ed. 1975. *Toward an Anthropology of Women*. New York: Monthly Review Press.

Rosaldo, Michelle, and Louise Lamphere, eds. 1974. *Woman, Culture and Society*. Stanford, CA: Stanford University Press.

Rylko-Bauer, Barbara, Merrill Singer, and John van Willigen. 2006. "Reclaiming Applied Anthropology: Its Past, Present and Future." *American Anthropologist* 108 (1): 178–190. doi:10.1525/aa.2006.108.1.178.

Scheper-Hughes, Nancy. 1995. "The Primacy of the Ethical: Propositions for a Militant Anthropology." *Current Anthropology* 36 (3): 409–440. http://www.jstor.org/stable/2744051.

Scott, James C. 1985. *Weapons of the Weak: Everyday Forms of Peasant Resistance*. New Haven, CT: Yale University Press.

Scott, James C. 1986. "Everyday Forms of Peasant Resistance." *Journal of Peasant Studies* 13 (2): 5–35. doi:10.1080/03066158608438289.

Scott, James C. 2009. *The Art of Not Being Governed: An Anarchist History of Upland Southeast Asia*. New Haven, CT: Yale University Press.

Shear, Boone W., and Angelina Zontine. 2010. "Reading Neoliberalism at the University." *Learning and Teaching* 3 (3): 32–62. doi:10.3167/latiss.2010.030303.

Shukaitis, Stevphen, David Graeber, and Erika Biddle, eds. 2007. *Constituent Imagination: Militant Investigations, Collective Theorization*. Oakland, CA: AK Press.

Shweder, Richard A. 2006. "Protecting Human Subjects and Preserving Academic Freedom: Prospects at the University of Chicago." *American Ethnologist* 33 (4): 507–518. doi:10.1525/ae.2006.33.4.507.

Sluka, Jeffrey A. 2000. "Introduction: State Terror and Anthropology." In *Death Squad: The Anthropology of State Terror*, edited by Jeffrey A. Sluka, 1–45. Philadelphia, PA: University of Pennsylvania Press.

Stacey, Judith. 1988. "Can There Be a Feminist Ethnography?" *Women's Studies International Forum* 11 (1): 21–28. doi:10.1016/0277-5395(88)900040.

Tedlock, Barbara. 2005. "The Observation of Participation and the Emergence of Public Ethnography." In *The Sage Handbook of Qualitative Research*, edited by Norman K. Denzin and Yvonna S. Lincoln, 3rd ed., 467–481. London: Sage.

Tsing, Anna Lowenhaupt. 2005. *Friction. An Ethnography of Global Connection*. Princeton, NJ: Princeton University Press.

Urla, Jacqueline. 1995. "Outlaw Language: Creating Alternative Public Spheres in Basque Free Radio." *Pragmatics* 5 (2): 245–261. http://elanguage.net/journals/pragmatics/article/view/405/337

Urla, Jacqueline. 2012a. *Reclaiming Basque: Language, Nation and Cultural Activism*. Reno: University of Nevada Press.

Urla, Jacqueline. 2012b. "Total Quality Language Revival." In *Language in Late Capitalism: Pride and Profit*, edited by Monica Heller and Alexandre Duchene, 73–92. Oxford: Routledge.

Visweswaran, Kamala. 1994. *Fictions of Feminist Ethnography*. Minneapolis: University of Minnesota Press.

Weldes, Jutta, ed. 1999. *Cultures of Insecurity: States, Communities, and the Production of Danger*. Minneapolis, MN: University of Minnesota Press.

Willis, Paul. [1977] 1981. *Learning to Labor: How Working Class Kids Get Working Class Jobs*. New York: Columbia University Press.

Wolf, Eric R. 1982. *Europe and the People Without History*. Berkeley, CA: University of California Press.

Zulaika, Joseba. 1995. "The Anthropologist as Terrorist." In *Fieldwork under Fire: Contemporary Studies of Violence and Survival*, edited by Carolyn Nordstrom and Antonius C. G. M. Robben, 206–222. Berkeley, CA: University of California Press.

Zulaika, Joseba, and William A. Douglass. 1996. *Terror and Taboo: The Follies, Fables and Faces of Terrorism*. New York: Routledge.

Upending Infrastructure: *Tamarod*, Resistance, and Agency after the January 25th Revolution in Egypt

Julia Elyachar

In this paper, I review recent contributions to theories of resistance and agency in the context of anthropology of Egypt. Drawing on ethnography conducted in Egypt after the January 25th Revolution and then after the election of Mohamed Morsi as President, I analyse the mass mobilization movement in Egypt called Tamarod. Tamarod *led the effort to have twenty-two million Egyptians sign a call for President Mohamed Morsi of the Muslim Brotherhood to step down, and mobilized an estimated twelve million to come on the street for a mass demonstration on 30 June, after which Morsi was removed from power. Rather than critique the notion of* Tamarod *as resistance, as a dupe of the Military, or as the legitimate voice of the Egyptian people and their agency, I argue that* Tamarod *made visible, and rendered available for political goals, a social infrastructure of communicative channels in Egypt. More generally, the paper shows concretely, and as concomitant processes, how agency is embedded in infrastructure and how infrastructure is upended in uprisings.*

After Structure and Agency

The relationship between structure and agency has haunted social theory from the start. But what happens to agency when we shift focus from structure to infrastructure?[1] In this article, I pursue this question by revisiting resistance. My interest is not to defend or critique the concept of resistance. Nor is it to use resistance as a diagnostic of power (Abu-Lughod 1990), to use ethnography to reveal political resistance in practices of everyday life (Comaroff 1985; Scott 1985), or as a substitute for in-depth ethnographic analysis (Ortner 1995). I draw on ethnographic fieldwork in Egypt conducted in a time when the concept of "resistance" proliferated as a mode of political action and political analysis to examine the relation between massive revolt, infrastructure, and social theory. To speak of theory in a time of such continuing upheaval, uncertainty, and death may seem pretentious or frivolous. I take inspiration to do so from my colleague Hanan Sabea, who called for analysis of the implications of the revolution for social theory in a brilliant article written at the end of 2011 (2012).

At the centre of my analysis is the mass mobilization movement in Egypt called *Tamarod*. *Tamarod* led the effort to have twenty-two million Egyptians sign a call for President Mohamed Morsi of the Muslim Brotherhood to step down, and mobilized twelve million to come on the street for a mass demonstration on 30 June, after which Morsi was removed from power.[2] Rather than critique the notion of *Tamarod* as resistance, as a dupe of the Military, or as the legitimate voice of the Egyptian people and their agency, I argue that *Tamarod* rendered visible, and upended for political goals, a social infrastructure of communicative channels in Egypt. Such an approach, I suggest, allows us to focus on agency as distributed, dialogic, and historically constituted. It furthermore allows us to pose different questions than whether or not the revolution "failed" or "succeeded".

These are admittedly big questions. To consider them, I will make a number of moves. First, I review key questions raised in the anthropology of resistance and agency in the Middle East. Second, I delink agency from structure to consider how what I call "social infrastructures" are upended and integrated into socio-technical platforms of revolt. Third, I note precedents for taking up the challenges posed to social theory by widespread revolt, in particular the analysis of political theorist Karuna Mantena in her book *Alibis of Empire: Henry Maine and the Ends of Liberal Imperialism*, where Mantena argues that the 1857 revolts against the Rule of the East India Company led to a massive shift in imperial social theory away from liberal utilitarianism. Fourth, I explore the implications of my approach to infrastructure for rethinking agency.

Let me start with resistance in the Middle East. In a classic article, "The Romance of Resistance", Lila Abu-Lughod draws on Foucault's observation that "where there is power, there is resistance" and that resistance "is never in a position of exteriority in relation to power" (1981, 95–96; cited in Abu-Lughod 42) to challenge romantic notions of resistance in the everyday (Comaroff 1985; Scott 1985). As such, Abu-Lughod argues, resistance offers an empirically tractable way to study power and is thus a "diagnostic of power" (1990, 42). Some twenty years later, in her powerful and influential ethnography of women's piety movements in Egypt, Mahmood showed the extent to which studies of resistance were linked to a problematic thematization of agency in poststructuralist feminist theory, in which "agency is conceptualized on the binary model of subordination and subversion" (Mahmood 2011, 14).

The problem of agency and resistance took on new urgency since the January 25th Revolution in Egypt. One of Abu-Lughod's secondary questions, about the "relationship between scholarship or theorizing and the world-historical moment in which it takes place", became even more relevant (1990, 42). Sabea raised this issue as well in her 2012 article that I referred to above (2012). According to Karuna Mantena, in fact, widespread revolt poses challenges to theory whether we are aware of them or not at the time.

Between 2010 and 2013, no one needed tools of critical analysis to reveal resistance in Egypt. Resistance had become a native concept for countless activists and academics, in Egypt and around the world. "Resist Everywhere!", for example, was the title of a subpage of the website *Jadaliyya*, in which instances of resistance were documented and described from across the Middle East, most prominently in Istanbul's Taksim Square and Cairo's Tahrir Square. The concept of resistance proliferated in sites that extended, like *Jadaliyya*, across the activist/academic boundary (Haddad 2012). What does it mean to have long-standing themes of resistance and agency reappear as part of academic-activist discourse?

In and Off the Street, July 2012

My appointed ethnographic field in July 2012 was former Yugoslavia, where protests against austerity and theft by corrupt government officials were widespread. Enraged citizens in Croatia and Slovenia, like in Greece and in Spain, echoed calls on the streets of Tahrir back in January 2011: elected leaders had stolen their national wealth and robbed them of their birthright. Protests kicked off during the January 25th Revolution had set a precedent and a challenge taken up the world over. I did not plan to go to Egypt for fieldwork per se: I went first and foremost to see friends who were ill, recovering from the revolution, and engaging in the mundane. I was reticent to relate to my friends as informants in a time of bullets, jail, and death. And yet, over time, I realized that those weeks by the wayside, during a pause in what had seemed to be the main action, during apparent non-events, had their own importance.

I landed in Cairo that July of 2012 soon after Mohamed Morsi had been elected President.[3] Street battles were over, for now; streets quiet—for now. But eloquent signs of the revolution were etched in my friends' bodies. Ahmed's hands told tales of what had passed. They shook, especially before his morning coffee and cigarette, usually in the early afternoon. We met for the first time around a small rickety metal table at one of the coffeehouses along a small cobblestone street of downtown Cairo. Soon into our talk, a bottle clattered to the ground from a table nearby. To me it was just one sound among many of a busy Cairo street. But Ahmed jumped in his chair, with the classic startle reflex of post-traumatic stress disorder. Street battles downstairs from what had been calm homes set on fire nerve endings damaged in years past. Under Nasser and Sadat, arrests and torture had logic: if you spoke out, you risked arrest and torture. But under Mubarak in the later years especially, security proliferated and became random; young men going out on the street increasingly feared that they could be picked up at random and tortured, even to death (Ghannam 2011, 2012; Kandil 2012). Such was the case with Khaled Said, whose brutal beating to deal on the streets of Alexandria was one spark for the January 25th Revolution.[4]

If Ahmed's hands told tales, it was Omar's eyes that spoke. Or rather his eye that was not there, and the other one that was there but could not see. Omar had been blinded by Egyptian police during one of the evenings of street clashes when a reported eighty Egyptians were blinded by the police.[5] I met him one evening at a gathering at a friend's house. He came in quietly, sat down, and played his 'oud for hours. I listened to his music with joy and silence; his friends were solicitous that he not be bothered with conversation with a stranger.

Downtown streets told other tales. Traders selling wares on the main streets of downtown Cairo crowded the sidewalks and spilled onto the street, in a triumph of the "informal economy" that Mubarak had kept so assiduously at bay in places of symbolic power of the state. Streets that had seemed impossibly crowded in the 1990s now inspired nostalgia, from a time as far away as images from 1960s Egyptian films, in which a car or two or three would glide blissfully down wide empty streets. Tahrir was blocked off much of the time that July, full of monuments and clusters of people sitting in and peddlers selling revolution memorabilia. Artists congregated on the square, for a festival, making the streets public, blocking the traffic from one direction or another. Driving south one day to visit my sick friend Lamia, we passed by a hospital where Mubarak was reputed to lay. But no one knows if he is really there, said Said, a friend of a friend who was driving me there. No one knows where he is. Further down the street, lawyers held a protest spilling onto the street. And in a refrain one heard often that month, "Why did we make the revolution? Salaries are low, and prices are higher. What is going to happen? What was the point?"

Strikes and takeovers were everywhere, in the universities, in factories, on the streets. We drove through New Ma'adi, by the offices of telecom, the sandy expanse of land from which sprouted massive dishes of Telecom, and then down Palestine street by the offices of GUPCO (Gulf of Suez Petroleum Company, a joint venture between BP and the Egyptian General Petroleum Company). Streets were far less crowded here but marked by revolution as well. As we approached the entrance to GUPCO, chants rang out, and we came to a halt on a smoothly paved street, grass and small trees growing behind brick walls in front of neat five-story family buildings. "The people want the downfall of the regime! The workers want resignation of the management!" Workers were occupying the administration offices at the end of the working day.

Sounds of the street faded away as I entered Lamia's house. Rays of the late afternoon sun turned a deep yellow through the dust panes of neglected windows. Lamia was a doctor who had saved many lives and served many Egyptians rich and poor; her life was now coming to an end from a metastasized cancer. Here, the revolution appeared differently: in the medicine she needed disappeared from the pharmacies, in her fear of entering the hospital, and in the quantities of tubes of crème for joint inflammation she handed me from her sickbed in a rumbled plastic bag one day. I laughed at her excess, as she told me about the multiple treks of her *bowab* (doorman) to pharmacies all over southern Cairo, in search of stock. All too soon, I came to appreciate her foresight: the German-Egyptian factory that produced the medicine had shut down in Cairo, perhaps for good.

Passing by GUPCO on the way back to downtown that day, the workers had all home. Along the low brick walls around the entire area owned by Telecom splashed graffiti of the Ultras, Egypt's football support clubs who took to the streets to support the revolution and paid a high price with their lives. A sign warning the public to stay away merged into drawings of a fist, the image of a martyred young revolutionary, and the phase: "Long life the revolution". That night I joined friends at an impromptu club where every Tuesday, a well-known DJ played music through the night, and the veterans of street battles and organizing took a respite from the year that had gone by, and the year to come: "Welcome to Egypt under the Rule of the Muslim Brothers!", Ahmad joked.

Neoliberalism and Resistance under Mubarak

Could these details of life on the street in Cairo in the summer of 2012 be understood in terms of resistance? The temptation is there. From strikes in the headquarters of GUPCO, to the graffiti of Ultras on the walls of Telecom, to the organizing of art events in Tahrir, to the joyous release of dancing together under the rule of the Muslim Brothers on a street where friends had died and battles been fought—all could be read as resistance. But resistance against what? If, as Abu-Lughod suggested, resistance is a diagnostic of power, what is the form of power against which that resistance is shaped? In many critical studies of the past twenty years, resistance is often revealed in juxtaposition to impositions of "neoliberalism". Resistance can then match the diffuse nature of neoliberal power, in which violence is not directly exercised, but forms of conduct instilled. But events of these years exceed the frame of neoliberalism as it has been conceived in social analysis of the Middle East (Ambrust 2012; Denis 2010; Elyachar 2005; Mikdashi 2011; Mitchell 2011).

Development programmes advanced by international organizations, NGOs, and the state in Egypt in the 1990s to promote microenterprise and microlending were a laboratory for experiments in neoliberal remaking of law, finance, and subjectivities (Elyachar 2005). In that experiment, new kinds of financial products, legal devices, banking instruments, and economic rationalities were created and subsequently drawn on in a much broader effort to "neoliberalize" strategic sectors of the Egyptian economy such as finance and telecommunications. In the 2000s, these efforts were led by Gamal Mubarak, son of President Hosni Mubarak, who was educated in economics at the American University in Cairo and abroad, had worked in London in investment banking, before returning to Egypt. As is now well known, he and his allies were given power to remake markets according to the precepts of neoliberal economic theory and, concomitantly, to sell off assets of the public sector, including vast swathes of public lands, to friends and allies at fire-sale prices, in a pattern repeated around the Mediterranean region in the name of neoliberalism and austerity, and related to waves of protest cum resistance there as well.

Implementation of structural adjustment agreements and neoliberal policies was spotty under Mubarak through the 1990s. Agreements were often agreed to but not carried out. As late as 1998, four state-owned banks in Egypt still accounted for 80% of commercial deposits in Egypt (OECD n.d., 1, I.4). Ten years later, privatization had put "about half of the banking sector in private hands" (International Monetary

Fund 2007, cited in Elyachar 2012). When Mubarak agreed to plans that he did not implement for privatization of financial services, for example, this could be seen as a kind of "resistance" without outright defiance to dictates of a "strong" USA and International Monetary Fund (IMF). But in relation to its own citizenry, the Egyptian state was the "strong" player in relation to a "weak" Egyptian citizenry, which had acceded to a trade-off of political acquiescence in return to relative economic stability since Abdul-Nasser (Kandil 2012). Here, too, it was possible to analyse manoeuvring without outright political defiance among Egyptian citizenry as "defiance" or "weapons of the weak". Use of "trickery" and "ruse" (*hiyla*) was common under Mubarak, and drew on long semiotic and linguistic resources (Elyachar 2005). Stories of the great Egyptian writer 'Abdallah al-Nadam (1994) noted a rich tradition of trickery or resistance by the poor and downtrodden, a tradition documented across the Arab world by al-Najar (1981) and Khawwam (1992).

When development organizations worked together with the Mubarak regime to "empower the poor" through self-reliance and microenterprise, Egyptian borrowers used their loans for ends different than those intended: they used loans that would have gotten them into hopeless debt with no chance of repaying to buy apartments and get married; they forged order forms from public sector stores to get their loans released from the bank; and made their microenterprises into shells for wealthy businessmen seeking new ways to escape government taxes (Elyachar 2005, 216). This proliferation of trickery could also be seen as weapons of the weak and resistance (Scott 1985). Apparently technical fights over business arrangements and the flow of loans were simultaneously a struggle over power; empowerment debt was itself a mode of reconfiguring fields of power (217). And yet, events since 2010 exceed the framework of neoliberal forms of development, in which mechanisms of persuasion, the creation of new economic subjectivities, and new socio-technologies of empowerment are more prominent than violence in the exercise of power.

Writing the Revolution

I was not in Egypt during the revolution. It felt more appropriate to help organize channels for others to bring together their ethnographies and analyses of what was underway than to write myself. Together with Jessica Winegar, Farha Ghannam, and Angelique Haugerud, I helped organize conference panels at the American Ethnological Society Spring Conference, and then at the American Anthropological Association Annual Meeting (AAA), regarding the Egyptian Revolution and the Arab Spring in 2012.[6] Winegar and I then assembled the outcomes of that AAA panel, and other writings, in a "Hotspot" on Egypt for the website of the journal *Cultural Anthropology*. We did not realize it at the time, but our efforts were part of an emergent shift towards new kinds of infrastructures of knowledge creation and dissemination characteristic of this period (Anderson 2013; Muehlebach 2013).

The notion that President Morsi would be elected, let alone removed from power, was impossible to contemplate in 2011, the year of the January 25th Revolution. Anthropologists trying to write about the revolution faced dilemmas and sometimes anguish. How to write when so many voices—of friends, relatives, and acquaintances—had been silenced forever? Uncertainty prevailed, for those living in Cairo as well as abroad. Comments about uncertainty of the kind I heard from friends and informants in July 2012 were pervasive in 2011 as well. How to know what was going on? Dominant concepts in social sciences about the Arab world—that Arabs were passive, that Egyptians were patient, that Arab states were "too strong"—had all collapsed. What analytic frames would take their place? It is striking to note that resistance was not prominent here. Some anthropologists had spent years, months, or weeks organizing the events leading up to the Revolution—some had felt impelled to fly in for the occasion and write up what they found. Some found it hard to leave home, and just went to Tahrir and back again every day. Others turned to the piled-up tasks of junior faculty anywhere: classes that had to be taught, grades that needed to be turned in, tenure files that had to be assembled, bills that needed to be paid, and parents whose health crises needed to be attended to—all this fit into days otherwise occupied with organizing strikes at the university, volunteering at clinics for victims of SCAF violence in Tahrir, of virginity tests, and testifying at hearings.[7]

Colleagues returned to the day-to-day job of getting institutions functioning again. Some turned back to books and articles set aside for a year. For some, activism had become a full-time occupation. It was hard to turn the Revolution into the means of academic reproduction: papers, conference presentations, and books. For some it felt like exploitation of those who had sacrificed so much to even try to write. For others, writing ethnography while taking part in historical events felt impossible. For those who tried, it was hard to finish a paper taken up, over and over again, in moments wrested from days each radically different from the day before. The establishment of narrative becomes a problem.

The founding of *Jadaliyya*, around the time of the January 25th Revolution, marked a crucial shift in the infrastructure of knowledge creation and dissemination about the region. Jadaliyya brought together the immediacy of the blog with the scholarly apparatus of a journal and the politics of committed public intellectuals writing in English, Arabic, and French (Haddad 2012). Others wrote new blogs, books of blogs, and analysed the output of others (Anderson 2013). The lines between scholarly research and the individual blog became blurred.

In Egypt, ethnography showed how theft by the Mubarak regime was experienced as a violent attack on the nation and the body. Ghannam's ethnography drew on the notion of exemplary figures of Egyptian popular culture, and the ways in which they animated long-standing experiences of violence on the street, in the home, and in the market. She analysed the *baltagiyya*, or thugs, who were brought by to attack protestors in Tahrir, in a decisive day of the Revolution (Ghannam 2011, 2012). Native concepts of manhood, such as *baltagiyya* and *gada'*, are socially and historically constituted exemplaries of social action in the present (Elyachar 2005; Ghannam 2012). *Baltagiyya* use violence in daily life to bully, coerce, or extort. The *gada'*, by way of contrast, is an exemplary figure, a young man of the popular classes whose social action is oriented around the protection of his community and community resources (Elyachar 2005; Ghannam 2012). Ghannam's informants in 2011 were sympathetic to Mubarak when they heard his penultimate speech on state TV; but when Mubarak had lost their allegiance due to his use of the *baltagiyya* on unarmed protestors, the same images on state TV could no longer move them (2012).

When the Mubarak regime became identified among Ghannam's informants with the *baltagiyya* it hired, it lost legitimacy (*shara'iya*; a term that would become crucial in 2013) among her informants who had, just one day before, remained sympathetic to Mubarak. These Egyptian notions of legitimate and illegitimate forms of exercising violence and control over women's bodies and over the street were a harbinger of trends in the years to come, leading up to 30 June 2013. Ghannam's research illustrated the extent to which indigenous categories such as the *gada'* are exemplaries and a part of the semiotic resources of the Egyptian people (Agha 2002; Elyachar 2011; Kockelman 2010). The indexical quality of these exemplaries gave them more power in action aimed at influencing the near future (Guyer 2007).

If Ghannam's research showed symbolic constitution of violence, Walter Ambrust analysed violent attacks on symbols, and attempts to determine their interpretive range by fiat. Ambrust's research focused on martyr images, of those whose lives were lost in the course of the revolution, and the image of the martyr Sally Zahran in particular (2012). At the beginning of Ambrust's paper, Sally Zahran's image on a "martyr poster" without a headscarf is being scratched out. A shouting match ensues. Why? Martyr images were a key medium for political contests in the months following the revolution, Ambrust shows. Sally Zahran was perhaps the most recognizable martyr, and a "productive prism" through which social tensions festering in the Mubarak era and brought into "active play in the revolution" became clear. The martyrs, bodies on whom the violence of Mubarak's regime was projected, are symbols channelling action in the motivation of social action in the present. Any image of a martyr "projected into discourse or public space" was an "implicit invitation to anyone viewing it to declare a position on what it signifies" (Ambrust 2012).

To look at the signs, relationships, and channels through which the contests of the Egyptian Revolution have been fought out, to take seriously contests over symbols as a crucial arena of politics, and to pay attention to the peculiar temporality in which people acting in a revolutionary situation find themselves need not erase from view the emotions, arguments, fears, and bloody bodies in the various squares of Cairo. It was difficult for anthropologists—foreigner and Egyptian alike—to write of all this and to effectively convey the power of the outrage, distress, and disappointment. The growing violence and chaos were frightening, the lack of effectiveness of the Muslim Brotherhood government in solving basic problems of infrastructure, livelihood, and security frustrating. Political hope and imagination had been aroused, and then crushed.[8] If we analyse the signs and channels through which the outrage was conveyed, does that mean neglecting the outrage itself? I think not.

Tamarod as Infrastructure

Resistance, I have said, was not an important native or analytic concept in early ethnography of the January 25th Revolution of 2011. The situation was different in 2012.

Resistance was everywhere—but more in the "field" than in academic journals. The most clear case, once again, is "*Tamarod*", or "*tamarrud*", usually translated as "Rebel" (or rebellion). *Tamarod* led the extraordinary mobilization of some twenty-two million Egyptians to sign a call for President Mohamed Morsi of the Muslim Brotherhood to step down or call early elections, and to come on the street for a mass demonstration on 30 June, of which twelve million did so (though these numbers are the subject of political contestation). Organizers of *Tamarod* took inspiration from two earlier petition drives in Egypt, one in support of Saad Zaghloul in 1919, one led by El Baradei in 2009 and 2010, and also from the work of the community advocacy group Askar Kazeboon (Askandar, Jadaliyya, 30 June 2013). *Tamarod* claimed to have gathered twenty-two million discrete signatures with national ID numbers on forms calling for Morsi to step down or call early elections. Organizers of *Tamarod* recount having learned from the shortcomings and successes of the January 25th Revolution, and the ways in which its mobilization was heavily centred in cyberspace, without deep connection to embodied mobilization on the street (Iskandar 2013).

To deploy the tools of critical analysis and social theory for analysis of *Tamarod* raises certain problems, some of which have been characterized as challenges of "paraethnography", when "native" concepts of informants so closely overlap with those of ethnographers. This challenge is in addition to some of the other issues raised in Egypt since the revolution about the politics of social science research—who are informants versus who has the privilege of writing and publishing. But rather than critiquing the notion of *Tamarod* as resistance, or as an instance of naïve and apolitical, or misguided revolutionary Egyptian youth being taken advantage of by the military and Mubarak *fuloul*, as proliferated in media analyses in July 2013, I would like to think about these events from a different frame of reference, and to consider the youth of *Tamarod* as workers in what I have called elsewhere a social infrastructure of communicative channels (Elyachar 2010).

Infrastructure is something we tend to think about when it breaks down—when bridges collapse, when roads have potholes, when telephones do not work. A new body of work on infrastructure influenced by the perspective of science and technology studies loosely conceived has shown this in varying ways (Barry 2005, 2006; Larkin 2008; Otter 2004, 2002). The near collapse of the financial system in the USA in 2008 helped bring the question of financial infrastructures into public debate; ongoing crises in public finance have helped keep it there. Infrastructure is a classic "public good", a set of resources available to all and the use of which does not decrease its availability to others (Samuelson 1954; Stigliz 1999). At the same time, infrastructure can fail to fulfil the promise of connectivity (Harvey and Knox 2012); be designed to block, impede, or exclude flows of people, goods, and resources, as is most clear in apartheid South Africa and Israel/Palestine; or privatized in part or in whole, through the building of toll roads or the securitization of rising tuition in a public university.

Economies cannot function without infrastructure. This commonplace is known in all kinds of economic theory. In Volume II of Marx's *Capital* ([1885] 1956), for example, Marx devotes a great deal of attention to how infrastructure is central to the circulation and realization of value: the creation and maintenance of infrastructure is not itself directly productive of value and yet is essential to the capitalist system of production. Nor, from the standpoint of a neoclassical theory of value, does infrastructure create price. But if you cannot link a product to the market, then that product will spoil and become worthless. If you cannot link a buyer to a seller, then a market cannot function. Infrastructure—roads, airports, ports, and bridges—allows producers to realize the potential economic value of a product. Linking buyers and sellers entails more than physical transportation of goods in space over roads and railroads, as in classic accounts of the role of railroads in nineteenth-century economic expansion. More is entailed than the transport of signals across telephone lines or mobile phones. Infrastructure matters for rethinking social theory after 2010.

When talking about connections and their importance, Cairenes often use the words ʿalaqat (relations) or wasta (intermediaries). The concept of wasta is pervasive in Egypt and many other Middle Eastern societies. Cultivating wasta entails great investments of time and energy among poor people but is not a phenomenon of the poor alone: Wasta is central to life among elites as well (Inhorn 2004). A concept similar to wasta is found in other cultures: the native concepts of guanxi in China (Hutchings and Weir 2005; Kipnis 1997) and nepotism in the USA (Bellow 2004) both refer to the importance of cultivating networks of personal connections in order to get things done. Wasta was sometimes glossed in social science research as corruption or patronage and was an object of concern for those studying the conduct of business in the Middle East (Hutchings and Weir 2005; Loewe, Blume, and Speer 2008).

Anthropologists often glossed this phenomenon in terms of networks. Some used spatial metaphors to denote different kinds of networks: there are both "horizontal networks" and "vertical networks" (Hoodfar 1997, 229–230; Singerman 1995). Wasta can denote a vertical network that reaches into state or other powerful bureaucracies. The notion that networks created by poor women of Cairo are at the core of the political life of Egypt has been argued by political scientist Singerman (1995). In Singerman's view, informal networks "organize, coordinate, and direct individual actions … they aggregate the interests of the shaʿb [the people]" (1995, 133). Such indirect ways of expressing needs and interests were a key part of social analysis about Egypt under Mubarak.

Here, my interest is not in looking at networks as an interlocking web of individuals, as a coordinator of individual interests, or as a framework for action. Instead, I am interested in communicative channels that I maintain are an outcome of practices of sociality on their own terms, as a distinct object of inquiry. There are a number of clues within and around anthropology to how such an approach might look. The first possibility is to think of channels in a way similar to how Bourdieu writes about practical reason, in terms of "beaten tracks" or "pathways that are really maintained and used" (1990, 35). If we take an approach common in linguistics since Jakobson, then we can think of channels as existing wherever there is physical proximity and psychological contact between a speaker and addressee that allows them to send and receive messages ([1960] 1990). We could also take an approach common in communications theory, where a channel usually refers to the medium used to convey information, or to transmit a signal of some kind from a transmitter to a receiver

(Shannon 1948). More recent work in network theory refers to channels without the concept of a fixed transmitter or receiver and builds instead on a random network model constructed with theories from statistical physics (Franceschetti and Meester 2007, 1–2).

But once we recognize that channels can rest on social convention as much as a specific one-to-one physical or psychological connection, we can understand "channel" as anything that relates a signer to an interpreter "such that a sign expressed by the former may be interpreted by the latter" (Kockelman 2009). Understood in this way, we can see communicative channels as a collective resource for all kinds of semiotic communication in addition to language per se (Elyachar 2010; Kockelman 2009). And once we shift focus away from *humans* brought together in networks to analysis of *channels* themselves as a relatively stable outcome of human practices, then different kinds of metaphors come to mind as to what this might imply. Specifically, we can think of *sets* of channels as infrastructure. These infrastructures, I want to suggest, were a central part of the January 25th Revolution and of events since. And this approach to infrastructures and channels provides a way to think about sign, meaning, agency, and political economy in Egypt in the same analytic field.

The Politics of Platforms

When technologies such as mobile phones and Internet services were shut down by the Mubarak regime in January 2011 in an attempt to halt social action, Egyptians turned to and patched together alternative platforms that were less visible under neoliberal reform but which remained nonetheless. Here I refer to traditional forms of communicative infrastructures such as landlines, but also to communicative channels created and maintained through visits, gossip, and socializing and discussed in local concepts such as *wusta* or connections. This multi-layered infrastructure of communicative channels played into and became visible in the January 25th Revolution, and then around the world. Communicative infrastructures became available to people with highly divergent agendas across the political spectrum. Resistance and revolution come into view as social technologies that lend themselves to use towards quite different ends. This is a different perspective than the early story of the January 25th Revolution as a Facebook Revolution.

Social media in Egypt emerged in the context of a broad restructuring of telecommunications, including the licensing of private companies to provide mobile phone and Internet services. Remaking telecommunications infrastructure was instituted as an essential element of creating a neoliberal free market economy in Egypt in the 2000s. This entailed more than engineering decisions. Competing models of the market, socio-technologies of market life, technological innovations, engineering dilemmas, and historical layering of infrastructures in Egypt came together to create a functioning platform for communications and telecommunications.

The January 25th Revolution was the first time that the Internet and mobile phone services in a country were shut down. Platforms and communicative infrastructures become visible in moments of breakdown (Larkin 2008; Star 1999). When Mubarak turned off the Internet and mobile phones, he inadvertently made visible the relational and multi-layered nature of infrastructures of communicative channels. Egyptians activated older technologies like boat phones and satellite communications. They created pirate and alterative infrastructures (Simone 2004), patching together whatever worked to keep up contact with each other and with the outside world. It became possible to see how mobile phones, Internet, landlines, patterns of sociality in neighbourhoods, and marches that called neighbours and friends down to the street were working together as a communicative infrastructure.

One powerful image from the Revolution shows a group of young men in Tahrir Square at night, crouched over a group of mobile phones "in a tangle of extension cords" wired into stores opened up by owners around Tahrir Square, under spotlights patched by activists into the state grid of streetlights, charging their mobile phones. This image captures the way in which poor people in Cairo and other cities of the global South patch their way into infrastructure of the state on a daily basis (Elyachar 2005; Simone 2004). The Revolution showed how these practices are linked into geek networks and other forms of expert computer and engineering knowledge as well. These capacities represent the extraordinary knowledge base of Egyptian youth, and the ways in which those capacities are being completely wasted by Egypt and many countries facing the structural unemployment of a generation of indebted and educated young people with few if any job prospects.

Organizers of *Tamarod* built on this infrastructure with skill and tenacity. In fact, we can see them as workers in the maintenance and extension of the massive social infrastructure of communicative channels in Egypt already drawn on in the January 25th Revolution. *Tamarod* worked to make visible and create new means to express outrage among most sectors of Egyptian society with the way that Morsi and the Muslim Brotherhood had abused the aims and aspirations of the Egyptian people in the January 25th Revolution. In the process, they created new means to achieve the long-term aims of the January 25th Revolution—bread, freedom, and justice—with a shorter term goal: removing Morsi from power through early elections.

Creation of new means does not fully control composition of ends (Kockelman 2007). Others had greater power to mobilize these communicative infrastructures as a means for the achievement of their own short- and medium-term ends. Accounts in July 2013 after Morsi was removed from office often portrayed the organizers of *Tamarod* as dupes, either through inexperience or political naïveté. But this is too simple. The social infrastructure mobilized and extended by *Tamarod* to express political will was, like any infrastructure, available for utilization by other users with greater agency over composition of ends: here, most notably, the Egyptian military, and wealthy Egyptian businessmen associated with the Mubarak regime, such as Coptic businessman Nabil Sawaris, who gleefully told of having anonymously funded *Tamarod* to help overthrow Morsi. *Tamarod* made visible and thus accessible to others with different political agendas a vast communicative infrastructure they did not control. But that in no way eliminates the astonishing accomplishment, technical skills, and wasted economic potential of Egyptian youth. With *Tamarod*, to use another kind of analytic language, gesture as dialogic action became overt political symbol turned to political aims (Mead [1934] 1967). Here, I also draw on Taylor's analysis of dialogic action and its turn to political ends in the case of Tiananmen Square (1991), and as has happened in other cases of political revolt in Egypt, ranging from the 'Orabi Revolt, the Bread Riots, and others. The fact that particular agendas controlled the composition of ends does not mean that there is no agency in the composition of means.

Temporality, Crisis, and the Time that Never Comes

One of the most powerful ethnographies of revolution after January 25th came from anthropologist Hanan Sabea. Sabea's writing for the AAA in 2012, subsequently part of the *Cultural Anthropology* 2012 Hotspot on Egypt, conveyed something of the intensity of the experience of the iconic eighteen days, and the challenges the Revolution posed for social theory. From this perspective, once again, the problem is not to see how to explain the January 25th Revolution and to see how to make sense of it in terms of our social science concepts, but rather to see what challenges the Revolution and its aftermath pose for theory itself, even while honouring and mourning all of those who have lost their lives.

It was no easier to write about the revolution a year later, with its "more dramatic events of loss, death, violence, exhaustion, incomprehension, yet also of hope, creativity, resilience, and determination" (Sabea 2012). Sabea turned to Law to open her piece: "pains and pleasures, hopes and horrors, intuitions and apprehensions, losses and redemptions, mundanities and visions, angels and demons, things that slip and slide … change shape or don't have much form at all, unpredictabilities" (2004, 3). We need to change focus, away from resistance as we usually conceive of it, away from social structure and the apparent main action. How do we analyse things that slip and slide, change shape, or do not have much form at all?

Sabea begins by bringing out temporal aspect of the revolution, as what she called time out of time. The revolution—an event—reappears as an iteration of Fridays, each named. Here, already, we see the extent to which the "event" is embedded in its own implicit extended temporality, in a logic we cannot see in our anthropological analyses of "the social" (cf. Caton 2006). An Egyptian participant observer in 2011 makes sense of events in terms of events gone by last week, last Friday, and events in years past leading up to the revolution (Sabea 2012). And those events, in turn, make sense in a longer history of revolt and revolution in Egypt: the Bread Riots of 1977, the Free Officers coup of 1952, the Revolution of 1919, and the Orabi Rebellion of 1881–1882. For members of the Muslim Brothers, events fall in a different geography, beyond the boundaries of the Egyptian nation-state, before the colonial era. Months of mobilization, the demonstrations of 30 June, the coup/popular removal of Morsi, and immediately the past year appears as a time of calm, with the upswing of violence after 1 July.

Contingency, and the full specificity of localized detail, emerges as a crucial player in Sabea's account of decisive moments of the Revolution. Most important for social theory is that the "decisive moment" which everyone waits for—the moment when life settles into a new steady state—never arrives. The "rupture" of crisis, deeply linked as it is to critical inquiry itself (Roitman 2013), when all is revealed and the future arrives, is ever postponed. The revolution and the years to follow reveal a radical instability in the relation of meaning, event, and social structure.

In a field of knowledge predicated on notions of the social, social structure, and a relatively stable equilibrium or social reality to analyse, what kind of social theory can help us make sense of a world in which crisis never resolves, and the tail event of the impossible and unimaginable has become the stuff of everyday life? Here, I draw on the words of Mohamed el-Erian, who lends coherence to some of his and others' musings about the nature of financial markets after 2008, in which the "unimaginable and the unthinkable" had become the stuff of the everyday, to find insights for thinking, together with John Law, about Egypt after January 25th. Rather than being exceptions or "noise" to the underlying signal of meaning uncovered by critical inquiry, these unstable moments, or "transients" (Kockelman 2010), turned out to be crucial for the new world in which we live. And in this world, we need to turn to different methodologies for making sense of the noise and the irreconcilable contrasts.

Communicative systems are built in order to transmit signal, which we can then receive and interpret as meaningful (Shannon 1948). Channels help keep out "noise", which distract us from meaningful signal. This notion of signal and noise has been finding huge application within the financial world in the wake of the 2008 crash. Much of what had been tuned out as "noise" became the main deal. For example, el-Erian wrote about Occupy Wall Street as important "noise" that had to be listened to, and taken seriously, by financial markets and politicians (2011). In the Middle East as well as in financial markets, outlier events tuned out as "noise" turned out to be indicative of the everyday to come. In both finance and politics, the "outlier event" or tail event that was statistically irrelevant in our models of social structure or normal distribution curves has come to proliferate, to dominate new realities, and to pose questions for theory as well.

Revolt, Agency, and Social Theory

There are precedents for Sabea's challenge to take up the implications of widespread revolt for social theory. A brilliant example is the work of historian of political thought Karuna Mantena in her analysis of the "Indian Rebellion of 1857" against the rule of the East India Company and the challenges the rebellion posed for imperial social theory. While I cannot here review the details of Mantena's brilliant argument in *Alibis of Empire: Henry Maine and the Ends of Liberal Imperialism*, for my purposes what matters is the link she shows between revolt, strategies of rule, and rethinking of social theory (2010, 49).[9] The fact that the rebellion could be sparked by a rumoured use of pork and beef fats to grease newly issued cartridges for rifles, offending both Hindu and Muslim sensibilities, revealed what Henry Maine wrote of as "terrified fanaticism" springing from "inscrutable sentiments" (Mantena 2010, 49–50). The rebellion challenged utilitarian liberal theories that had been, until then, inextricably linked to the logic of empire, progress, and development of the natives. Late empire then saw the rise of a culturalist model developed by Maine, as the basic mode of explanation of difference. Social theory of late empire then "sought to project a model of the social as the privileged arena for understanding the nature and dynamics of society" (Mantena 2010, 49–50). Reading Mantena on India, we are reminded of the extent to which anthropological theories of resistance still tend to assume that "political institutions and structures of authority … express, rather than constitute, underlying social relations" (2010, 68).

Anthropologists and other social analysts have inherited that privileging of the social. What to do with our proclivities for social structure or culture as the implicit pair of agency when control of political institutions is the object of contestation on the street? How to proceed when agency over interactions and their outcomes is at least as important as agency over actions? What happens to writing when what you thought you had to write seems, now, to be so different than what you need to see, to grasp, to take part in, to live through. When the intensity of that underway seems a rupture from all we were thinking and analysing before?

I offer some initial suggestions by following Kockelman and Agha, who suggest that we see agency as a "name for a variable dimension of human conduct, a capacity whereby social actors … effectively transform a context of action and thereby enlarge the sphere of their enablements" (Agha 2007, 387). The Egyptian Revolution and its aftermath can then be seen from a theoretical perspective as a (bloody, embodied, tragic, confusing and frustrating) process through which a collective, distributed, historically constituted subject transforms the very context of social action, and "thereby enlarge[d] the sphere of their enablements" (Agha 2007). Here, we can see how agency is embedded in infrastructure. And we can see as well how infrastructure is upended in uprisings—especially when we recall that infrastructure encompasses more than pipes and wires.

Sabea is here once again helpful. She turns to the work of John Law, and his own use of Wittgenstein's concept of the hurly-burly to make sense of the revolution. When so much is thrown in the air, in this as in other revolutionary times, it becomes hard to fix meaning to the ongoing course of daily life. Those living through the events come to find aspects of life that were once regularized and predictable completely unended. They become part of what Wittgenstein called, in a famous passage, the "hurly-burly" of life. We can only describe human behaviour, Wittgenstein writes, by

> sketching the actions of a variety of humans, as they are all mixed up together. What determines our judgment, our concepts and reactions, is not what one man is doing now, an individual action, but the whole hurly-burly of human actions, the background against which we see any action'. (Wittgenstein 1981, no. 567)

In the hurly-burly, we have bloody battles that also involved control over what Kockelman calls "representational agency" in a time when the "epistemological norms of a community and different communities have [radically] different understandings of what counts as a good reason for one's representations" or analyses or explicitly stated explanations of what is underway (Kockelman 2007, 383). This we saw, in 2012 and 2013, in fierce battles over the meaning of key terms such as coup or revolution, in conflicting explanations of what happened after 30 June 2013, or in the fights over numbers of demonstrators on the street, and petitions signed, during the experience of the *Tamarod* mobilization. It could be heard in arguments about whether or not the Revolutions "achieved anything", such as sceptical statements often heard on the street that the revolution "brought nothing" (*magabitsh 7aga*).[10]

Who will have the power of representational agency over the events of the past years in Egypt? What are the implications of the different claims being made, of who "takes up the claim, and presume[s] different actions" (Kockelman 2007, 384)? These questions are life and death issues. The revolts of the Arab world since 2010 and their bloody aftermaths pose as great a challenge to social theory as those posed by the revolt of 1857. We are left trying to think the unthinkable through concepts that cannot adequately explain what is going on. How can social theory address the apparent permanency of a prolonged impermanency in the face of ongoing reconfiguring of power? What kind of theory can make sense of these ongoing historical events, as those events are unfolding?

Power, social theory tells us, is hidden; it needs to be signified. Resistance, in turn, has been almost too readily accessible as a sign. Can we find new indices of resistance, not just in dragged heels (as in the resistance literature of the1980s) or raised fists (as in the revolts of 2011)? That said, power is rarely hidden on the streets of Cairo today; The subtleties of neoliberal persuasion are hard to come by in what is left of Syria or Iraq. The proliferation of resistance as political slogan is not matched by its power as an analytic for making sense of the world remade by the January 25th Revolution. In that world, it helps to recall, agency is also embedded in infrastructures upended in revolt and always distributed.

Acknowledgements

Partial funding for the research on which this article is based was provided by the Institute for Money, Technology, and Financial Inclusion, University of California, Irvine. Thanks to audiences at Harvard University and the "Retreat on Foundations of Social Agency," Max Planck Institute, as well as to Lila Abu-Lughod, Nathan Coben, Essam Fawzi, Paul Kockelman, Sean Mallin, Tomaz Mastnak, Bill Maurer, Ajantha Subramanian, and two anonymous reviewers for their help and comments on earlier drafts. All remaining errors are my own.

Notes

[1]   My thanks to Ajantha Subramanian for this formulation.
[2]   As I show below, these numbers are the object of intense debate.
[3]   I have conducted fieldwork in Cairo since 1993, for four years in the 1990s, and then on regular shorter visits since, and keeping up with friends and informants by phone and Internet.
[4]   For one account, see http://english.ahram.org.eg/NewsContent/1/0/43995/Egypt/0/Khaled-Said-The-face-that-launched-a-revolution.aspx.

[5]   For one account of these battles and attacks on heads and eyes by the police, see http://www.
        egyptindependent.com/news/police-reportedly-shoot-out-activists-right-eye-mansour-
        street-clashes.

[6]   This section is adopted from "Writing the Revolution", online "Hotspot" on Egypt, edited by
        Jessica Winegar and myself, which in turn built on a panel about Egypt we co-organized at the
        AAA in 2012, as part of a double panel together with Farha Ghannam on the Arab Spring.

[7]   SCAF, or the Supreme Council of the Armed Forces, is made up of senior officers in the Egyp-
        tian Army. SCAF assumed power in Egypt after President Hosni Mubarak's resignation on 11
        February 2011, and again on 3 July 2013, when Morsy was deposed. SCAF did not formally
        rule Egypt after 3 July: the military leadership used a civil government with a formal head of
        the state as a legal front. I am grateful to an anonymous reviewer for reminding me of this
        important fact.

[8]   I am indebted to Lila Abu-Lughod for the line of thought and formulation in this paragraph.

[9]   In the wake of the rebellion, the Crown assumes direct responsibility over the Company's
        former Indian territories and, in its first official act, "explicitly put forth a doctrine of non-
        intervention as the direct principle of British rule" (Mantena 2010, 40).

[10]   I am indebted to an anonymous reviewer for this insight, and for pointing me to Laidlaw's
        work on agency, ontology, and efficacy (Laidlaw 2010).

References

'Abd Allah, Yehiya al-Tahir. 1994. *Al-Kitabat at-kamila*. Al-Qahira: Dar al-Mustaqbal al-'Arabi. al-
        Nadim.

Abu-Lughod, Lila. 1990. "The Romance of Resistance: Tracing Transformations of Power Through
        Bedouin Women." *American Ethnologist* 17 (1): 41–55.

Agha, Asif. 2002. "Honorific Registers." In *Culture, Interaction and Language*, edited by Kuniyoshi
        Kataoka and Sachiko Ide, 21–63. Tokyo: Hituzisyobo.

Agha, Asif. 2007. "Comment." *Current Anthropology* 48 (3): 387–388. (Comment on Kockelman,
        Agency, 2007).

al-Nadim, 'Abdallah. 1994. *'Abdallah al-Nadim: al-'Adad al-kamila li majallat alustadh*. Cairo: al-
        Hi'ya al-'amma l-il-kitab.

al-Najar, Mohamed Rajib. 1981. *Al-shuttaar wa al-'ayyarun fi al-turaath al-'arabi*. Al-Kuwait: Al-
        maglis al-watani lil-thaqafa wa al-fanoun wa al-aadaab.

Ambrust, Walter. 2012. "The Ambivalence of Martyrs and the Counter-Revolution." In *Revolution
        and Counter-Revolution in Egypt a Year after the January 25th Revolution*, edited by Julia Elya-
        char and Jessica Winegar. Hotspot on Egypt, *Cultural Anthropology*. http://culanth.org/
        fieldsights/213-the-ambivalence-of-martyrs-and-the-counter-revolution

Anderson, Mark Allen. 2013. "Writing Ethnography in Post-Mubarak Egypt." Connected in Cairo.
        Accessed April 10, 2013. http://connectedincairo.com/2013/04/10/writing-ethnography-in-
        post-mubarak-egypt/

Barry, Andrew. 2005. "The British-Georgian Case: The Baku-Tbilisi-Ceyhan Pipeline." In *Territoires,
        environnement et nouveaux modes de gestion: La gouvernance en question*, edited by B. Latour
        and C. Gramaglia, 105–118. Paris: Centre National de la Recherche Scientifique.

Barry, Andrew. 2006. "Technological Zones." *European Journal of Social Theory* 9 (2): 239–253.

Bellow, Adam. 2004. *In Praise of Nepotism: A History of Family Enterprise from King David to George
        W. Bush*. New York: Anchor.

Bourdieu, Pierre. 1990. *The Logic of Practice*. Translated by Richard Nice. Stanford, CA: Stanford Uni
        versity Press.

Caton, Steven. 2006. *A Yemen Chronicle: An Anthropology of War and Mediation*. New York: Hill and
        Wang.

Comaroff, Jean. 1985. *Body of Power, Spirit of Resistance: The Culture and History of a South African People*. Chicago, IL: University of Chicago Press.

Denis, Eric. 2006. "Cairo as Neoliberal Capital? From Walled City to Gated Communities." In *Cairo Cosmopolitan: Politics, Culture, and Urban Space in the New Globalized Middle East*, edited by Diane Singerman and Paul Amar, 47–72. Cairo: American University in Cairo Press.

El-Erian, Mohamed A. 2011. "Listen to the Occupy Wall Street Movement." *Huffington Post*, October 11. http://www.huffingtonpost.com/mohamed-a-elerian/occupy-wall-street-_b_1004222.html

Elyachar, Julia. 2005. *Markets of Dispossession: NGOs, Economic Development, and the State in Cairo*. Durham, NC: Duke University Press.

Elyachar, Julia. 2010. "Phatic Labor, Infrastructure, and the Question of Empowerment in Cairo." *American Ethnologist* 37 (3): 453–464.

Elyachar, Julia. 2011. "The Political Economy of Movement and Gesture in Cairo." *Journal of the Royal Anthropological Institute* 17 (1): 82–99.

Elyachar, Julia. 2012. "Before (and After) Neoliberalism: Tacit Knowledge, Secrets of the Trade, and the Public Sector in Egypt." *Cultural Anthropology* 27 (1): 76–96.

Foucault, Michel. 1981. *The History of Sexuality. Volume One: An Introduction*, translated by R. Hurley. Harmondsworth: Penguin Books.

Franceschetti, Massimo, and Ronald Meester. 2007. *Random Networks for Communication: From Statistical Physics to Information Systems*. Cambridge: Cambridge University Press.

Ghannam, Farha. 2011. "Mobility, Liminality, and Embodiment in Urban Egypt." *American Ethnologist* 38 (4): 790–800.

Ghannam, Farha. 2012. "Meanings and Feelings: Local Interpretations of the Use of Violence in the Egyptian Revolution." *American Ethnologist* 39 (1): 32–36.

Guyer, Jane. 2007. "Prophecy and the Near Future: Thoughts on Macroeconomic, Evangelical, and Punctuated Time." *American Ethnologist* 34 (3): 409–421.

Haddad, Bassam. 2012. "Jadaliyya: A New Form of Producing and Presenting Knowledge in/of the Middle East (Interview with Julia Elyachar)." In *Revolution and Counter-Revolution in Egypt*, edited by Julia Elyachar and Jessica Winegar. Cultural Anthropology, Hotspots, January. http://www.culanth.org/?q=node/486

Harvey, Penny and Hannah Knox. 2012. "The Enchantments of Infrastructure." *Mobilities* 7 (4): 521–536.

Hoodfar, Homa. 1997. *Between Marriage and the Market: Intimate Politics and Survival in Cairo*. Berkeley, CA: University of California Press.

Hutchings, Kate and David Weir. 2005. "Guanxi and Wasta: A Comparison." *Thunderbird International Business Review* 48 (1): 141–156.

Inhorn, Marcia D. 2004. "Privacy, Privatization, and the Politics of Patronage: Ethnographic Challenges to Penetrating the Secret World of Middle Eastern, Hospital-Based In Vitro Fertilization." *Social Science and Medicine* 59 (10): 2095–2108.

International Monetary Fund. 2007. "Arab Republic of Egypt—2007 Article IV Consultation Preliminary Conclusions of the IMF Mission." Accessed October 20, 2007. http://www.imf.org/external/np/ms/2007/091207.htm

Iskandar, Adel. 2013. "Tamarod: Egypt's Revolution Hones Its Skills." *Jadaliyya*, June 30. http://www.jadaliyya.com/pages/index/12516/tamarod_egypts- revolution-hones-its-skills

Jakobson, Roman. [1960] 1990. "The Speech Event and the Function of Language." In *On Language*, edited by Linda R. Waugh and Monique Monville-Burston, 69–79. Cambridge, MA: Harvard University Press.

Kandil, Hazem. 2012. *Soldiers, Spies, and Statesmen: Egypt's Road to Revolt*. London: Verso.

Khawwam, Rinih. 1992. *Al-Siyasah wa al-hilah 'inda al-'Arab: Raqa'iq al-hilal fi daqa'iq al-hiyal*, al-Tab'ah 2. London: Dar al-Saqi.

Kipnis, Andrew B. 1997. *Producing Guanxi: Sentiment, Self, and Subculture in a North China Village*. Durham, NC: Duke University Press.

Kockelman, Paul. 2007. "Agency: The Relation Between Meaning, Power, and Knowledge." *Current Anthropology* 48 (3): 375–401.

Kockelman, Paul. 2010. "Enemies, Parasites, and Noise: How to Take Up Residence in a System Without Becoming a Term in It." *Journal of Linguistic Anthropology* 20 (2): 406–421.

Laidlaw, James. 2010. "Agency and Responsibility: Perhaps You Can Have Too Much of a Good Thing." In *Ordinary Ethics: Anthropology, Language, and Action*, edited by Michael Lambek, 143–64. New York: Fordham University Press.

Larkin, Brian. 2008. *Signal and Noise: Media, Infrastructure, and Urban Culture in Nigeria*. Durham, NC: Duke University Press.

Law, John. 2004. *After Method: Mess in Social Science Research (International Library of Sociology)*. New York: Routledge.

Loewe, Markus, Jonas Blume, and Johanna Speer. 2008. "How Favoritism Affects the Business Climate: Empirical Evidence from Jordan." *Middle East Journal* 62 (2): 259–276.

Mahmood, Saba. 2011. *Politics of Piety: The Islamic Revival and the Feminist Subject*. Princeton, NJ: Princeton University Press.

Mantena, Karuna. 2010. *Alibis of Empire: Henry Maine and the Ends of Liberal Imperialism*. Princeton, NJ: Princeton University Press.

Marx, Karl. [1885] 1956. *Capital: A Critique of Political Economy, vol. 2*. Edited by Frederick Engels. Translated by I. Lasker. Moscow: Progress.

Mead, George Herbert. [1934] 1967. *Mind, Self, and Society: From the Standpoint of a Social Behaviorist (Works of George Herbert Mead)*. Chicago, IL: University of Chicago Press.

Mikdashi, Maya. 2011. "Neoliberalism's Forked Tongue." Jadaliyya. Online publication, Accessed May 17, 2011, http://www.jadaliyya.com/pages/index/1606/

Mitchell, Timothy. 2011. *Carbon Democracy*. New York: Verso.

Muehlebach, Andrea. 2013. "On Precariousness and the Ethical Imagination in Sociocultural Anthropology." *American Anthropologist* 114 (2): 297–311.

OECD. n.d. "Egypt National Investment Reform Agenda Workshop Privatisation Session: Reforming State Owned Banks, Draft Background Document, OECD/MENAOECD Investment Programme." Accessed June 2006. http://www.oecd.org/dataoecd/18/57/36807408

Ortner, Sherry B. 1995. "Resistance and the Problem of Ethnographic Refusal." *Comparative Studies in Society and History* 37 (1): 173–193.

Otter, Christopher. 2002. "Making Liberalism Durable: Vision and Civility in the Late Victorian City." *Social History* 27 (1): 1–15.

Otter, Christopher. 2004. "Cleansing and Clarifying: Technology and Perception in Nineteenth Century London." *Journal of British Studies* 43 (1): 40–64.

Roitman, Janet. 2013. *Anti-Crisis*. Durham, NC: Duke University Press.

Sabea, Hanan. 2012. "A 'Time out of Time': Tahrir, the Political and the Imaginary in the Context of the January 25th Revolution in Egypt." In *Revolution and Counter-Revolution in Egypt*, edited by Julia Elyachar and Jessica Winegar. *Cultural Anthropology* Hotspots. Accessed July 2014. http://culanth.org/fieldsights/211-a-time-out-of-time-tahrir-the-political-and-the-imaginary-in-the-context-of-the-january-25th-revolution-in-egypt

Samuelson, Paul A. 1954. "The Pure Theory of Public Expenditure." *Review of Economics and Statistics* 36 (4): 387–389.

Scott, James. 1985. *Weapons of the Weak: Everyday Forms of Peasant Resistance*. New Haven, CT: Yale University Press.

Shannon, C. E. 1948. "A Mathematical Theory of Communication." *Bell System Technical Journal* 27: 379–423, 623–656.

Simone, AbdouMaliq. 2004. "People as Infrastructure: Intersecting Fragments in Johannesburg." *Public Culture* 16 (3): 407–429.

Singerman, Diane. 1995. *Avenues of Participation: Family, Politics, and Networks in Urban Quarters of Cairo*. Princeton, NJ: Princeton University Press. http://archive.today/mq3D7

Star, Susan Leigh. 1999. "The Ethnography of Infrastructure." *American Behavioral Scientist* 43 (3): 377–391.

Stiglitz, Joseph E. 1999. "Knowledge as a Global Public Good." In *Global Public Goods: International Cooperation in the 21st Century*, edited by Inge Kaul, Isabelle Grunberg, and Marc A. Stern, 308–325. New York: Oxford University Press.

Taylor, Charles. 1991. "The Dialogical Self." In *The Interpretive Turn: Philosophy, Science, Culture*, edited by D. R. Hiley, 304–314. Ithaca, New York: Cornell University Press.

Wittgenstein, Ludwig. 1981. *Zettel*. 2nd ed. (Edited by G.E.M. Anscombe and G.H.V. Wright). Oxford: Blackwell.

Resistance and the City

Dan Rabinowitz

The mass demonstrations that took place in 2011 in major cities worldwide, dubbed here Contemporary Metropolitan Protest (CMP), varied in terms of the issues tackled and the political efficacy attained, but featured similarities in style, mobilization patterns and the use of traditional and social media. The similarities explain the tendency among commentators and researchers to treat CMP as a coherent category. The variation, on the other hand, raises questions about conceptual and theoretical idioms used so far in the analysis of CMP. The article begins by scrutinizing "resistance"—an idiom introduced to anthropology in the 1980s to theorize peasant response to metropolitan policies—and its recent emergence in the depiction and analysis of CMP. Highlighting the strengths and limitations of the term, I use the rise and fall of CMP in Tel Aviv in 2011 and 2012 as an example of how the implicit logic of aggression and response, so central to earlier employment of the notion of resistance, can be hijacked by defensive regimes that seek to delegitimize and criminalize critique, thus forcing CMP to decline and implode.

Introduction

The mass demonstrations, rallies and sit-ins that took place in 2011 in, among others, Tunisia, Morocco, Egypt, Portugal, Spain, Greece, Israel and the USA, labelled herein Contemporary Metropolitan Protest (CMP), saw one-off gatherings rapidly transforming into weeks-long processes involving millions of real and virtual participants. Characterized *inter alia* as "protest", "resistance", "struggle", "movement", "mobilization", and associated with verbs such as "indignation", "occupation", and "contention", CMP has since attracted considerable attention from social scientists (see, for example, Collins 2012; Juris 2012; Razsa and Kurnik 2012; Schechter 2012; Knight

2013; Marom 2013; Moghadam 2013; Perugorria and Tejerina 2013; Rosenhek and Shalev 2013; Sotirakopoulos and Sotiropoulos 2013; Tejerina et al. 2013; Theodosso-poulos 2013; Elyachar 2014; Gledhill 2014; Theodossopoulos 2014).[1]

The quick succession of CMP events in 2011, and their rapid domination of political arenas and mediascapes-inspired activists, supporters, sympathizers and voyeurs onlookers at local levels as well as internationally. A view of CMP as a coherent entity, perhaps even a singular event with different localized manifestations, became widespread.[2]

Simultaneity and inspiration notwithstanding, the 2011 events were by no means homogenous. In Tunisia, the self-immolation of a street vendor harassed by a police officer in a small town on 17 December 2010 soon inspired mass rallies against repres-sion and a general strike by lawyers. Within a month the president departed and an interim government took office, leading later to the abolishment of the secret police and to extraordinary general elections. In Egypt mass rallies advocating the end of tyranny and nepotism began on 25 January 2011, leading to the resignation of the pre-sident seventeen days later, the drafting of a new constitution and first-ever meaningful general elections within a year. Morocco saw demonstrations that began on 20 Febru-ary 2011 and focused on the lack of civil liberties, failures in the education and health-care systems, inequalities, corruption and an exclusionary executive system (Desrues 2013). Months of unrest followed, eventually prompting the king to offer constitutional reforms.

In Portugal, 300,000 demonstrators marched in Lisbon and elsewhere on 12 March 2011 to protest EU directives of austerity measures, the economic crisis and to promote reforms in labour laws. The prime minister resigned eleven days later, giving currency to new patterns of political participation and awareness (cf. Baumgarten 2013). In Spain, 15 May 2011 became a day of mass demonstrations and sit-ins in Madrid and over sixty other locations. Protests, which focused on unemployment, welfare cuts and the ailments of the stagnant two-party political system (Perugorria and Tejerina 2013), continued throughout 2011 and eventually involved millions. In Greece, mass protest against political corruption and austerity measures demanded by the EU on 25 May 2011 grew exponentially. By June they drew crowds estimated at 500,000 coun-trywide (BBC 2011). Protestors rejected cooperation with all political parties and trade unions, but the energy they generated soon infiltrated mainstream politics, leading to the resignation of the prime minister on 10 November. Italy saw 200,000 demonstra-tors gather on 15 October 2011 in Rome and other cities[3] to express solidarity with the Spanish protestors, to rally against inequality, Berlusconi's policies and the dispropor-tional clout of international financial institutions on Italian politics.

In Israel, a case which I shall analyse with more detail in the analytic section of this article, tents set up in Central Tel Aviv on 14 July 2011 by youngsters indignant with housing prices and the shrinkage of the welfare state soon became the nucleus of the largest, longest and most geographically diverse protest the country ever saw. 2 Septem-ber saw 450,000 participants—an impressive 6% of the entire population—demon-strating in many towns across the country (see Marom 2013; Greenberg 2013; Herzog 2013; Misgav 2013; Ram and Filk 2013; Rosenhak and Shalev 2013; Shenhav

2013). A Reform Commission established by the government submitted a comprehensive report to the ministry of finance six weeks later.[4] Discernible shifts occurred in public debates on the economy and social justice, and the protest is widely seen as the main factor behind the success two years later of "Yesh Atid", a new centrist-right party that secured 16% of the parliamentary vote in 2013, following which its leader Yair Lapid became the minister of Finance. On 17 September 2011 protestors came to Zuccotti Park near Manhattan's Wall Street, sparking a movement known as Occupy Wall Street (OWS), branding the slogan "We are 99%." Rallying against social and economic inequality, corruption and the undue power of financial corporations over government, protestors were eventually forced out of the park in November, whereby some of them attempted to temporarily occupy banks, corporate headquarters, colleges and university campuses. And while the impact of "Occupy" on mainstream US politics remains unclear, the OECD's move in July 2013 to curb tax havens in an attempt to force multinational corporations to pay more taxes[5] has been directly attributed to the protest of 2011.

The temporal proximity of the events of 2011 and the central role played in them by young urbanites partly explain the tendency of journalists and other commentators to represent CMP through a unifying narrative. But the considerable diversity of the issues raised in them and the uneven impact they had on the respective political arenas where they played out across the globe suggest that the phenomenon is better analysed as an amalgam of morphologically analogous events, akin mostly in terms of mobilization patterns, expressive style and organizational outlines.

Those who see CMP as a wholesome movement with a clear trajectory, able and willing to overthrow tyranny, undo corruption, restructure dysfunctional politics and defeat neoliberalism and capitalism in the process might find this sceptic view of CMP's homogeny ideologically flawed. But if political efficacy is genuinely sought, hopes and wishes must not interfere with analytical lucidity. Seeing CMP as local variants of a coherent global campaign is unwarranted and risky. In Egypt in 2012, a conservative clerical regime took over a protest movement initially staged by secular liberals. In Israel in 2013, a party with a stark neoliberal agenda reaped the benefits of a protest initially designed to represent underprivileged strata and the welfare state. These are but two of many cautionary tales. They indicate that obscuring ideational differences and overemphasizing internal unity in CMP can play into the hands of agents harbouring divergent, sometimes conflicting, values and political agendas.

The first part of this article seeks to address this conundrum by examining "resistance". The term, first introduced to anthropology by James Scott in the 1980s, became a linchpin in an imaginative and timely attempt to theorize indigenous peasant responses to market-oriented, neoliberal dictums in "developing" countries, both before and after decolonization (Scott 1979, 1985). Its (re)emergence as a recurring analytical tool in recent social scientific work on CMP, including in the present volume, merits critical attention.

The second part of the article, which focuses on the dynamics by which the extraordinary wave of protest that swept Israel in the summer of 2011 was hijacked into insignificance by the hegemony, illustrates the ease with which the logic of "resistance", complete with the emotional load and intuitive sensibilities which it evokes, can be turned on its head by those who seek to marginalize dissent into submission. The article concludes with a call for more conceptual work, backed by better ethnographic effort that might enable to avoid such hijack, enhance CMP's potential and improve its chances to bring positive change.

Resistance Revisited

Resistance made its debut as an analytical concept in anthropology in the late 1970s, as part of the Foucauldian turn. Foucault's famous assertion "where there is power there is resistance" reverberates through Scott's pioneering work on peasants in recently deco-lonized states in South East Asia (1979, 1985). Scott looked at the response of village communities to metropolitan forces seeking to commandeer their land, exploit their labour and manipulate them to toxic dependencies on seed supplies, agricultural credit and markets they could neither shape or influence. Standing up to these encroachments, he argued, is seldom overt. Rather, it is built on strategic, passive-aggressive non-compliance: faked incompetence, deliberate miscommunication, foot-dragging, orchestrated laziness, chronic disregard to time frames and a general aura of unpredictability. Such tactics may appear docile and compliant in public, but in the safety of more congenial circumstances they become hubs of dissent and insu-bordination.[6] Conscious of the need to conceal the actual drive behind their ploys, sub-alterns are nevertheless lucidly cognizant of what in fact goes on as they lead smug masters and officials up the garden path. These are the features of the syndrome Scott deftly labelled "resistance".

The influence of Polanyi's attentiveness to local traditions is apparent. Resistance, Scott asserts, is often premised on local moral economies, and may in fact prolong and strengthen traditional patterns of patronage and inequality. He takes issue, however, with Gramsci's view of subaltern consent. While Gramsci sees hegemony as built on people's inclination to suspend critique of power, thus imbuing the prevail-ing structure with inertia and legitimacy, Scott leaves little room for such concurrence. Villagers, he argues, are keenly and consistently aware of the injustices that shape their lives. It is their limited ability to challenge power—not some inadvertent mechanism that begets accord—which channels them towards tacit subversion.

Scott's attribution to subalterns of willingness to stand up to coercion and ability to respond to it with passive-aggressive subtlety was welcomed by anthropologists, many of whom had come across these patterns in their own field researches but lacked the theoretical framework to articulate them. The notion of "the weapons of the weak" was similarly ideologically appealing to a discipline committed to the discovery of inge-nious and progressive institutions among indigenous communities (see Brown 1996). It also suited anthropology's ideological preoccupation with the downtrodden, sooth-ing nagging guilt among researchers whose careers benefit from representing poverty and subjugation, but who rarely have the opportunity to help those represented.

The 1990s saw "resistance" becoming a popular theoretical and analytical social scientific concept in the 1990s (see, for example, Price 1983; Gal 1995; Hirsch 1995; Merry 1995; Starn 1995; Rabinowitz 1997; Levi 1998), and the emergence of a body of work some have since dubbed "resistance studies".[7] But proliferation did not necessarily bring theoretical lucidity. Ortner, referring to the issue almost two decades ago, blamed the lack of rigour in resistance studies on what she saw as an absence of ethnographic perspective (Ortner 1995). Hollander and Einwohner's subsequent essay "conceptualizing resistance", which reviews a decade and a half of works by anthropologists, sociologists and political scientists, laments the fact that

> many writers using the language of resistance may not in fact be talking about the same thing. Scholars have used the term "resistance" to describe a wide variety of actions and behaviors at all levels of human social life (individual, collective, and institutional) and in a number of different settings, including political systems, entertainment and literature, and the workplace. Indeed, everything from revolutions […] to hairstyles […] has been described as resistance. (Hollander and Einwohner 2004, 533–534)

This theoretical slackness partly explains the tendency to depict all action on the part of disenfranchised communities and individuals as one and the same. Put crudely, the implication is that come the right moment, all downtrodden persons anywhere will find a voice, express their pent-up sensibilities, unite around new identities, discover their capacities to act and finally take action to destabilize the system that oppressed them.[8] This composite approach to resistance, and its tendency to essentialize both agents of domination and their victims, is perilous. Flattening ideological, operational and constitutive variations on either side of the divide, it tends to overlook the complicity, collaboration and hybridization so often bred by power structures (Brown 1996).

Virtually all research on resistance recognizes that action on the part of subalterns comes as a response to aggression on the part of those in power. The result is a knee-jerk emotional affinity with the subaltern and an idealized sense of "justice for the weak" that compliments the more descriptive "weapons of the weak". But the presence of a power gradient between aggressor and respondent, important as it may be for the initial settings for defiance, does not cover the entire spectrum that constitutes resistance. Scott's work was in fact so influential precisely for its willingness to go beyond the basic structural imbalance and for its ability to highlight two additional facets of resistance: the serendipitous concealment on the part of those resisting; and the ignorance, misapprehension and smug naiveté of those resisted.

Between Resistance and CMP

CMP of course is about people speaking truth to power and standing up to injustice, sometimes putting themselves at harm's way in the process. As such it has some similarities with the phenomena observed and theorized by Scott and other social scientists who worked in similar circumstances. First, in both contexts, predatory forces of domination pose as promoters or at least defenders of ostensibly benign policies such as "land reform", "modernization", "abundant agricultural credit", "economic restructuring", "free market", "growth" and "mobility", to name but a few. Second, in CMP as well as in peasant resistance, activists are fuelled by disillusionment with such promises, which they identify as hollow at best, duplicitously abusive at worst. Third, in either context, activists perceive and articulate their political objectives as comprehensive and systemic. Seeking to transcend locality and temporal specificity, they see themselves as committed to redressing root causes of injustice, not only their symptoms. They are convinced, in short, that their protests are relevant to many.

But CMP, typically organized and attended by young, well-educated urbanites, is also significantly different from the prototypes that served as models for Scott's theory. First, most participants in CMP are rights-holding citizens or residents of states purporting to be liberal and democratic. Public protest is but one of a variety of means for political expression and agency potentially available to them. The metropolitan settings in which they operate, particularly social media, afford them easy access to wide audiences, and initial protection from real-time attempts by the authorities to silence them. This of course contrasts with settings of the type analysed by Scott, where peasants are excluded from metropolitan politics, have limited opportunities to shape their own fate and enjoy little protection from predatory regimes and the retribution they are able to inflict.

Second, compared to peasant resistance, which tended to emphasize quite focused issues and was anchored in more uniform and stable local identities, affiliations and cultural inventories, CMP is infinitely more diverse and heterogeneous. The events of 2011 saw anti-capitalism indignation alongside social-democratic sensibilities. Progressive socialists marched along distributive justice welfarists, reformers of electoral systems collaborated with environmentalists, protectors of consumer rights heuristically joined unionists and so the list goes on. This variety of issues has obvious strategic value. It forges new alliances which, even if conjunctural, often inspire solidarity and fires up participants' imaginations with promises of mass empowerment and imminent change. Its homogenizing force attracts the popular media, emancipating it from the tedious task of analysing nuance. Last but not least, its inclusivity brings numbers.

But diversity can also be fragile. The unity of purpose and performative coherence that was abundant in the early phases of the wave of protest in 2011, when ruling politicians and regimes were targeted as stereotyped nemesis, began disintegrating as soon as real political opportunities emerged and more concrete demands and strategy had to be formulated. When such moments appeared, the lack of representational governance which characterized so many CMPs became a hindrance. Political momentum soon crumbled into procedural mayhem, in some cases unleashing competition between individual leaders and activist formations over symbolic and political capital. This threw into relief the analytical and operational limitations of buzzwords such as "reform", "transformation", "resistance", "horizontal democracy", "mobilization" and "rebellion", to name but a few.

A third set of differences has to do with the role played by race and ethnicity. Self-evident and self-explanatory in the context of colonized and recently de-colonized regions, ethnicity and race as it were came with the territory; not so in CMP. Few campaigns in 2011 acknowledged race, ethnicity or religion as major signifiers. Some in fact intentionally obfuscated them. Protests in Cairo in early 2011, for example, initially heralded slogans like "we are all Egyptians," designed to stir away from ethno-religious pitfalls, especially the Muslim versus Coptic divide. The leaders of the three-month-long protest in Tel Aviv in the summer of 2011 were similarly adamant in their insistence not to condemn or otherwise refer to Israel's occupation of the West Bank and Gaza or the long-standing discrimination and alienation of Mizrahim—Israelis with roots in Arab countries (see Misgav 2013; Shenhav 2013). These critiques were silenced even though many activists believed they should be voiced, probably due to the prevailing thought that mobilizing numbers—the most significant sign of momentum and success—demands avoiding issues that might divide a crowd that came out to support a "social" (read: socio-economic) protest.

Fourth are differences in the choreography and orchestration of defiance. The subalterns depicted by Scott were masters of covert resistance. Seldom resorting to declarative rebellious acts, their retort to domination prioritized passive non-compliance, miscommunication, ostensible stupidity, incompetence and indolence. Their public displays were cover-ups for sentiments of insubordination, acted out in the safety of their own milieus. CMP, in contrast, clearly prefers exposure, energetically advertising its critique, exaggerating calls for reform and accentuating cries for confrontation and rebellion. Loud and often deliberately provocative, its compelling need to broadcast, coupled with its novel and dynamic patterns of recruitment, has become its main defining feature.

Finally, there are important differences in the use of territory and space. CMP comes at the heels of a long tradition of modern urban protest and unrest. The 1848 spring of nations was instigated by a network of cities that included Frankfurt, Milan, Warsaw and Paris, the latter featuring again in 1870 with the famous commune. St. Petersburg in 1917; Seattle and Shanghai in 1919; Chicago, Mexico City, Bangkok and Paris in 1968; the recent chronology of urban protest in Latin America, the hundreds of cities that held simultaneous marches against the war on Iraq in February 2003 and many others are some of the precursors of the phenomenon recently labelled rebel cities (Harvey 2013). In short, modern cities, their political legacy and their sociocultural facilities offer brilliant public *fora* and excellent meeting opportunities for massive protest.

Land rights and agricultural practices were of course seminal also for peasant struggles, with space and territory assigned significant symbolic load and political import. This notwithstanding, particular rural locations did not often become emblematic "places" in the sense alluded to by Lefebvre (1991) or by McCannel (1999). If anything, symbolic gestures that took place in rural peripheries—Gandhi's and Mao's marches in the 1940s come to mind—homogenized space, using its volume, uniformity and relevance to millions as a powerful but ultimately abstract mobilizing device. CMP, on the other hand, often has protestors taking over major metropolitan landmarks, transforming them in the process into symbolic place-making junctures. Parks, squares, boulevards, roundabouts and bridges were invaded, turning to iconic emblems in the process. Acts of occupation and take-over were imbued with transcendental meanings. Place names, followed by temporal reference—a year, a month, a day—became metonymies of processes and visions activists, supporters and onlookers could identify with. Tahrir Square (Cairo, Egypt) January 2011, Pearl Roundabout (Manama, Bahrain) February 2011, Puerta del Sol square (Madrid, Spain) May 2011, Syntagma Square (Athens, Greece) June 2011, Rothschild Avenue (Tel Aviv, Israel) July 2011, Zuccotti Park, then Battery Park, then Wall Street (New York City, USA) September 2011, University Square (Bucharest, Romania) February 2012 and many others have emerged as hyphenated lexical components of a new language of space–time indices.[9]

A summary so far: contemporary urban protest diverges from earlier instances of resistance in at least five dimensions: affiliation and identity of participants; diversity of issues tackled; the role of race and ethnicity; concealment versus broadcast; and the use of space and territory. These differences, compounded by the analytical ambiguity of the term "resistance", underline the limitations of this idiom as a tool for more lucidity regarding CMP.

Now to a further twist: if "resistance" is indeed popular and useful mainly due to its ideological—rather than analytic—efficacy, then is there not a danger that its targets— those in power—might be tempted to capture some of its emotional load and turn it against those criticizing them? A brief account of recent events that played out in Tel Aviv on the heels of the 2011 protest illustrates this vividly.

The Logic and Sentimental Load of Resistance Hijacked

In April 2012 the mayor of Tel Aviv Ron Huldai—a retired Air Force General, then in his fourteenth year in office—gave an exclusive interview to the weekend supplement of *Yedioth Aharonot*, Israel's most widely circulated daily newspaper. This was a rare occasion: mayor Huldai has only been on direct record (that is, speaking personally to members of the press rather than issuing releases through his spokespersons) a handful of times during his long period in office. He often says that he prefers doing to talking.

The reason for this uncharacteristic openness became apparent in the four-page story based on the interview, as well as in subsequent TV appearances the mayor made the following week. Most of the content had little interesting insights and hardly anything that could pass as news. One recurrent theme however was significant. The mayor, propped by sympathetic reporters and helpful editors, made sure the quotes by him which featured in the article were replete with strongly worded warnings directed at the leaders of the mass protest that had taken place in Tel Aviv the previous summer.

A lifelong member of the Labour party, Huldai portrayed himself in this article, as well as in a TV interview that coincided with its publication, as a champion of free speech and civil protest. He repeatedly took credit for "facilitating" and "graciously allowing and assisting" the protest of 2011. These statements however came with a twist: having issued them, Huldai quickly moved on to express his mayoral commitment to the residents of Rothschild Avenue, taken over the previous summer by the tent city that became the epicentre of the protest. Their lives, he said "became a misery". As mayor, he proclaimed, his responsibility to the residents compels him to prevent "those irresponsible kids" from taking over public turf again.

The weeks that followed saw leaders of the 2011 protest—many of them now house-hold figures in Israel despite their tender ages—summoned to interviews at police stations, where officers demanded them to disclose their "plans" for the approaching summer. The view of the protest which officers projected during these interrogations was analogous to most people's imagined effigy of government in general or the police: a hierarchical, coherent organ, with effective planning, a high degree of readiness, compliance and executive prowess. Activists who emerged from these interviews told reporters they could hardly recognize themselves and the protest they had been part of in the questions they were asked and conversations that ensued.

Mayor Huldai's warnings and the anticipatory mood of the police came full circle two months later. On the weekend of 21–23 June, a few dozen activists attempted to pitch tents on Rothschild Avenue again, only to meet shocking police brutality. Dafni Leaf, the 27-year-old video editor who had sparked the 2011 protest by pitching the first tent on Rothschild Avenue in July 2011, was attacked by six male policemen, thrown to the ground, had her arm broken and was whisked to a police car and on to custody. Her clearly stated indications to the officers as she was lying on the ground of having no intention to resist arrest went deliberately unheeded. Ninety protestors were held and brought to police headquarters for interrogation. Fourteen of them were brought to court the next day, to hear the police prosecutor requesting their arrest until legal procedures were concluded. This is a penalty reserved for suspects of violent and dangerous crimes with hefty records, prior indictments and sentences against them (none of which of course Leaf and her friends ever had) and which, in this case, would have had them locked up for almost two years. The prosecutor's request was rejected by the judge, who voiced criticism of the police's disproportionately harsh treatment of protestors he depicted as perfectly normative members of the public. The protestors walked that day, but nine of them, including Leaf, were later indicted for "assaulting a police officer". The charge was rejected in court in February 2014 amidst more criticism, this time by another judge, of the police and the prosecution decision to press charges in the first place.

Leaf's belated victory in court received considerable media attention. But it could hardly do away with the signal the police and the prosecution, like Mayor Huldai, sent the protestors in 2012, when the indictment was conducted: the sympathetic treatment the protestors enjoyed in the summer of 2011 is not to be repeated.

But there was something else about the incident of June 2012: the police was not the only law and order agency involved in the harassment and futile arrest of the veteran protestors and their leaders. They were flanked by two additional forces. One consisted of teams belonging to Israel's infamous Border Patrol—a military unit formally under police command, which in recent decades became the avant-garde of Israel's brutal suppression of Palestinian civilians in the occupied territories. The second, for which that weekend signalled a debut, was a first-ever coercive force established by, and answerable to, an Israeli municipal council. Officially dubbed "municipal wardens"—a title reserved in Israel to men and women individually patrolling streets and neighbourhoods looking for parking, littering and noise offenders—these athletic new recruits, almost exclusively male, were present that weekend in numbers, and were deployed as a cohesive regiment. Looking and operating like a well-trained cohort, with a military-like chain of command and their own communications network, they displayed agile proficiency in manoeuvres designed to isolate protestors, overpower them and whisk them to police custody.

Taking everybody by surprise, and working in synchrony with the local chiefs of the regular Police (which in Israel is answerable to the Ministry of Internal Security, not to municipal government), Mayor Huldai established this new disciplinary organ in anticipation of another summer of protest. His rare media appearances described above were initiated by his office only after the new force had been recruited and prepared. It later transpired that this had taken place with no due legal basis, without even a semblance of formal decision-making or other accountable process in the city council. A few days later the deputy mayor, an elected politician representing Meretz, a social-democratic party who had been part of the mayor's municipal coalition since 2008, resigned in protest, claiming a red line had been crossed.

Huldai is not the first mayor to resort to such coercion at times of social discontent. In 1919, Seattle's mayor Ole Hanson took credit for ending the famous general strike staged in his city, an act which gained him popularity in many media outlets and in right-wing bastions countrywide. Hanson soon resigned and went on a lecture tour about "domestic bolshevism", for which he earned much more that his former salary as mayor. For him, the strike had been a revolutionary event, the fact that it was peaceful only further proof of its revolutionary intent. In his words:

> The intent, openly and covertly announced, was for the overthrow of the industrial system; here first, then everywhere [...] True, there were no flashing guns, no bombs, no killings. Revolution, I repeat, doesn't need violence. The general strike, as practiced in Seattle, is of itself the weapon of revolution, all the more dangerous because quiet. To succeed, it must suspend everything; stop the entire life stream of a community ... That is to say, it puts the government out of operation. And that is all there is to revolt —no matter how achieved. (Zinn 1995, 370–371)

The repressive episode in Tel Aviv in June 2012, like the one in Seattle almost a century earlier, should come as no surprise to those who followed the protests of 2011 and the repressive means they met in many places. In May 2012 David Graeber recounted how, since the events in Zucotti Park and Battery Park in September 2011, repression against protestors in the USA has become considerably more brutal and determined, while at the same time growing almost entirely transparent to the media. The indifference on the part of media outlets, Graeber argued, was particularly noticeable when emanating from the same reporters, editors and broadcast organs who in 2011 meticulously cited much slighter violations, displaying genuine commitment to the freedoms of speech, association and political expression.[10]

Garland, following Bauman, suggests that apprehensions on the part of government to lose control triggers "liquid fear"—an obsession with security that often leads to calls for more stringent crime control and harder scrutiny of whole categories—the poor, the foreign, the protestor—now effortlessly depicted as undeserving underclasses. Then, when attention has already shifted from crime to the criminal, every breech of any law, including petty misdemeanour, can be construed as threatening all individuals, including those not present and, even more importantly, the social order generally (Welch 2002).

Waever and others identified securitization (Buzan, Wæver, and Wilde 1997) as the justification, through an appeal to security, of the deployment of excessive means—a practice which the public and the media can hardly discern, let alone supervise. Elsewhere, Buzan and Weaver equate securitization as a successful speech act in which "intersubjective understanding is constructed within a political community to treat something as an existential threat to a valued referent object, and to enable a call for urgent and exceptional measures to deal with the threat" (2003, 491).

Huysmans (2000, 758) illustrates how securitizing discourse segregates migrants in Europe, reifying them as a hazard, thus encouraging internal frameworks of security that include regimes of work permits, residence licences, welfare grants, etc. which control and manage migrants independently of borders and the technologies deployed to seal them. Wacquant's discussion of the contemporary penal state likewise invokes the image of a powerful Leviathan which, having destroyed the welfare state, then turns against the remnants of the social services, transforming them to mechanisms of surveillance, repression and control that target those who dare criticize authority or challenge bureaucratic practices.

Protest, particularly when it becomes effective, obviously triggers defensive and repressive response from those targeted by it. Laclau (2005), in *On Populist Reason*, analyses forms of anti-hegemonic mobilization, and the strategies and vocabularies often employed by forces of reaction to adopt their terminology and turn it against them. For Laclau, populism often throve on "empty signifiers": idioms and representations that forge a false equivalence between sensibilities emanating from vastly different, at times indeed diametrically opposed, valences and values.

Significantly for the present context, reactionary responses on the part of mayors, police chiefs, public prosecutors and pundits well versed in moral panic are often backed and justified by language resembling the idioms so often valorized in many studies of resistance. Police chiefs, cabinet ministers and municipal officials do not often use the R word.[11] But the vocabularies invoked by them to justify repression often reflect their "duty" to "respond" when ostensible "aggression" from forces imagined as malicious and transgressive threatens civilians formally under their "care". Employment of such empty signifiers, to use Laclau again, is of course as effective as it is strategic. It shifts attention from the real issues and demands protestors raise—that is, from primary political concerns—to the secondary questions where law and order and its protectors will always have the upper hand: protestors' right to use public space, the legitimacy of voicing criticism in the first place or the ever popular theme of clandestine motives and conspiratorial networks that lurk behind dissent.

It is, to be sure, a most effective strategy. It can easily put off individuals who see themselves as part of the mainstream, and who may have been initially inclined to sympathize with the protest, and nudge them to withdraw support. When this begins to happen, the centre stage of the protest becomes available to smaller and more ideologically radical individuals and groups. Local and national government agencies and the police then find themselves much closer to their comfort zone, with more perceived justification to use repressive means, and the flatter but immensely more potent wave of political energy tends to subside.

Conclusions

The need to better understand CMP, a fascinating central element of contemporary politics, and its potential to further influence the socio-economic and governance reality in many places, is acute. To meet the challenge, social scientists, not least anthropologists, have reached for existing theoretical tool boxes in search of a suitable instrument for the task. Resistance, a concept that successfully captures and explains incidents of slow-moving non-violent attempts on the part of subalterns to upset repressive regimes, presents itself immediately. It has featured regularly since 2011 in the discourse surrounding CMP.

The genealogy of the concept goes back to the time in which revolution—a secular version of redemption promising a placid, a-political ever-after—transpired as no longer tenable in either analytical or sociopolitical terms. A seemingly more doable and effective approach to current politics, resistance became a substitute idiom, purporting to represent a more realistic, down-to-earth approach to change. Given the common features shared by many cases of CMP, and the similarities between them and cases of peasant struggles that served as models for the initial coining of the term, the choice of resistance as analytical tool is not a bad one. But the considerable internal variation of CMP, between countries and within them, with activists sharing the same platforms often raising different issues, presenting different demands, using different strategies and tactics and achieving different results, raises questions about the analytical approach best suited for this syndrome. The significant dissimilarities between the circumstances, participation profiles and modus operandi of CMP and those prevailing in the situations on which resistance theory were modelled thirty and forty years ago, through the limitations of applying resistance theory to CMP into even more dramatic relief.

CMP could be described as a belated outcome of the demise of labour movements generally and trade unions specifically since the Second World War. The second half of the twentieth century saw labour politics retreat to what most unions now see as their core business: collective bargaining for formally designated constituents in an attempt to secure better shares of the spoils of an economic system that promises to grow forever and to allow more individuals to enjoy this growth. When this took place, responsibility for general, non-sectorial social needs was handed over, by default more than by design, to the state. And when the welfare state began to wither, perhaps due to an inherent inability on the part of states to substitute society, a vacuum was created that becomes the stomping ground of the populist merchants of false equivalences.

The twenty-first century, seen from the perspective of youngsters preparing for adult life, looks bleak. Economic safety nets, even in affluent countries with a substantial heritage of social-democratic values, by now have more loopholes than fibres. And an entrenched individualistic ethos leaves every person to his or her own devices at a time when inequality in capital accumulation and in the distribution of opportunity is more extreme and skewed than it has ever been in human history.

This is the context into which CMP emerges. But its current move into the void created as pre-war versions of the labour movement were eclipsed takes place today without the solidarity and infrastructure that once provided affordable housing, health insurance, vibrant welfare institutions, newspapers and organized access to leisure and high culture. Now, when the relics of these old institutions disappoints so many and no longer enjoys their public, those aspiring to represent the politics of solidarity find themselves doing this almost from scratch. They need to produce a vision of collective action that appeals to many, convince them it is doable, create the opportunities to mobilize public support, demonstrate its presence on the streets and over cyberspace, hold it together long enough to make it a critical mass, and then confront the toughest challenge: convert the protest energy into a force capable of political electoral success, reasonable performance in parliamentary settings and, if given a chance, efficacy in the executive realm.

All this must happen in extremely short time frames, and must survive the vast disparities between the rules of play of public protest and the ones that govern politics. This gap is anything but trivial. More often than not in 2011, it barred the persons who rose to prominence during the protest to be the ones who carry the baton into the corridors of formal politics. This conversion was of course difficult in peasant struggles too. But the subtle interplay involving identity, affiliation, interests and representation carried a simpler tenor in community-based struggles of the type that grabbed Scott's attention. The complexities involved with CMP obviously require an enhanced theoretical horizon.

This article has demonstrated that like "revolution", "resistance" can be idealized, idolized and ideologized, thus becoming insignificant and even dangerous as an analytic tool. It is in this respect that more sophisticated ethnographic work could become useful. Events of CMP are witnessed by large numbers of intelligent, conscientious, critical participant observers, many of them engaged in on-line, real-time cyber commentary on what they see, they feel and apprehend of processes they are so integrally part of. Their innovative modes of virtual participation in and contribution to CMP via cyberspace has been alluded to, sometimes in detail. The contents of their input, which could assist anthropologists in enhancing the apparatus available to them for more advanced theorization of the syndrome, are yet to be more systematically tapped.

Finally, my critique of "resistance" as an analytical term, and my call to theoretically refine it as part of the attempt to elucidate what CMP is and how it works, must not be confused with the respect I have for resistance as a mobilizing device, however ideologized. In the important realm whereby theoretical idioms and analytical contraptions get translated into the emotional language of political mobilization and activism, resistance has a brilliant intuitive appeal. Those who believe, like me, that the worlds of theory and action can be kept cognitively separate, should not discard the political efficacy of "resistance", as long as they take into account events such as the one recorded here of Tel Aviv 2012, which demonstrates the double-sword quality of ideological buzzwords and the manner in which they can be turned against the people who had forged them in the first place.

Notes

[1]   Similarly, *Cultural Anthropology*'s hot-spot project, led by Juris and Razsa (2012), featured over 20 short interventions by anthropologists offering impressions and analysis of the 2011 events, more than twenty essays by leading public intellectuals and links to seven books and twenty-six websites and blogs that offer analysis and insight of these events.

[2]   The entry "The Occupy Movement" on Wikipedia (http://en.wikipedia.org/wiki/Occupy_movement, accessed July 22, 2013) is a vivid illustration of this view. Its opening paragraph reads:

> The Occupy movement is an international protest movement against social and economic inequality, its primary goal being to make the economic and political relations in all societies less vertically hierarchical and more flatly distributed. Local groups often have different foci, but among the movement's prime concerns is the belief that large corporations and the global financial system control the world in a way that disproportionately benefits a minority, undermines democracy and is unstable.

Other commentators similarly treat CMP as a single process, embodying a unified trajectory (see Chomsky 2012; Juris 2012; Tejerina et al. 2013).

[3]   http://en.wikipedia.org/wiki/2011_Rome_demonstration; Vicari (2013).

[4]   Ministry of Finance, 27 September 2011.

[5]   http://www.oecd.org/newsroom/oecd-calls-on-g20-finance-ministers-to-support-next-steps-in-clampdown-on-tax-avoidance.htm.

[6]   Said (1989), in the one essay he explicitly dedicated to anthropology, admired the brilliant recognition of these subaltern ploys on the part of ethnographers, but questioned the ethics of exposing the very secrets resistance and its tactics were striving to conceal.

[7]   See Ortner (1995) and Seymour (2006) for explicit usage of the term "resistance studies".

[8]   The tendency to see resistance everywhere as following a single pattern was summarized succinctly in a sentence included in the entry "James Scott" on Wikipedia, which captures Scott's three books on resistance in the following words: these three books have been summarized humorously with the description "Peasants in Malaysia, peasants everywhere, everyone everywhere" http://en.wikipedia.org/wiki/James_C._Scott (accessed July 30, 2013).

[9]   In early 2013 Harvey demonstrated the rising salience of cities for CMP by relating how British union leaders, who had built careers on sectorial struggles – separate campaigns for the rights and benefits of miners, transport workers, nurses, teachers and so on – sought guidance from social scientists on how to run, manage and sustain integrated city-wide protests. See Marom (2013) for an analysis of the role of space in the Israeli protests of 2011.

[10] http://www.youtube.com/watch?v=eAzUQlSR6NQ.

[11] An interesting exception whereby the term "resistance" was explicitly invoked by the extreme right is the British National Party, which in 2011 renamed its youth section "Resistance" (it had been called Young BNP, then "Crusaders"). http://en.wikipedia.org/wiki/Resistance_(YBNP) (accessed July 31, 2013).

References

Baumgarten, Britta. 2013. "Geração à Rasca and Beyond: Mobilizations in Portugal after 12 March 2011." *Current Sociology* 61 (4): 457–473.

BBC. 2011. "EU Leaders Urge Greek Politicians to Support New Cuts." *BBC.* June 24, 2011. Accessed July 22, 2013. http://www.bbc.co.uk/news/world-europe-13900008

Brown, Michael F. 1996. "On Resisting Resistance." *American Anthropologist* 98 (4): 729–735.

Buzan, Barry, and Wæver, Ole. 2003. *Regions and Powers: The Structure of International Security*. Cambridge: Cambridge University Press.

Buzan, Barry, Wæver, Ole, and Wilde, Jaap de. 1997. *Security: A New Framework for Analysis*. Boulder, CO: Lynne Rienner Publishers.

Chomsky, Noam. 2012. *Occupy!* New York: Penguin.

Collins, Jane. 2012. "Theorizing Wisconsin's 2011 Protests: Community-Based Unionism Confronts Accumulation by Dispossession." *American Ethnologist* 39 (1): 6–20.

Desrues, Thierry. 2013. "Mobilizations in a Hybrid Regime: The 20th February Movement and the Moroccan Regime." *Current Sociology* 61 (4): 409–423.

Elyachar, Julia. 2014. "Upending Infrastructure: Tamarod, Resistance, and Agency after the January 25th Revolution in Egypt." *History and Anthropology*. doi:10.1080/02757206.2014.930460.

Gal, Susan. 1995. "Language and the 'Arts of Resistance' (Review of 'Domination and the Arts of Resistance: Hidden Transcripts' by James Scott)." *Cultural Anthropology* 10 (3): 407–424.

Gledhil, John. 2014. "Indigenous Autonomy, Delinquent States, and the Limits of Resistance." *History and Anthropology*. doi:10.1080/02757206.2014.917087.

Greenberg, Lev Luis. 2013. "The J14 Resistance Mo(ve)ment: The Israeli Mix of Tahrir Square and Puerta del Sol." *Current Sociology* 61 (4): 491–509.

Harvey, David. 2013. *Rebel Cities: From the Right to the City to the Urban Revolution*. New York: Verso.

Herzog, Hanna. 2013. "A Generational and Gender Perspective on the Tent Protest." [In Hebrew.] *Theory and Criticism* 41 (Summer): 66–85.

Hirsch, Arnold R. 1995. "Massive Resistance in the Urban North: Trumbull Park, Chicago, 1953–1966." *The Journal of American History* 82 (2): 522–550.

Hollander, Jocelyn A., and Rachel L. Einwohner. 2004. "Conceptualizing Resistance." *Sociological Forum* 19 (4): 533–554.

Huysmans, J. 2000. "The European Union and the Securitization of Migration." *Journal of Common Market Studies* 38 (5): 751–777.

Juris, J. 2012. "Reflections on Occupy Everywhere: Social Media, Public Space, and Emerging Logics of Aggregation." *American Ethnologist* 39 (2): 259–279.

Juris, Jeffrey, and Maple Razsa. 2012. "Occupy, Anthropology and the 2011 Global Uprisings." Accessed February 15, 2014. http://www.culanth.org/fieldsights/63-occupy-anthropology-and-the-2011-global-uprisings

Knight, Daniel Martyn. 2013. "The Greek Economic Crisis as Trope." *Focaal: Journal of Global and Historical Anthropology* 65: 147–159.

Laclau, Ernesto. 2005. *On Populist Reason*. London: Verso.

Lefebvre, Henry. 1991. *The Critique of Everyday Life*. London: Verso.

Levi, Jerome. 1998. "The Bow and the Blanket: Religion, Identity and Resistance in Rarámuri Material Culture." *Journal of Anthropological Research* 54 (3): 299–324.

Marom, Nathan. 2013. "Activising Space: The Spatial Politics of the 2011 Protest Movement in Israel." *Urban Studies* 50 (13): 2826–2841.

McCannel, Dean. 1999. *The Tourist: A New Theory of the Leisure Class*. Berkeley: University of California Press.

Merry, Sally Engle. 1995. "Resistance and the Cultural Power of Law." *Law & Society Review* 29 (1): 11–26.

Misgav, Chen. 2013. "'Shedding Light on Israel's Backyard': The Tent Protest and the Urban Periphery." [In Hebrew.] *Theory and Criticism* 41 (Summer): 86–120.

Moghadam, Valentine. 2013. "What Is Democracy? Promises and Perils of the Arab Spring." *Current Sociology* 61 (4): 393–408.

Ortner, Sherry. 1995. "Resistance and the Problem of Ethnographic Refusal." *Comparative Studies in Society and History* 37 (1): 173–193.

Perugorria, Ignacia, and B. Tejerina. 2013. "Politics of the Encounter: Cognition, Emotions, and Networks in the Spanish 15M." *Current Sociology* 61 (4): 424–442.

Price, Richard. 1983. *First-Time: The Historical Vision of an Afro-American People*. Baltimore, MD: Johns Hopkins University Press.

Rabinowitz, Dan. 1997. *Overlooking Nazareth: The Ethnography of Exclusion in Galilee*. Cambridge: Cambridge University Press.

Ram, Uri, and Daniel Filk. 2013. "The 14th of July of Daphni Leef: The Rise and the Fall of the Social Protest." [In Hebrew.] *Theory and Criticism* 41 (Summer): 17–43.

Razsa, Maple, and Andrej Kurnik. 2012. "The Occupy Movement in Žižek's Hometown: Direct Democracy and a Politics of Becoming." *American Ethnologist* 39 (2): 238–258.

Rosenhek, Zeev, and Michael Shalev. 2013. "The Political Economy of the 2011 Protest: A Class and Generational Analysis." [In Hebrew.] *Theory and Criticism* 41 (Summer): 45–68.

Said, Edward. 1989. "Representing the Colonized: Anthropology and Its Interlocutours." *Critical Inquiry* 15 (2): 205–223.

Schechter, A. 2012. *Rothschild: Chronicle of the Protest*. [In Hebrew.] Tel Aviv: Hakibbutz Hameuhad.

Scott, James. 1979. *The Moral Economy of the Peasant: Subsistence and Rebellion in Southeast Asia*. Newhaven, CT: Yale University Press.

Scott, James. 1985. *Weapons of the Weak: Everyday Forms of Peasant Resistance*. Newhaven, CT: Yale University Press.

Seymour, Susan. 2006. "Resistance." *Anthropological Theory* 6 (3): 303–321.

Shenhav, Yehouda. 2013. "The Carnival: Protest in a Society with No Oppositions." [In Hebrew.] *Theory and Criticism* 41 (Summer): 121–145.

Sotirakopoulos, Nikos, and George Sotiropoulos. 2013. "'Direct Democracy Now!': The Greek Indignados and the Present Cycle of Struggles." *Current Sociology* 61 (4): 443–456.

Starn, Orin. 1995. "To Revolt Against the Revolution: War and Resistance in Peru's Andes." *Cultural Anthropology* 10 (4): 547–580.

Tejerina, Benjamin, Ignacia Perugorría, Tova Benski, and Lauren Langman. 2013. "From Indignation to Occupation: A New Wave of Global Mobilization." *Current Sociology* 61 (4): 377–392.

Theodossopoulos, Dimitrios. 2013. "Infuriated with the Infuriated? Blaming Tactics and Discontent about the Greek Financial Crisis." *Current Anthropology* 54 (2): 200–221.

Theodossopoulos, Dimitrios. 2014. "On De-Pathologizing Resistance." *History and Anthropology*. doi:10.1080/02757206.2014.933101.

Vicari, Stefania. 2013. "Public Reasoning Around Social Contention: A Case Study of Twitter Use in the Italian Mobilization for Global Change." *Current Sociology* 61 (4): 474–490.

Welch, David. 2002. *The Third Reich: Politics, and Propaganda*. London: Routledge.

Zinn, Howard. 1995. *Self Help in Hard Times. A People's History of the United States*. Revised and updated edition. New York: Harper and Collins.

The Ambivalence of Anti-Austerity Indignation in Greece: Resistance, Hegemony and Complicity

Dimitrios Theodossopoulos

This article engages with a contradiction that can help us appreciate the ambiguity and complexity of indirect resistance as this is articulated in informal everyday contexts: many citizens in Greece boldly challenge the antisocial austerity measures that have plagued their lives, highlighting how these represent a hegemonic imposition led by foreign centres of economic power. Their anti-hegemonic critique, however, often recycles a dislike for foreigners and xenophobia, echoing more pervasive hegemonic narratives (for example, a crypto-colonial identification of Greece with the West). To deal with this contradiction, I stress the need to (1) de-pathologize local indignant discourse (avoiding the orientalization of anti-austerity discourse as emotional or inconsequential) and (2) acknowledge that indirect resistance may represent an astute critique of visible inequalities, but is not isolated from overarching hegemonic ideological influences that shape local interpretations of historical/economic causality.

I have recently discussed indignation with austerity in Greece as a master trope of protest that communicates a concern with accountability (Theodossopoulos 2013a, 2014a). In this article, I extend this analysis beyond the figurative, interpretive or exegetical dimension of indignation-discourse, to evaluate its emancipatory potential and its ambivalent relationship to power (or its complicity with it). The case of anti-austerity indignation in Greece allows us to evaluate the transformative potential and effectiveness of indirect resistance, but also its limitations. For example, to what extent does local discontent depart from previous established hegemonic narratives? What is the relationship between indirect resistance, defensive nationalism and electioneering populism?

I address these questions with reference to the increasing voicing of indignation with austerity (as a measure of economic recovery) in Greece, focusing on local indignant narratives that represent an everyday form of indirect resistance to neoliberal economic priorities. This timely example of widespread popular discontent provides an opportunity to explore the transformative power of indirect resistance, the challenges it poses to the priorities set by the financial establishment, but also the constraints of indignant discourse and its relationship with defensive nationalism. In this exploration, I use as a point of departure the influential work of Scott (1985, 1990), to analyse anti-austerity indignation as a form of indirect resistance, yet one that does not represent an autonomous social field (Keesing 1992; Gledhill 1994, 2012; Moore 1998; Fletcher 2001), untouched by pre-existing hegemonic master narratives. In this respect, my analysis provides a context-specific critique of Scott, to complement my more extensive appraisal of his work in the introductory essay of this special issue.

On the one hand, I acknowledge that indirect resistance encourages a great deal of critical thinking that engages with the structures of power in creative ways (including irony and innovative adaptations of previous arguments and ideas). Rhetoric, irony, ambiguity and metaphor play an important role in negotiating the causality and eventfulness of political life (Carrithers 2009; Fernandez 2009; Herzfeld 2009), and may even temporarily destabilize—as Greek indignation demonstrates—pre-existing political structures. Yet, on the other hand, I recognize that indirect resistance is often constrained by pre-existing explanations of causality in politics—including ethno-nationalist narratives—an observation that encourages us to depart from Scott's (1990) vision of subaltern discontent as an a "hidden" transcript independent of power-holders. In the case of anti-austerity indignation in Greece, indirect resistance often stumbles upon, and becomes confined by (or complicit to) nationalism, ethnocentric interpretations of history, political-party rhetoric and electioneering campaigns.

These limitations pose the following analytic problem: how can a social analyst reconcile the obligation to expose and deconstruct defensive nationalism (or political-party interests) that may figure prominently in indirect resistance, with the equally important commitment to acknowledge the logic of local anti-hegemonic narratives and the astute awareness of inequality among peripheralized subjects (who may also be complicit in reproducing nationalism or political-party lines)? Anti-austerity discourse in Greece—which is anti-hegemonic in its orientation, but still partially complicit to hegemonic narratives—provides us with a very good opportunity to explore this challenging dilemma.

The anthropological analysis that follows does not attempt to explain the causes of the crisis or summarize its consequences within a single, unilinear narrative of events. I privilege instead some local views—fragmented and unofficial—that capture the frustration of local actors with the official policies of austerity that have been presented to them as a remedy to the financial crisis. These local views come from Patras, a medium-sized Greek town in South Greece, and for me, a site of ongoing fieldwork since 1999. My indignant respondents are middle and working-class citizens from Patras (the *Patrinoí*); they have shared their explanations of political and economic life with me during this and previous crises (see, for example, Brown and Theodossopoulos 2000, 2003; Theodossopoulos 2004, 2007a, 2007b; Kirtsoglou and Theodossopoulos 2010a, 2010b), and recognize me as a locally born academic and a mirror—the anthropological listener who occasionally provokes—through which they reflect upon timely issues. Their arguments have provided me with a partial but nuanced account of the local indignant discourse, the ambivalences that it engenders, and the aetiology of the crisis as this is debated in everyday, unofficial social contexts (see Theodossopoulos 2013a, 2013b).

De-Pathologizing Indignation

Far from denoting merely a sentiment, indignation in crisis-afflicted Greece is a potent metaphor that links different narratives of accountability together. In local conversation about austerity, indignation conveys messages and supports arguments about austerity; some remain unsaid but locally understood, while other arguments rely on indignation's figurative potential. In either case, the image of injustice so vividly conveyed by indignation becomes an opening and closing point in many conversations: "I am indignant because ..." [argument] " ... hence, we are indignant".[1] In appreciation of this metaphorical rootedness, and drawing from Fernandez (1986), I have previously referred to anti-austerity indignation in Greece as a trope that communicates a variety of indirect, but also straightforwardly expressed messages (Theodossopoulos 2013a, 2014a; see also Knight 2013a). The powerful imagery of the powerless indignant citizen—victim of "the mistakes of others", "those bankers, politicians, unscrupulous capitalists", as my respondents say—validates a moral standpoint for eliciting a critique of the consequences of austerity in everyday life.

In its metaphorical capacity, indignation links different narratives of accountability together. These include, first and foremost, the representation of being taken by surprise, as most crisis-afflicted respondents in Patras did not expect this turn of events (cf. Douzinas 2013, 31). In this particular respect, the figurative use of indignation communicates anger towards those politicians who were aware of the nation's bad economic state, and kept this information hidden from the public until one day the bad news suddenly exploded into the public sphere. Indignation also targets those many politicians in successive governments who created the conditions of debt (and lack of transparency) that resulted in the current situation. Overall, politicians (in general) and their responsibility has been a central feature in the negotiation of accountability (of the crisis) in Greece (Herzfeld 2011; Theodossopoulos 2013a, 2014a) and internationally (Knight 2013a).

As the play of different figurative images associated with indignation unravels in everyday discourse, it engenders identifications with new subject positions: the indignant protestor, who may also be the indignant young unemployed, the indignant pensioner (whose pension has been devalued), the indignant parent (previously encouraged to bear many children to counter the nation's demographic decline, and who has now lost several child-related benefits), the indignant shop owner (whose clientele is now diminished) and the indignant tax-payer (whose reduced salary cannot accommodate the increased rate of taxation). Such new and old identities of indignation communicate, in turn, with familiar figurative permutations of political subjects: the indignant conservative (who sees stability falling to pieces), the indignant socialist (who sees hard won benefits vanishing one after the other), the indignant communist (who says "I told you about capitalism before, but you didn't listen"), and, to add a sinister figurative distortion, the indignant fascist (who hates "the migrant for having a job while 'he' hasn't").

Indignation, in its many and constantly transforming figurative combinations, links the current predicament of austerity with previous crises experienced in the past; for example, memories of famine, war, poverty and social inequality in the twentieth century (Knight 2012a, 2012b). Suffering, as many anthropologists maintain, is a major theme in the modern Greek moral imagination (Dubisch 1995) and resonates with an "agonistic" ethos (Herzfeld 1985) and a view of life as a constant struggle (Friedl 1962; Du Boulay 1974; Kenna 1990; Hart 1992; Dubisch 1995; Theodossopoulos 2003b). In its re-emergence as a metaphor of indignation, the suffering of the austerity-afflicted community provides a solid foundation for criticizing visible examples of injustice and inequality in the World economic order (such as the current economic crisis).

Seen from this point of view that stresses accountability, indignation frames local discussions about austerity, but also invites an explanation of the crisis. Indignant conversations about austerity have an interpretive dimension, one that is almost existential, in the political sense. Such an exegetical orientation in local conversation—especially conversation about timely developments in politics—has been noticed and analysed by anthropologists writing about Greece before the debt crisis (see Herzfeld 1992, 1997; Sutton 1998, 2003; Brown and Theodossopoulos 2000, 2003; Papadakis 2004; Kirtsoglou 2006; Kirtsoglou and Theodossopoulos 2010a, 2010b). Herzfeld (1992), in particular, has referred to the secular theodicy of the ordinary Greek citizens: their search for explanations and meaning against the indifference of bureaucracy and the injustices perpetrated by politicians or state officials.

Evidently, as Herzfeld (1982, 1992) himself has stressed, local commentary in Greece may embrace a good deal of defensive nationalism—a problem I will address later in this article—especially when local actors attempt to exonerate themselves by targeting more or less powerful cultural Others (see also Theodossopoulos 2003a, 2007a). However, the anthropological emphasis given to the creative adaptations and irony of blame-oriented discourse also highlights its alternative (non-hegemonic) orientation (Sutton 2003) and subversive potential (Kirtsoglou 2006), and the ability of peripheral subjects to cut down to size and discuss as equals those perceived as more powerful than the Self, including powerful nations such as USA (see Brown and Theodossopoulos 2000, 2003; Kirtsoglou and Theodossopoulos 2010b).

In all these respects, the anthropology of informal political discourse in Greece has established a tradition of studying blame without turning the study of blame into a practice of blaming (Theodossopoulos 2014a). This has contributed in de-pathologizing vernacular political discourse, by encouraging social analysis to move beyond the functional instrumentality of blaming—or its denigration as irrational or pathological in "pseudopsychological terms" (Sutton 2003, 197)—highlighting instead the cultural worldviews that render justice and injustice meaningful on a local level. In this respect, the de-pathologization of local commentary about international politics opens the way for appreciating its contribution to processes of resistance, as in the case of indignation with austerity, which presents us with a good example of indirect resistance.

In the *Weapons of the Weak*, Scott (1985) marked out the concept of indirect resistance as a legitimate sub-topic of resistance studies; most manifestations of resistance, he explains, take a less dramatic form. For example, those Greek local actors who resist austerity discursively—by denigrating powerful politicians who impose on them harsh economic policies—can be seen as following a tactic quite similar to the Malaysian peasants studied by Scott, who subvert the power of their landlords through slander and character assassination. From this perspective, ordinary citizens in Greece who evaluate timely political or economic events in peripheral conversational contexts, indirectly resist the imposition of undesirable measures on their lives, arguing from the relative safety of—what Scott (1990) describes as—autonomous contexts of social life (of subordinate groups), or what Herzfeld (1997)—much more aptly, and without isolating local political discourse—calls contexts of cultural intimacy.

Those powerful politicians or institutions that do shape economic policy—for example, with respect to Greece's recovery from debt—are seen by local actors as choosing to ignore local indignation for being too sentimental or apparently irrational, and prioritize instead what my respondents call "the cold language of numbers". In sharp contrast to the rationality of budgeting and spreadsheets, anti-austerity discourse, as this is voiced in unofficial contexts, often promotes alternative narratives about the crisis that prioritize social concerns and a focus on accountability. In this respect, indignation with austerity operates as an alternative "sense-making" practice (Sutton 2003, 192) that challenges dominant—presented as "transparent" (Sanders and West 2003)—discourses about economic recovery. For example, many Greek local (and indignant) actors insist that austerity is not the only possible route for escaping from the crisis, while austerity is probably the path that bears the most undesirable social consequences. Such views often reflect an astute awareness of the systemic inequalities that shape economic policies, yet their vernacular and emotion-laden articulation encourages their easy dismissal by the elites.

A restaurant owner in Patras, exasperated with the widespread dismissal of public indignation, reflected upon this:

> Who listens to what we say? Those who take the decisions about the economy do not care about you and me, the [ordinary] people (*ton laoutzíko*): they speak another language; the language of the technocrats and say that the Greeks want to take out their own eyes; the Greeks are crazy, they say ... what do *you* think?

The Spectre of Austerity: Reification, Subversion, Transformation

Austerity has a name in Greece: *Mnimónio*. The term itself means "memorandum", and when used in ordinary prose carries an overtone of de-humanizing bureaucratization. It has been used to refer to the particular memorandum that outlines the Economic Adjustment Programme for Greece, a bailout aiming to save the country from bankruptcy, or ideally to lead towards economic recovery. In everyday discourse, *mnimónio* is taken to signify an agreement imposed on Greece by its foreign lenders, and is seen as representing a foreign imposition. As such, it is detested, or at best, tolerated, at least by the overwhelming majority of Greek citizens, who refer to it frequently in day-to-day conversation. Often, and especially in heated debates, the *mnimónio*, is treated in a reified manner, as a societal force that haunts the lives of the poorer citizens (Theodossopoulos 2014a).

In its reified use, *mnimónio* is treated as the source of all evils that come with austerity: the cancellation of one's dreams, the difficulties in providing for one's family, the lack of employment opportunities or the threat of losing existing jobs. *Mnimónio*, the spectre of austerity, is seen by many in Greece as a perversion of the natural order of things; it negates a basic expectation in post-Second Wold War Greece: the idea that life becomes more comfortable over time, as succeeding generations move further away from the difficulties of the post-war period. Early anthropological accounts identified the struggle of Greek society to recover from post-war poverty and the emerging social aspirations of the peasantry (see Friedl 1969). With increasing prosperity, subsequent generations negotiated "distinctions of wealth, class, prestige" (Cowan 1990, 62), for the most part through consumption patterns (see Bousiou 2008; Knight 2013b; cf. Argyrou 1995), and especially in the last two decades of the twentieth century.[2] As a result, the young Greek adults of today expect to enjoy a life much better than their grandparents (the generation of the 1950s and 1960s), "even better" than that of their parents (the generation of the 1970s and 1980s). Sadly, the unexpected arrival of *mnimónio*—the spectre of austerity—has thwarted this unidirectional (and naturalized) perception of improvement in one's (or everyone's) life.

The effects of such a grand scale cancellation of ordinary expectations are discussed by many citizens in Patras in terms of comparisons of life before and after *mnimónio*. Until recently, university graduates invested in postgraduate studies abroad hoping to qualify for a "better job"; in the life after the *mnimónio*, "there are no jobs". Before the *mnimónio*, the employed expected a raise in salary, or a promotion; now "there are only salary cuts". In the years before the *mnimónio*, those who ran small or larger business dreamed about expansion or new opportunities; yet now, after the imposition of austerity, businesses are shrinking or closing down. Until a couple of years ago, pensioners had a smaller income than their employed children; nowadays, the old are providing for the young sharing their reduced pensions. In these and so many other respects, my respondents argue, *mnimónio* has overturned "the course of their lives".

No wonder then that austerity has inspired so much indignation. In fact, since the beginning of the crisis, growing discontent with austerity has transformed a previous empty and bureaucratic term, the *mnimónio*, into a concept that denotes not merely austerity, but also points towards the direction of responsibility. As such, the term *mnimónio*, loaded with meaning derived from the concrete experience of austerity in everyday life, is used in conversation as a versatile discursive weapon to criticize the idea of austerity and its sources: politicians, political parties and foreign institutions and all those responsible for unleashing the *mnimónio*-monster and its unsociable consequences. Some citizens may reluctantly tolerate this newly introduced austerity—in the guise of neoliberal economic rationality—but an overwhelming majority question if its imposition was absolutely necessary. Many conservative and left-leaning respondents in Patras argue that there can be no economic recovery based on austerity. So, the *mnimónio* was an unnecessary evil!

Having closely studied local discontent with neoliberal politics in Greece in the period preceding the financial crisis (Theodossopoulos 2010; Kirtsoglou and Theodossopoulos 2010a), I was accustomed to the critical spirit of local political discourse, but I had also underestimated its potential for stimulating direct political change. Before the financial crisis, local discontent appeared to offer only ephemeral and rhetorical empowerments. Independently of how critically local actors discussed neoliberalism and Westernization in peripheral contexts, the political-party landscape in Greece remained fairly static for at least thirty years: two major political parties, the conservatives (New Democracy) and the socialists (PASOK), dominated official politics, and took turns in exercising the power to govern and provide their supporters with favours (which further cemented their electorate support).

Anti-austerity indignation has challenged this constellation of political power, leading to the partial restructuring of official political representation in the parliament, as this emerged from the elections of 6 May and 17 June 2012. The subversive potential of massive popular indignation led to the collapse of one of the two political parties, PASOK, which happened to be the party on power when the truth about the dire financial situation of Greece was announced to the (unaware) Greek public, and the first austerity measures were introduced. Thus, we may say that the monster called *mnimónio* crashed this mighty political party, which has not yet recovered from its association with the first wave of salary cuts and unpopular reductions in Greek social infrastructure. Another political party, SYRIZA, has absorbed a substantiate proportion of PASOK's electoral support and has become the official opposition in the Greek parliament. A central feature in SYRIZA's political campaign is its firm anti-austerity (anti-*mnimónio*) stance, which has captured (and benefited from) the public's growing indignation with the consequences of the crisis.

SYRIZA's sudden and spectacular rise to power (from 4.6% to 26.8%), representing primarily indignant voters oriented towards the left or centre-left, was paralleled by the unexpected electorate success of two anti-austerity political parties from the right wing: a politically conservative-*cum*-nationalist party ("Independent Greeks") and an unashamedly fascist political formation (the infamous, "Golden Dawn"). Golden Dawn, in particular, "soared from 0.29 per cent in the 2009 elections 6.9 per cent" (and eighteen seats in the parliament), while most recent opinion polls show a further increase in the party's projected popularity (Kirtsoglou 2013). Interestingly, the results of the 2012 elections demonstrate that the build-up of public discontent can subvert existing political structures, and bring about change in politics that might affect anti-austerity politics. Indignation, in this respect, is a transformative political "weapon" for crisis-afflicted local (and peripheralized) actors in Greece.

Yet, to complicate this picture further, I will briefly reflect on the commentary of my respondents in Patras, who maintain that the electorate transformations outlined above partly mirror the previous political landscape, with SYRIZA, as they say, merely replacing PASOK, to restore a two party political structure. A communist supporter summarized this position by stating that "the new SYRIZA is the old PASOK". Critical evaluations such as this, which are also shared by conservative citizens (arguing from an opposite, but equally critical angle), allude to the history of PASOK, which entered the Greek political scene as a radical political party, critical of Western hegemony (Verney 2011), but after its first electorate success, shiftily transformed to a moderate social-democratic party (unable to challenge, as my communist respondents argue, the neoliberal status quo).

Local critical commentary of this sort, had led me to argue in a recent article (Theodossopoulos 2014a) that the spontaneous[3] and anti-structural spirit of the first wave of Greek anti-austerity indignation, has now become appropriated by (and complicit to) political-party politics. The "officialisation" of indignation via parliamentary representation (following the 2012 elections) sharply contrasts with the public protest of summer 2011 (mostly in front of the Greek parliament), which was, as with the Spanish indignant movement (Postill 2014), initiated by social media (Papailias 2011a, 2011b; Theodossopoulos 2013a) and communicated indignation in dialogical form, mostly beyond the narrow constraints of political-party priorities (Gourgouris 2011; Panourgia 2011; Dalakoglou 2012; Theodossopoulos 2014a).

The original anti-structural spirit of anti-austerity protest may now contrast sharply with formalized political-party indignation, a contrast that is most visible in the case of the fascist party, which has appropriated public discontent—hijacking the politics of spontaneity (Dalakoglou 2012)—to promote sinister anti-migrant provocation (a topic I will discuss in the following section). However, several respondents in Patras do not see the emergence of the new political parties as the replication of one structure by another. Those who support SYRIZA, for example, explained that their new party represents a new dynamic that will bring into power a new generation of politicians (néa prósopa) who will subvert or cancel the mnimónio. Some even admitted that they hope that SYRIZA will be transformed itself into a less "radical" party—as did PASOK in the 1980s—but one strong enough to deliver them for the plague of austerity (Theodossopoulos 2013b), "We don't care if SYRIZA is the old PASOK", said the owner of a small commercial business, "we want SYRIZA to take power and stop austerity for ever!"

Anti-Hegemonic Indignation Meets Defensive Nationalism

Having already outlined some layers of cultural meaning negotiated by anti-austerity indignation, I will now confront an analytical problem that has troubled me from the first moment I attempted to write about the social consequences of the debt crisis in Greece. This relates to the relationship between (a) anti-hegemonic discourses that expose inequality and (b) defensive nationalism, including populist narratives that exploit anti-hegemonic sentiments for electioneering purposes. While hegemonic power is perceived as representative of foreign tutelage, anti-hegemonic discourse may incite nationalist sentiments, including ideological associations or arguments representing "patriotic" or deeply conservative ideological positions. The latter can be easily unearthed and introduced in current conversations that criticize the role of foreign powers. This aetiology of blame, as Herzfeld (1982, 1992) has perceptively observed, can be manipulated in local conversation to exonerate the ethnic self and transfer responsibility by blaming ethnic Others.

The problem I have sketched out poses serious challenges for the social analyst, who is often called to walk the thin line that separates two contrasting features of indirect resistance: (a) a critically predisposed local awareness of inequality (expressed as a desire to challenge a world of post-colonial relationships) and (b) a uncritical recirculation of nationalist arguments and xenophobic tendencies. In everyday discourse, and especially within the context of anti-austerity indignation in Greece, these two tendencies co-exist, and manifest themselves simultaneously in unofficial narratives and dialogues articulated in informal contexts. In fact, the two features of indirect resistance mentioned above articulate with each other, as very often the visible power inequalities in international politics fuel defensive nationalism.

One of the central causes of exacerbation for my crisis-afflicted respondents in Patras is the realization that austerity is imposed hegemonically by foreign centres of power— for example, the European commission and the International Monetary Fund (IMF)— and implemented in a top down manner by Greek government bureaucracy. The overwhelming majority of the indignant narratives I witnessed in Greece implicitly or explicitly challenge hegemony. Yet, this predisposition towards indirect resistance—which reflects an awareness of the systemic inequalities of international politics—communicates and often articulates with blatant manifestations of defensive nationalism, or even, as in the case of ultra-right discourse, with a generalized mistrust for both powerful and powerless ethnic Others.

To complicate this problem further, indignation with foreign hegemony in Greece has been adopted and used as a political agenda by anti-austerity political parties that represent leftist, but also rightist (and extreme right) positions. In fact, some ultra-right voices protest against the patronizing interventions of EU or the IMF (or German and French politicians) in a manner that resembles—and borrows from— the analytic sharpness of a leftist critique. Such narratives are often manipulated to fit the purposes of political-party rhetoric, but inspire, in turn, through the circulation of political-party views in the media, local adaptations of anti-hegemonic (but also xenophobic) arguments. These are creatively adjusted to fit the purposes of particular discussions in the everyday, and are voiced by citizens that may not be closely affiliated with extreme rightist parties.

"I am not racist" many citizens would say before blaming directly or indirectly the foreign migrants, who are now ubiquitous in Greece, and often become a convenient scapegoat for the ills of the economic crisis (see also Herzfeld 2011). Herzfeld refer to this type of disclaimers as a form of polite racism (2007, 255, 263). During fieldwork in Patras, I heard many times the "I am not a racist, but ..." clause. The town attracts great numbers of illegal migrants hoping to embark on ferries departing for Italy. These desperate migrants, whom I have seen running behind lorry trucks so that they can cling onto the undercarriage (and thus pass the border control at the port undetected), live in deplorable conditions in segregated areas and derelict buildings. The overwhelming majority of my respondents in Patras—independently of their political affiliation—are threatened by the presence of so many destitute people in their hometown, and would not hesitate to accuse them of contributing to (what the Patrinoi perceive as) a generalized "feeling of insecurity".[4] Even Patrinoi, involved in charitable activity in support of the migrants, would not hesitate to charge the latter for all sorts of misbehaviour or petty crimes. "Our town has changed", they argue, due to this "serious problem", "the problem of the migrants".

"It is a problem created by the powerful of Europe", commented a forty-year-old woman, who is a SYRIZA supporter: "the rich countries in the North have left Greece unsupported to deal with the consequences of the illegal migration"; and after a brief moment of reflection she added: "this is how the powerful perpetuate inequality". Her interlocutor, a moderately socialist woman, in her thirties, added: "I am not a racist, but the migrants are an unbearable problem; the Europeans expect us to support them with the very little we have". Citizens of conservative predilections would share this generalized view, but switch it to serve a more nationalist agenda: they focus on the perceived "injustice" of seeing Greeks being unemployed or suffering from severe cuts in their salaries, while government bureaucrats (and the rich nations of Europe) "keep the migrants on their doorstep". "They do so to destabilize our nation", said a Golden Dawn sympathizer, "it is all part of larger plan".

Citizens inclined towards the Left dissociate themselves from Golden Dawn with principled and confident disdain, but they also use the "destabilization argument" to explain the crisis, and the insistence of Northern politicians to promote austerity—although evidently austerity withholds economic recovery. As a communist friend confided in me, "the Golden Down supporters (*oi hrysaygítes*) have twisted some of our arguments to serve their sinister purpose; the problem is not the migrants, but capitalism". "The stronger nations of the North create problems for the South", said a sixty-year-old doctor sympathizing with the left, "they brought the austerity measures to cripple our economy, to colonize us, for ever! How do they expect us to recover when we face so many austerity measures!" Even Patrinoi with conservative views will not completely disagree with the idea that austerity is a foreign imposition; many of them maintain that "Europe", and, in particular, German politicians, are imposing on Greece "harsh" measures, that partly serve Northern or German interests; "we have not seen Germany suffering", said a committed Conservative Party supporter, "they get stronger and stronger".

When my respondents search for a convenient joke to relax the tone of conversations about austerity, or a concrete image to punctuate their arguments, they frequently employ familiarly mediatized figures of foreign politicians, such as the German Chancellor, Angela Merkel, the IMF director, Christine Lagarde or the German Minister of

Finance, Wolfgang Schäuble. Enormous wax caricatures of the aforementioned figured prominently in the carnival of Patras (in 2013), paraded as satirical representations of the harshness and unsociable nature of neoliberal economics: "the monsters of austerity!" (see Figure 1). "Merkel and Schäuble are indifferent to the sufferings of the ordinary people" remarked a couple of bystanders. In the context of everyday conversation, Angela Merkel, in particular, has been the recipient of an avalanche of ironic remarks, mostly used as punch lines of critical arguments focusing on the unrelenting economic policies pursued by the German Chancellor. Irony, Fernandez and Huber remark, "can be expected in situations of unequal power" (2001, 4); and in fact, since the beginning of the crisis, inequality is the idea most prominently underlined in local discussions about Greece's relationship with Germany. In 2013, many Patrinoi, from both leftist and rightist political affiliations, regularly refer to Merkel as "Hitler" (see Figure 2) or "the godmother" (alluding to a female version of a mafia leader).

On other occasions, associations are drawn between foreign politicians and their Greek counterparts. In most cases, local commentary criticizes, often with humorous but pointed remarks, the subordinate position (*shesi ypotélias*) of Greek politicians and their perceived lack of power to challenge externally imposed dictums of austerity. The current and previous prime ministers of Greece (Antonis Samaras, Lukas Papademos and George Papandreou) have been the targets of such criticism (the latter even by disaffected supporters of his own party). Nevertheless, shrewd local commentary that unravels systemic inequalities and patterns of hegemony is not solely expressed by citizens affiliated with the left. An increasing number of right wing crisis-afflicted citizens

Figure 1. Carnivalesque caricatures of Angela Merkel and Wolfgang Schäuble.

Figure 2. Impersonations of the Greek prime minister and the German Chancellor in Nazi uniform in the Carnival parade; the sign "DIAPLOKI" can be translated as "intertwining interests".

articulate a critical predisposition towards Western hegemony, one that does not target neoliberal policies, but rather the historical role of Germany and other Western nations in shaping the fate of Greece.

Conveniently, the German occupation of Greece during World War II provides ample opportunity for drawing metaphors or "lessons from history", a practice to which Sutton (1998) refers as "analogic thinking".[5] In this particular version, the German military invasion in the past is compared to the imposition of austerity in the present, "an invasion of harsh economic measures". These are implemented, some of my respondents argue, with "characteristic German harshness", "just as in the war", without consideration for "the non-combatant civilians", that is, the poor, the old and the underprivileged. "Germany destroyed Greece during the war", argued a respondent who is moderate conservative, "they took the nation's gold, and never paid the war reparations". I have recorded similar variations of this argument in the narratives of respondents from literally all political affiliations, but also in the rhetoric of politicians from most Greek political parties.

Remarks with nationalistic overtones—that frequently rely on "naturalised" stereotypes (for example, the "harshness" of the Germans) or lessons from history (for example, the "unjust" treatment of Greece by foreign nations in previous eras)— provide a platform for the convergence of leftist and rightist arguments, allowing interlocutors from different political affiliations to draw a more amicable closure to a

discussion; one that may underline the perceived hegemony of the West, and the inter-
ference of foreigners in the attempts of Greece to achieve economic recovery. Citizens
leaning towards the left might use arguments with nationalist overtones to conclude on
the unscrupulousness of Western capitalism,[6] while citizens from most political affiliations do not hesitate to highlight a perceived sense of loss of sovereignty in Greek economic policy. Finally, those who appear to be partially sympathetic to ultra-rightist
rhetoric issue patriotic warnings against all foreigners: the economically powerful Wes-
terners, but also the destitute migrants who live next door.

Conclusion: Anti-Hegemonic Indignation Confined by Hegemony

In my first accounts of the Greek anti-austerity indignation, I attempted to shed some
light on the ambivalence of local discontent and its many contradictions (Theodossopoulos 2013a, 2013b, 2014a). These become apparent in the ambivalent—and, in Herzfeld's (1987, 1997) words, *disemic*—desire of so many Greeks to remain in the
Eurozone (and in the consumerist sphere of the West) but defy the constraints
imposed by the EU, the IMF, and the international financial establishment. To
capture ethnographically this ambivalence, I engaged with the complexity of the emerging indignation—the internal politics and fragmented (often self-critical) views of
those afflicted by austerity—"filling in the black hole" (Ortner 1995, 190), the interpretative vacuum created by homogenizing depictions of the crisis. The anthropological perspective, with its attention on the local diversity of views, can contribute to the
de-orientalization (and de-pathologization) of indirect resistance, by moving beyond
its easy dismissal as irrational, incoherent or inconsequential. Recent anthropological
accounts of the Greek crisis have contributed to this effect (Herzfeld 2011; Papailias
2011a; Dalakoglou 2012; Kalantzis 2012; Knight 2012a, 2012b, 2013a, 2013b; Hirschon
2013; Rakopoulos 2014).

In this article, I have argued for the need to explicitly de-pathologize local discontent
with the financial crisis. Far from representing an inchoate, emotional or irrational discourse, indignation with austerity promotes a sustained critique of visible inequalities
in the World economic order. Thus, moving one step further from my initial interpretative analysis (See, Theodossopoulos 2013a, 2014a), I am now—two years after the first
wave of popular mobilization against austerity—in a better position to fully acknowledge the transformative potential of local anti-austerity discourse, and its ability to
unite diverse (even international) social groups in discontent with the World economic
order (see Theodossopoulos 2010). Indignation with austerity is not merely a trope, a
figurative communication of meaning, but also a guiding principle of emancipatory
imagination (Appadurai 1996, 2001) leading towards (or requesting) change in
social life. Testaments of its transformative power are the dramatic shifts in political-
party politics in Greece that I have outlined earlier.

Considerations such as this allow us to appreciate that anti-austerity discourse does
not only offer discursive empowerment in peripheral conversational contexts, but also
frames local anti-hegemonic narratives within an everyday pursuit of accountability.
This persistent search for meaning may provide alternative readings of causality—for

example, via the exploration of recurring patterns in history (cf. Sutton 1998, 2003; Stewart 2012; Knight 2012a, 2012b)—which lead to explanations of the crisis that differ from hegemonic narratives; for example, "the powerless should not pay for the mistakes of bankers or politicians", "austerity is not the only way out of the crisis". In this emancipatory role, indignation with austerity represents a very timely example of indirect resistance: it proliferates in unofficial, everyday contexts of social life, sometimes beyond the direct observation of power-holders (Scott 1985, 1990). However, unlike Scott's view of indirect resistance, anti-austerity indignation in Greece directly aspires to communicate an explicit message to power-holders (critically engaging with the exercise of power, especially with regard to economic policies).

It is also important to acknowledge that indirect resistance to austerity may realize its most creative and original forms in informal contexts, but it is not merely an "off-stage" discourse, confined to—what Scott (1990) perceives as—autonomous contexts of subordinate sociality; in fact, it is doubtful if such isolated social contexts really exist (Gledhill 2012; Theodossopoulos, 2014b). On the contrary, anti-austerity indignation (so far) has been informed by, and has also inspired political-party rhetoric; it has been voiced in public protest and championed by elected politicians; it has numerous advocates among left leaning highly educated elites; and, far from being independent (or autonomous) from wider ideological, political or economic visions, it plays a formative role in the imagination and reproduction of such visions, often moving—via social networks—beyond national borders (Papailias 2011a, 2011b; Postill 2014).

In all these respects, anti-austerity resistance provides us with a scope to reflect upon the pervasiveness of hegemonic narratives, even within anti-hegemonic critique; an issue underestimated by Scott in *hidden* transcripts (1990). Even though indignant (anti-austerity) discourse consciously confronts hegemonic master narratives, it remains constrained by overarching ideological influences, which are not uncontaminated by hegemony. For example, anti-austerity indignation in Greece, despite its explicit critique of Western imperialism, is confined to a nationalist (and hegemonic) conceptualization of history, which, as many anthropologists have pointed out, has been originally inspired by a Western vision of classical Greece, and imported to Greece as a nation-building construct (Herzfeld 1982, 1987; Just 1989, 1995; Faubion 1993; Stewart 1994; Hirschon 2000; Brown and Hamilakis 2003; Theodossopoulos 2007a). The resulting idealization of classical antiquity in Greek nationalism represents a good example of colonized historical consciousness—an example of what Herzfeld calls crypto-colonialism[7] (Herzfeld 2002). Crypto-colonial narratives, "appear to resist domination, but do so at the cost of effective complicity", often through "the aggressive promotion of their claims to civilizational superiority or antiquity" (Herzfeld 2002, 902–903).

In consequence, Western hegemony is deeply embedded in the identification of the West with classical Greece, an identification adopted and reproduced uncritically by Greek national narratives. Trapped within such a persistent (and pervasive) conceptual framework, Greek anti-austerity narratives, although critical to Western power, do not completely escape from Western hegemony (which has so effectively colonized Greek national consciousness). The unconstrained xenophobia of the Greek ultra-right provides the most unattractive example of how nationalism springs from indignation with foreign intervention, yet nationalist undertones are also hidden in the anti-hegemonic critique of left-leaning indignant citizens. Anti-austerity political parties (from the left and right) have capitalized upon this fusion of nationalism with anti-hegemonic critique, and have adapted their rhetoric accordingly, to fit electioneering purposes.

The analytical trajectory I have outlined so far opens the way for resolving a dilemma I posed earlier in this article. This emerges from the contradictions inherent in indirect resistance, and, in particular, our commitment (as social analysts) to acknowledge the critically astute (non-pathological, and often radical) nature of indignant narratives, while simultaneously confronting the proliferation of nationalism (old-fashioned, banal and hegemonic) within the same narratives. Clearly, the solution lies in acknowledging that indirect resistance, even in its most creative form, is not completely isolated from overarching ideological influences and culturally established patterns of explaining causality. In vernacular political discourse, pre-existing interpretations provide the building blocks for new challenging explanations of timely events (and their relationship with power).

In his earlier work, Scott (1990) attempted to isolate the narratives of discontent within "hidden transcripts" and autonomous context of subaltern sociality. The example of anti-austerity indignation in Greece shows that this compartmentalization is not a wise analytic strategy, a point that echoes previous critiques (Keesing 1992; Gledhill 1994; Moore 1998; Fletcher 2001). Indirect resistance is not immune to the recycling of wider (and occasionally hegemonic) ideological narratives (Keesing 1992), as does not exist in a power vacuum (see Gledhill 2012). For this reason, it would be wise to complement our analytic de-pathologization of resistance with an equal commitment to avoiding its idealization (Abu-Lughod's 1990; Keesing 1992; Ortner 1995), an approach to which I refer to the introduction to this issue, as the de-exoticization of resistance. The ambivalence of anti-austerity discourse in Greece lies within the very conditions that make it meaningful and persuasive at the local level: its embeddedness in social relations, cultural expectations and previous ideological narratives.

Acknowledgements

An earlier version of this article was presented at the seminar "Anthropological Perspectives on the crisis in Southern Europe" organized by Charles Stewart and Daniel Knight in London (28 June 2013). I am grateful to the participants of this seminar, as well as the three anonymous reviewers of *History and Anthropology* for their enthusiastic comments and suggestions.

Notes

[1]   My use of the term "indignant" as equivalent of *aganaktisménos/i/oi* bears tribute to the Spanish *indignados*, who started the movement that inspired the respective "Greek indignant movement" (*Kinima Aganaktismenon Politon*). This connection, as well as subsequent use by

protestors, protesting authors and journalists has widely established the terms indignation/ indignant as the English equivalent of the Greek *aganaktisi* (noun) and *aganaktismenos* (adjective), and this translation is favoured by most dictionaries. Anthropologists, in an attempt to capture the polysemy of the term, have used alternative terms to discuss Greek indignation: "exasperation" (Herzfeld 2011; Kalantzis 2012), "infuriation" (Theodossopoulos 2013a) and "rage" (Panourgia 2011). In fact, the terms outraged, exasperated and infuriated translate in Greek as *exorgismenos*, *exagriomenos*, *ekneyrismenos*, a lack of definitional precision, which facilitates the figurative and all-embracing relevance of indignation as trope in everyday conversation.

[2]   Anthropological accounts based on longitudinal fieldwork trace the transformation in Greek household strategies and economic status throughout the last four decades of the twentieth century; see for example the work of Kenna (1990, 2001).

[3]   In a recent article, Dalakoglou (2012) discusses the limits of "spontaneity" in anti-systemic resistance and the difficulty with differentiating clearly between spontaneous and non-spontaneous action in the context of the Greek anti-austerity movement.

[4]   Although aware of similar immigration problems in other EU nations, such Italy or Spain, my respondents in Patras maintain a rather inward-looking view when they discuss the impact of illegal immigration. Their references to other EU countries refer mostly to the responsibility of the industrialized North, with the intention of highlighting how the nations of the European South, and in particular Greece, pay the heaviest cost in dealing with the consequences of immigration.

[5]   For recent examples of "lessons from history as negotiated by Greek local actors in the context of the current financial crisis", see Knight (2012a, 2012b).

[6]   Even supporters of the communist party (which has retained an honest and steady anti-neo-liberal orientation for decades) use nationalist arguments to the dismay of a few older fellow-communists who have been indoctrinated to an internationalist (class-based) vision of comradery.

[7]   Herzfeld has used the notion of "crypto-colonialism" to refer to countries whose national ideologies and "modalities of independence have been defined by outsiders" (Herzfeld in Byrne 2011, 147), often by placing such countries and national cultures "on high cultural pedestals that effectively isolate them from other, more brutally material forms of power" (Herzfeld 2002, 902).

References

Abu-Lughod, Lila. 1990. "The Romance of Resistance: Tracing Transformations of Power Through Bedouin Women." *American Ethnologist* 17 (1): 41–55.

Appadurai, Arjun. 1996. *Modernity at Large: Cultural Dimensions of Globalization*. Minneapolis, MN: University of Minnesota Press.

Appadurai, Arjun. 2001. "Grassroots Globalization and the Research Imagination." In *Globalization*, edited by A. Appadurai, 1–21. Durham, NC: Duke University Press.

Argyrou, Vassos. 1995. *Tradition and Modernity in the Mediterranean: The Wedding as Symbolic Struggle*. Cambridge: Cambridge University Press.

Bousiou, Pola. 2008. *The Nomads of Mykonos: Performing Liminalities in a "Queer" Space*. Oxford: Berghahn.

Brown, Keith, and Dimitrios Theodossopoulos. 2000. "The Performance of Anxiety: Greek Narratives of the War at Kossovo." *Anthropology Today* 16 (1): 3–8.

Brown, Keith, and Dimitrios Theodossopoulos. 2003. "Rearranging Solidarity: Conspiracy and the World Order in Greek and Macedonian Commentaries of Kosovo." *Journal of Southern Europe and the Balkans* 5 (3): 315–335.

Brown, Keith, and Y. Yannis Hamilakis. 2003. "The Cupboard of the Yesterdays? Critical Perspectives on the Usable Past." In *The Usable Past: Greek Metahistories*, edited by K. S. Brown & Y. Hamilakis, 1–19. Lanham, MD: Lexington books.

Carrithers, Michael. 2009. "Introduction." In *Culture, Rhetoric and the Vicissitudes of Life*, edited by M. Carrithers, 1–17. Oxford: Berghahn.

Cowan, Jane. 1990. *Dance and the Body Politic in Northern Greece*. Princeton, NJ: Princeton University Press.

Dalakoglou, Dimitris. 2012. "Beyond Spontaneity: Crisis, Violence and Collective Action in Athens." *City: Analysis of Urban Trends, Culture, Theory, Policy, Action* 16 (5): 535–545.

Douzinas, Costas. 2013. *Philosophy and Resistance in the Crisis*. Cambridge: Polity Press.

Dubisch, Jill. 1995. *In a Different Place: Pilgrimage, Gender, and Politics of a Greek Island Shrine*. Princeton, NJ: Princeton University Press.

Du Boulay, Juliet. 1974. *Portrait of a Greek Mountain Village*. Oxford: Clarendon Press.

Faubion, James D. 1993. *Modern Greek Lessons: A Primer in Historical Constructivism*. Princeton, NJ: Princeton University Press.

Fernandez, James W. 1986. *Persuasions and Performances: The Play of Tropes in Culture*. Bloomington: Indiana University Press.

Fernandez, James W. 2009. "Rhetoric in the Moral Order: A Critique of Tropological Approaches to Culture." In *Culture, Rhetoric and the Vicissitudes of Life*, edited by Michael Carrithers, 156–172. Oxford: Berghahn.

Fletcher, Robert. 2001. "What are We Fighting for? Rethinking Resistance in a Pewenche Community in Chile." *The Journal of Peasant Studies* 28 (3): 37–66.

Friedl, Ernestine. 1962. *Vassilika: A Village in Modern Greece*. New York: Holt, Rinehart and Winston.

Friedl, Ernestine. 1969. "Lagging Emulation in Post-Peasant Society." *American Anthropologist* 66 (3): 569–586.

Gledhill, John. 1994. *Power and Its Disguises: Anthropological Perspectives on Politics*. London: Pluto Press.

Gledhill, John. 2012. "Introduction: A Case for Rethinking Resistance." In *New Approaches to Resistance in Brazil and Mexico*, edited by John Gledhill, 1–20. Durham, NC: Duke University Press.

Gourgouris, Stathis. 2011. "Indignant Politics in Athens: Democracy Out of Rage." *Greek Left Review*, 17 July 2011. http://greekleftreview.wordpress.com/tag/gourgouris (accessed 16 January 2014).

Hart, Laurie K. 1992. *Time, Religion, and Social Experience in Rural Greece*. Lanham, MD: Rowman & Littlefield.

Herzfeld, Michael. 1982. "The Etymology of Excuses: Aspects of Rhetorical Performance in Greece." *American Ethnologist* 9 (4): 644–663.

Herzfeld, Michael. 1985. *The Poetics of Manhood: Contest and Identity in a Cretan Mountain Village*. Princeton, NJ: Princeton University Press.

Herzfeld, Michael. 1987. *Anthropology Through the Looking-Glass: Critical Ethnography in the Margins of Europe*. Cambridge: Cambridge University Press.

Herzfeld, Michael. 1992. *The Social Production of Indifference: Exploring the Symbolic Roots of Western Bureaucracy*. Chicago, IL: University of Chicago Press.

Herzfeld, Michael. 1997. *Cultural Intimacy: Social Poetics in the Nation State*. New York: Routledge.

Herzfeld, Michael. 2002. "The Absent Presence: Discourses of Crypto-Colonialism." *South Atlantic Quarterly* 101 (4): 899–926.

Herzfeld, Michael. 2007. "Small-Mindedness Writ Large: On the Migrations and Manners of Prejudice." *Journal of Ethnic and Migration Studies* 33 (2): 255–274.

Herzfeld, Michael. 2009. "Convictions: Embodied Rhetorics of Earnest Belief." In *Culture and Rhetoric*, edited by I. Strecker & S. Tyler, 182–206. Oxford: Berghahn.

Herzfeld, Michael. 2011. "Crisis Attack: Impromptu Ethnography in the Greek Maelstrom." *Anthropology Today* 27 (5): 22–26.

Hirschon, Renée. 2000. "Identity and the Greek State: Some Conceptual Issues and Paradoxes." In *The Greek Diaspora in the Twentieth Century*, edited by R. Clogg, 158–180. London: MacMillan.

Hirschon, Renée. 2013. "Cultural Mismatches: Greek Concepts of Time, Personal Identity, and Authority in the Context of Europe." In *Europe in Modern Greek History*, edited by Kevin Featherstone, 153–169. London: Hurst.

Just, Roger. 1989. "Triumph of the Ethnos." In *History and Ethnicity*, edited by E. Tonkin, M. McDonald, & M. Chapman, 71–88. London: Routledge.

Just, Roger. 1995. "Cultural Certainties and Private Doubts." In *The Pursuit of Certainty: Religious and Cultural Formulations*, edited by W. James, 285–308. London: Routledge.

Kalantzis, Konstantinos. 2012. "Crete as Warriorhood: Visual Explorations of Social Imaginaries in 'Crisis." *Anthropology Today* 28 (3): 7–11.

Keesing, Roger M. 1992. *Custom and Confrontation: The Kwaio Struggle for Cultural Autonomy*. Chicago, IL: University of Chicago Press.

Kenna, Margaret E. 1990. "Family, Economy and Community on a Greek Island." In *Family, Economy and Community*, edited by C. C. Harris, 143–163. Cardiff: University of Wales Press.

Kenna, Margaret E. 2001. *Greek Island Life: Fieldwork on Anafi*. London: Routledge.

Kirtsoglou, Elisabeth. 2006. "Unspeakable Crimes; Athenian Greek Perceptions of Local and International Terrorism." In *Terror and Violence; Imagination and the Unimaginable*, edited by A. Strathern, P. Stewart, and N. Whitehead, 61–88. London: Pluto.

Kirtsoglou, Elisabeth. 2013. "The Dark Ages of the Golden Dawn: Anthropological Analysis and Responsibility in the Twilight Zone of the Greek Crisis." *Journal of the Finnish Anthropological Society* 38 (1): 104–108.

Kirtsoglou, Elisabeth, and Dimitrios Theodossopoulos. 2010a. "Intimacies of Anti-Globalisation: Imagining Unhappy Others as Oneself in Greece." In *United in Discontent: Local Responses to Cosmopolitanism and Globalization*, edited by D. Theodossopoulos & E. Kirtsoglou, 85–102. Oxford: Berghahn.

Kirtsoglou, Elisabeth, and Dimitrios Theodossopoulos. 2010b. "The Poetics of Anti-Americanism in Greece: Rhetoric, Agency and Local Meaning." *Social Analysis* 54 (1): 106–124.

Knight, Daniel M. 2012a. "Cultural Proximity: Crisis, Time and Social Memory in Central Greece." *History and Anthropology* 23 (3): 349–374.

Knight, Daniel M. 2012b. "Turn of the Screw: Narratives of History and Economy in the Greek Crisis." *Journal of Mediterranean Studies* 21 (1): 53–76.

Knight, Daniel M. 2013a. "The Greek Economic Crisis as Trope." *Focal: Journal of Global and Historical Anthropology*, 65: 147–159.

Knight, Daniel M. 2013b. "Opportunism and Diversification: Entrepreneurship and Livelihood Strategies in Uncertain Times." *Ethnos* 79 (2): 1–28.

Moore, Donald. 1998. "Subaltern Struggles and the Politics of Place: Remapping Resistance in Zimbabwe's Highlands." *Cultural Anthropology* 12 (3): 344–381.

Ortner, Sherry B. 1995. "Resistance and the Problem of Ethnographic Refusal." *Comparative Studies in Society and History* 37 (1): 173–193.

Panourgia, Neni. 2011. "The Squared Constitution of Dissent." In *Hot spots: Beyond the 'Greek crisis' Histories, Rhetorics, Politics*, edited by P. Papailias. *Cultural Anthropology*. http://culanth.org/?q=node/438

Papadakis, Yiannis. 2004. "Discourses of 'the Balkans' in Cyprus: Tactics, Strategies and Constructions of 'Others." *History & Anthropology* 15 (1): 15–28.

Papailias, Penelope, ed. 2011a. "Beyond the 'Greek Crisis': Histories, Rhetorics, Politics." Fieldsights —Hot Spots. *Cultural Anthropology*. http://www.culanth.org/fieldsights/243-beyond-the-greek-crisis-histories-rhetorics-politics

Papailias, Penelope. 2011b. "Witnessing the Crisis." In *Hot Spots: Beyond the "Greek Crisis": Histories, Rhetorics, Politics*, edited by P. Papailias. *Cultural Anthropology*. http://culanth.org/?q=node/432

Postill, John. 2014. "Democracy in the Age of Viral Reality: A Media Epidemiography of Spain's Indignados Movement." *Ethnography* 15 (1): 50–68.

Rakopoulos, Theodoros. 2014. "Solidarity Economy in Contemporary Greece: "Movementality", Economic Democracy and Social Reproduction during Crisis." In *Economy For and Against Democracy*, edited by Keith Hart and John Sharp. Oxford: Berghahn.

Sanders, Todd, and Harry G. West. 2003. "Power Revealed and Concealed in the New World Order." In *Transparency and Conspiracy: Ethnographies of Suspicion in the New World Order*, edited by H.G. West T. Sanders, 1–37. Durham, NC: Duke University Press.

Scott, James C. 1985. *Weapons of the Weak: Everyday Forms of Peasant Resistance*. New Haven, CT: Yale University Press.

Scott, James C. 1990. *Domination and the Arts of Resistance: Hidden Transcripts*. New Haven, CT: Yale University Press.

Stewart, Charles. 1994. "Syncretism as a Dimension of Nationalist Discourse in Modern Greece." In *Syncretism/Antisyncretism: The Politics of Religious Synthesis*, edited by C. Stewart and R. Shaw, 127–144. London: Routledge.

Stewart, Charles. 2012. *Dreaming and Historical Consciousness in Island Greece*. Cambridge, MA: Harvard University Press.

Sutton, David. 1998. *Memories Cast in Stone: The Relevance of the Past in Everyday Life*. Oxford: Berg.

Sutton, David. 2003. "Poked by the 'Foreign Finger' in Greece: Conspiracy Theory or the Hermeneutics of Suspicion?" In *The Usable Past: Greek Metahistories*, edited by K. S. Brown and Y. Hamilakis, 191–210. Lanham, MD: Lexington books.

Theodossopoulos, Dimitrios. 2003a. "Degrading Others and Honouring Ourselves: Ethnic Stereotypes as Categories and as Explanations." *Journal of Mediterranean Studies* 13 (2): 177–188.

Theodossopoulos, Dimitrios. 2003b. *Troubles with Turtles: Cultural Understandings of the Environment on a Greek Island*. Oxford: Berghahn.

Theodossopoulos, Dimitrios. 2004. "The Turks and Their Nation in the Worldview of Greeks in Patras." *History and Anthropology* 15 (1): 29–45.

Theodossopoulos, Dimitrios. 2007a. "Introduction: The 'Turks' in the Imagination of the 'Greeks'." In *When Greeks Think about Turks: The View from Anthropology*, edited by D. Theodossopoulos, 1–32. London: Routledge.

Theodossopoulos, Dimitrios. 2007b. "Politics of Friendship, Worldviews of Mistrust: The Greek-Turkish Rapprochement in Local Conversation." In *When Greeks Think about Turks: The View from Anthropology*, edited by D. Theodossopoulos, 193–210. London: Routledge.

Theodossopoulos, Dimitrios. 2010. "Introduction: United in Discontent." In *United in Discontent: Local Responses to Cosmopolitanism and Globalization*, edited by D. Theodossopoulos and E. Kirtsoglou, 1–19. Oxford: Berghahn.

Theodossopoulos, Dimitrios. 2013a. "Infuriated with the Infuriated? Blaming Tactics and Discontent about the Greek Financial Crisis." *Current Anthropology* 54 (2): 200–221.

Theodossopoulos, Dimitrios. 2013b. "Supporting a Party that You Don't Entirely Support." *Journal of the Finnish Anthropological Society* 38 (1): 109–111.

Theodossopoulos, Dimitrios. 2014a. "The Poetics of Indignation in Greece: Anti-Austerity Protest and Accountability." In *Beyond the Arab Spring: the Aesthetics and Poetics of Popular Revolt and Protest*, edited by Pnina Werbner, Martin Webb, and Kathryn Spellman-Poots, 368–388. Edinburgh: Edinburgh University Press.

Theodossopoulos, Dimitrios. 2014b. "De-pathologising resistance." *History and Anthropology*. Forthcoming.

Verney, Susannah. 2011. "An Exceptional Case? Party and Popular Euroscepticism in Greece, 1959–2009." *South European Society and Politics* 16 (1): 51–79.

Indigenous Autonomy, Delinquent States, and the Limits of Resistance[†]

John Gledhill

This paper focuses on struggles by Mexican indigenous communities to defend their patrimony and guarantee their own security in an environment dominated by the parallel power of organized crime, paramilitary violence, impunity, and a neo-extractivist economy. After reviewing the relationships between the radicalization of indigenous autonomy demands and transformations of the Mexican state, analysis focuses on recent developments involving a Nahua community on the Pacific coast of Michoacán state that has a long history of successful defence of its communal lands, alongside a Purépecha community in the central highlands that has been its longstanding ally. The violence of external actors reflects the penetration of all levels of government by organized crime, but violence is not a new historical experience in this region. What has changed is that the capacity of these communities to resist has been affected by their internal disarticulation by the same forces.

Introduction

In a recent survey of critiques levelled against the 1980s resistance studies literature, I observed that one reason for wanting to agree with anthropologists such as Ortner (1995) and Fletcher (2001) that resistance remains a meaningful object of analysis is that "resisting" may be "what our research subjects say they are doing when they struggle, to defend their lands, culture, or religion, or to achieve *new* rights and social dignity in situations of inequality and discrimination" (Gledhill 2012, 1–2). I

[†]The research on which this paper is based forms part of a larger project carried out with the aid of a Leverhulme Trust Major Research Fellowship, entitled "Security for All in the Age of Securitization?"

exemplified the point by referring to Ostula, an indigenous community that I studied on the Pacific Coast of Michoacán state in Mexico, at that time engaged in a high stakes struggle to defend its control over resources that had already cost lives, although the death toll was soon to mount further. This paper offers an updating of the Ostula story, in the context of developments that have led some commentators to argue that the situation in Michoacán threatens national security.

In my earlier essay about "resistance", I argued, in criticism of James Scott, that there are no spaces of social action that are totally insulated from dominant power relations. I also emphasized how emancipating oneself from one set of power relations very often produces subordination to a new set of power relations, as Abu-Lughod (1990) showed in her reworking of the Foucauldian account of the inevitable complementarity of power and resistance. Collective subjects engaged in acts that might be described as "resistance" are seldom internally homogeneous, and as Ortner (1995, 177) observes, the fact that "subalterns have their own politics" influences the long-term results of their struggles even if those struggles began from a provisional position of unity. Ignoring such divisions is politically and ethically problematic, particularly if it silences movements against new kinds of domination within the "subaltern" population itself, which are often engineered through new interventions by the state or private capital in response to the gains produced by subaltern activism (Jones 1995). Since "internal" divisions so often reflect the interventions of actors external to the group in question, I argued that much of what resistance studies discusses could be embedded in a more dialectical account of the relationship between hegemony and resistance that recognizes that Gramsci's account of hegemony cannot be reduced to either ideology or false consciousness since, as Crehan (2002, 174) points out, for Gramsci, hegemony "always involves practical activity, and the social relations that produce inequality, as well as the ideas by which that inequality is justified, explained, normalized, and so on". As Dimitrios Theodossopoulos notes in his introduction to this collection of papers, I also suggested that the issues on which "resistance studies" focus could be expanded to articulate better with the broader study of social movements and "contentious politics".

The case study that follows exemplifies how stories about resistance can be made more complicated, but it also offers strong support to Theodossopoulos's arguments against the "pathologization", "exoticization" and "depoliticization" of resistance. Although all forms of social protest now tend to be criminalized in Mexico, indigenous Mexicans like the Ostulans offer a perfect example of the kinds of populations whose actions have habitually been painted as "irrational". Outsiders generally do not understand indigenous conceptions of territoriality that clash with the practices and assumptions of official land reform. They have seldom noticed how such communities produced their own intellectuals and found their own ways of engaging with the state and external elites in a political way long before the modern period. What the Ostulans have been resisting in recent years is, however, a development model that has been provoking growing mobilization throughout the entire Latin American region. There are many fractures and contradictions within this new wave of mobilization. Tourism, mining or energy mega-projects tend to produce local winners as well as losers, thereby factionalizing local communities. Yet not recognizing that there is a wave of "resistance" as "contention" that is provoking a great deal of repression would seem absurd.

Ostula: History Repeating Itself?

At first sight, contemporary conflicts on the Michoacán coast seem to replicate past historical patterns. The lure of gold brought the Spanish conquistadores rushing to the coast as soon as they had subdued the Aztec empire in the Mexican central highlands. Yet although this initiated a traumatic first century of colonial conquest and exploitation for the indigenous people who survived it, neither mining nor cacao plantations were to provide the basis for a sustainable colonial economy, and by the second half of the seventeenth century, the majority of Spanish residents had withdrawn (Sánchez Díaz 2001). This created a space of relative autonomy in which an indigenous population greatly reduced from pre-colonial levels could return to some of their old ways of organizing their territories and managing economic resources, albeit within institutions of "self-government" that reflected their appropriation of European symbols and practices, especially in the field of religion (Gledhill 2004). Members of a post-conquest Náhuatl-speaking provincial world that stretched northwards into Jalisco state and southwards into Guerrero, the coastguard militia of Ostula played an active role in the regional movement for Independence from Spain, but the nineteenth century did not bring these indigenous inhabitants of the new Mexican republic the deliverance from subaltern status for which they had risen up in arms. On the contrary, it brought new threats of mass dispossession from their communal lands and forests as the remaining judicial constraints provided by colonial laws were abolished, and *criollo* regional elites based in the highland town of Coalcomán dreamed of fostering an industrial revolution on the basis of the area's rich deposits of iron ore (Sánchez Díaz 1979). Such elites saw collaboration with European and North American capitalists in a favourable light, but their racism towards Indians was now inspired by nineteenth-century models of biological inferiority that painted them as an obstacle to "development" that would be best addressed by their displacement and repopulation of the area with "white" immigrants.

Although the Mexican Revolution of 1910 prevented completion of this elite project, the indigenous communities of the coast continued to suffer invasions from non-indigenous ranchers descending from the highlands in search of new lands (Cochet 1991). By the time that the post-revolutionary state began to restore judicial recognition to indigenous communal landholdings in the region in the 1950s, four of the seven original colonial communities had been completely extinguished and their original residents mostly converted into landless workers in neighbouring agribusiness regions. A new mestizo village, La Placita, was established on the coast on the borders of Ostula's territory, and the old indigenous community of Maquilí and municipal seat in Aquila were almost completely taken over by mestizo invaders. Two of the surviving indigenous communities, Pomaro and Coire, were also obliged to tolerate a substantial presence of mestizos within their borders. Ostula, whose agrarian community possessed 19,000 hectares of land and a population of 3360 at the time of the 1991 agrarian census, was, however, distinguished by a dogged defence of its territory that meant that the community still kept its rights to communal land intact *de facto* before they were reaffirmed *de jure* by the official land reform apparatus in 1964. Furthermore, even after 1964, Ostula's communal assembly continued to dispute the boundaries assigned to the community under the agrarian reform process and to mobilize its members against invasions by outsiders (Gledhill 2004).

On the basis of this historical record, it is tempting to construct a narrative in which Ostula figures as what its leaders proclaimed it to be in 2006 when they aligned it with the movement led by the Zapatista Army of National Liberation (EZLN) in Chiapas, "a community in resistance" endowed with a millennial "culture of resistance" that had enabled it to defend its territory successfully. Yet such a narrative would be simplistic for precisely the kinds of reasons that anthropologists such as Ortner and Fletcher have revealed. As was the case with most other Mexican indigenous communities, Ostula's internal political life always involved a great deal of factional conflict and disagreement over strategy. Some of the community leaders who were linked to external actors, including, in the twentieth century, the state's agrarian reform apparatus and (illegal) logging interests, tried to use the power that those relationships brought to their personal advantage in order to subvert the communal order and transform themselves into local political bosses. What distinguished Ostula in the history that I documented in my 2004 book was the repeated failure of these kinds of efforts to subvert communal institutions, whose resilience repeatedly served to mobilize the majority of community members in defence of their land and assertion of sovereign control over their resources, including those subsoil resources that the national constitution claims as property of the nation. Nevertheless, developments since 2006 have brought changes to community life that threaten the reproduction of this tradition, despite the fact that Ostula is also an example of what, by 2013, had become a more widespread movement on the part of rural communities in several parts of the country to resort to armed self-defence in an effort to end the depredations of criminal organizations able to operate with impunity in their territories.

This paper therefore seeks to offer a diagnosis of the limits of community resistance at a moment in which there is not only an upsurge of resistance in Mexico to mining, energy and tourism projects that local people perceive as threatening their displacement,[1] but also an increasing recourse to armed local self-defence forces in an effort to deal with the problems posed by the nature of the Mexican state. These developments are not restricted to communities and regions that retain an indigenous identity. Western Mexico was the epicentre of the Cristiada rebellion of Catholics against the secularizing post-revolutionary government of Plutarco Elías Calles (Meyer 1976; Butler 2004),[2] and home to a host of lesser known insurgencies and millenarian movements. The government itself armed peasants who supported the land reform to defend themselves against the Cristeros. So some of what is going on today is not entirely lacking in historical precedent. It is, however, necessary to be circumspect, with regard to contemporary as well as past episodes, in analysing the meaning and significance of local conflicts, not simply because they are sometimes rooted in local problems, but because their non-local dimensions often further complicate their logic.

The *cristero* fighters were not different kinds of rural people from the peasants who fought against them on the side of the government because their priority was land reform, something only the state could deliver. Indeed, their similarity probably exacerbated the violence of their antagonism, although some individuals did actually change sides, generally from *agrarista* to *cristero*. Notions such as "resisting the state" never took us very far towards understanding what was going on in these kinds of contexts. But such problems magnify in a contemporary context in which mafias present themselves on YouTube as social movements and establish religious cults, and it has become increasingly difficult to conceal the profundity with which organized crime has penetrated the state security apparatus.[3]

Whatever historical precedents may exist for some of the processes described in this paper, recent history in Mexico has both awoken new hopes and aspirations and then tended to dash them in a way that produces consequences that it will become increasingly difficult to reverse. The nineteenth-century cycle of agrarian rebellions and resistance to dispossession did, after all, end in the most comprehensive agrarian reform ever undertaken in Latin America, even though Mexico retained a dualistic structure in which capitalist agriculture remained dominant over "the social sector" comprising the land reform communities called *ejidos* and the communal landholdings of indigenous communities. The danger is that the twenty-first century will replay the nineteenth with even greater levels of dispossession. Yet at first sight this seems paradoxical, particularly as far as indigenous people are concerned, because state-sponsored neoliberal multiculturalism in Mexico had scarcely been rolled out when it received an unexpected challenge from the armed rebellion of the EZLN against the Mexican government and global neoliberalism. In the next section, I will consider the broader ramifications of what happened in Chiapas, before turning in more detail to my case studies from Michoacán.

Neoliberalism and Indigenous Rights

Mexico was the second country, after Norway, to ratify International Labour Organization Convention 169, in September 1990, under the administration of President Carlos Salinas de Gortari. At that moment, two years after the elections that brought Salinas to power had been widely impugned as fraudulent, Mexico found itself in the middle of an accelerating transition towards a new neoliberal economic and political model over which there was little consensus even within the Institutional Revolutionary Party (PRI), the political machine that monopolized power for the seventy years before it finally conceded defeat to the right-wing National Action Party (PAN) in the presidential election of 2000. In 1992, an amendment to Constitutional Article 4 (relocated to Article 2 in 2001) declared Mexico "a nation that has a pluricultural composition originally based on its indigenous peoples". Yet despite the "progressive" appearance of its recognition of indigenous rights, the principal goal of the Salinas "reforms" was to strengthen Mexico's participation in neoliberal capitalist globalization: the government did not worry about whether its economic strategy was likely to conflict with the aspirations of the newly recognized "indigenous peoples".

The year 1992 also saw the revolutionary agrarian reform officially ended through amendments to Constitutional Article 27. These were accompanied by other judicial and institutional changes designed to facilitate the privatization of the lands granted by the state to the *ejidos*.[4] The end of land redistribution removed the material basis that had underpinned the post-revolutionary state's efforts to convince indigenous people to abandon their specific ethnic identities for a "national" peasant-mestizo class identity (Boyer 2003). Although specific claims on the part of indigenous people began to manifest themselves long before 1992, as a consequence of the failure of the post-revolutionary regime to fulfil its promises to the peasantry and the everyday experiences of racism and discrimination that many who did retain their indigenous identities continued to suffer, the juridical, economic and political transformations of the 1990s strengthened tendencies for agrarian and "peasant" demands to be reformulated as ethnic demands in states in which a significant minority of the rural population still identified itself as indigenous despite the fact that the majority had abandoned indigenous for mestizo identities (Overmyer-Velázquez 2010).

The Salinas government rapidly demonstrated that what was on offer to indigenous Mexicans was neoliberal multiculturalism, a regime of rights and recognition that would draw a clear line between what Charles Hale has distinguished as "permitted Indians" and "too radical Indians" who sought to add control over economic resources deemed valuable by capitalist markets to the right to preserve their cultures and languages (Hale 2006). In this sense, the regime extended a policy of control and co-optation that dated back to the beginnings of the independent political mobilization of indigenous actors in the 1970s. In many cases, the indigenous leaders who had pioneered this shift were motivated principally by their continued exclusion from local power by mestizo elites and had tended to remain within the "official" system of the PRI once they succeeded in improving their access to office. Nevertheless, the impact of the 1994 EZLN rebellion was soon to demonstrate that the neoliberal state had created new conditions that were propitious for the development of a much more radical indigenous movement than the architects of neoliberal multiculturalism had envisaged.

The Chiapaneco "neo-Zapatista" movement was the product of an historically unprecedented encounter between non-indigenous urban revolutionaries and indigenous peasant communities previously organized by clerics inspired by Liberation Theology and left-wing activists more orientated to electoral politics and capturing state power than the founders of the EZLN, subcomandante Marcos and his indigenous comrades in arms (Leyva Solano and Ascencio Franco 2002; Estrada Saavedra 2005). The leaders of the politico-military organization behind the village "support bases" of the EZLN dreamed, and have continued to dream, of the possibility of uniting the socially diverse expressions of discontent with neoliberal capitalism into a pluralistic and inclusive "rainbow coalition" that would revive the Mexican Left and transcend the social boundaries between indigenous people and mestizos that the state had so assiduously cultivated for many decades after the 1910 Revolution through assimilationist policies designed to turn "Indians into Mexicans". In reality, the movement failed to maintain its hegemony over the popular movement even in Chiapas, which resulted in a regional elite aligned with the PRI reconstituting its power. As an impressive "silent march" of young Zapatista militants through the principal regional cities of Chiapas in December 2012 demonstrated, the EZLN retains a significant local base. The Zapatistas continue to construct their practices of "autonomy" in regional spaces that they share with groups whose political allegiances are different, sometimes contentiously, under the shadow of continuing counter-insurgency tactics on the part of the state and threats from paramilitary forces with which the state denies any association, and sometimes relatively pacifically. Yet the construction of an effective national coalition of forces remains, at best, a work in progress, particularly following the PRI's recapturing of the national presidency in 2012, with a candidate, Enrique Peña Nieto, who is a scion of a political clique that came to prominence in the Salinas era.

Nevertheless, the EZLN not only succeeded in making itself a global symbol for antiglobalization activists, but also had a profound impact even on sectors of the national indigenous movement that did not wholly share its philosophy. Even groups that remained committed to working through institutional political and legal channels began to promote some kind of model of indigenous autonomy (Díaz Polanco 1997). Far from providing a definitive solution to the "Indian problem", the neoliberal regime therefore opened up a whole new area of dispute.

Controversies over Autonomy: From Chiapas to Michoacán

Part of the debate over autonomy relates to the distinction between projects that propose "self-determination" at the local or communal level and those that advocate models of autonomy that apply to regions, including multi-ethnic regions. The polemics over the federal indigenous law approved by the Mexican congress in 2001, under the PAN administration of Vicente Fox, were strongly focused on this distinction: all references to indigenous "territories" and rights to political association above the level of municipalities were removed by amendments made by the Senate to the original draft bill proposed by the multi-party Commission of Concord and Pacification (COCOPA).[5] The municipal level itself became a further bone of contention. Indigenous movements frequently proposed "remunicipalization" as a condition for exercising autonomy, that is, they proposed either the creation of new municipalities for indigenous populations hitherto dependent on mestizo authorities, or the restoration of municipal rank to indigenous communities that had lost that status as a consequence of the rise to dominance of non-indigenous groups. In the case of Chiapas, however, the state government converted remunicipalization programmes into another weapon of the low-intensity counter-insurgency campaign against the Zapatistas (Leyva Solano and Burguete Cal y Mayor 2007). The response of the EZLN to these provocations came in 2003, with establishment of its own scheme for organization above the municipal level, based on the "Good Government Councils", committees with a rotating membership of representatives of the Zapatista autonomous communities of the region that ran "autonomous" education and health projects and acted as tribunals in the settlement of disputes, offering their services to Zapatistas and non-Zapatistas alike.

Despite these imaginative responses, the federal and state governments possessed sufficient material resources and political guile to contain the EZLN advance. Nor did more radical autonomy projects fare well in the neighbouring state of Oaxaca, where indigenous people make up almost half the population. In 1995, a new state constitution gave official approval to the election of municipal authorities on the basis of "uses and customs" rather than voting for candidates of political parties in the standard system of individual secret ballots.[6] Although this produced a more tranquil political climate for a while, a bitter conflict did finally break out, in 2006, between the PRI state governor, Ulises Ruiz, and a disparate coalition of indigenous and non-indigenous social movements grouped into the Popular Assembly of the People of Oaxaca (Norget 2010). With the support of the Fox government, Ruiz won the battle by means of repression, although he was also able to take advantage of the divisions that existed within and between indigenous communities in an ethnically fragmented state whose 570 mostly tiny municipalities comprise almost a quarter of the national total. In this context, it was unsurprising that paramilitary groups enjoyed impunity when they harassed and besieged communities that expressed their demands for autonomy in terms of trying to secure greater local control over their resources.

In states with smaller indigenous minorities, even indigenous organizations that made more radical autonomy demands found themselves obliged to try to negotiate with state governments that were likely to be more preoccupied with other constituencies and interests in an effort to secure state legislation more favourable to their cause than the federal law. In Michoacán, the largest part of the indigenous population is concentrated in the central highlands and belongs to the Purépecha ethnic group, although the state has smaller populations of other ethnicities, including the Nahuas of the coastal regime that are the main focus of this paper. After the electoral fraud of 1988, a significant part of the Purépecha indigenous leadership abandoned the PRI to join the Party of the Democratic Revolution (PRD), a new party created by the candidate who lost the presidential election to Carlos Salinas, Cuauhtémoc Cárdenas, former PRI state governor and son of the michoacano Lázaro Cárdenas del Río, Mexican president from 1934 to 1940 and architect of the radical land reform and nationalization of the oil industry. The connection with the Cárdenas family is a special factor in Michoacán (Pérez Ramírez 2009). The 2002 state elections gave control of the state to the PRD and brought Cuauhtémoc's son, Lázaro Cárdenas Batel, into the governorship. Although these circumstances gave Purépecha leaders more reasons than ever to enter into dialogue with the state government, they were disappointed by its proposals. Despite having been trained as an anthropologist and frequently expressed his partisanship of indigenous rights, as a senator Cárdenas Batel had voted with the Right on the amendments to the COCOPA law. Although he subsequently apologized for this "error", he rejected proposals by the radical Purépecha Nation organization to create regional autonomies via remunicipalization and creation of levels of indigenous self-government above the municipal level (Gledhill 2004). Another contradiction in the political situation under the governorship of Cárdenas

Batel and his PRD successor, Leonel Gody, was the fact that the principal Purépecha leaders, many intellectuals quite socially distanced from the "bases" in whose name they spoke, had strong motives to continue to support the participation of their communities in conventional party-based electoral politics. Their party was in power regionally, and not only had power to implement social programmes, but also powers of patronage of interest to individuals (Jasso Martínez 2010).

Nevertheless, in recent years more sectors of Michoacán's indigenous movement have begun to follow the lead of Chiapas and Oaxaca in advocating the expulsion of conventional electoral parties from communal political life and elections by "uses and customs". This move has been taken furthest in the Purépecha municipality of Cherán, a community always noted for its internal disputes as well as for conflicts with neighbours over resources. Blaming escalating infighting between PRI and PRD factions for creating the situation that allowed organized crime to impose its grip on the divided community, the Cherán autonomists also opted for organizing an armed self-defence force as the only means of defending the community's forests, ending extortion and guaranteeing security to the local population. In this respect, they were following a path already taken in the Nahua community of Ostula on the coast, which was, in turn, following a tradition of using communal police forces as local self-defence forces that was already established in Guerrero state, where a regional coordinating association of communal police groups, the Coordinadora Regional de Autoridades Comunitarias (CRAC), was founded in 1995. By 2013, however, armed *autodefensas* were proliferating rapidly but also controversially in Michoacán and other regions in non-indigenous as well as indigenous communities.

State Transformation and the Rise of the *Autodefensas*

Although all those involved in such groups declared themselves to be ordinary citizens driven to self-defence by the incapacity of government to protect them from the depredations of criminals, some of the emerging groups were extremely well armed with sophisticated automatic weapons, exciting the suspicion that those weapons had been supplied by another of the drug cartels competing for control of their region. In the case of Colombia, the Spanish term *autodefensa* has the historical connotation of paramilitaries fighting left-wing guerrillas, on behalf of a government that they declared incapable of doing the job properly, but also linked to landlord interests and drug trafficking. The term "community police" (*policía comunitaria*) in Mexico has a less threatening air to it, because it has different historical associations in indigenous communities, where serving in the communal police was a form of service that most adults would perform at one or more points in their lives, without pay, and subject to election by community assemblies. Such organizations worked in terms of specifically indigenous concepts of security and the administration of justice, which take violence as an inevitable aspect of social life, and use a mixture of punishment and negotiation of settlements calculated to prevent conflict escalating (Speed and Collier 2000).

Democratically run local organizations of policing and the administration of justice that enjoy genuine popular support may offer a way forward to guaranteeing security to all in societies whose official justice systems are plagued by procedural inadequacies in terms of both North Atlantic legal norms and class and racial biases. Yet comparative historical evidence from organizations such as the Peruvian *rondas campesinas* (peasant patrols) suggests that even when they work in terms of reasonable deliberative procedures and even mimic official state practices to some extent, "autonomous" local policing and justice systems are not immune from external manipulation or a play of internal factionalism that can generate "boss rule" in the longer term (Starn 1999). In the case of Michoacán, some of the heavily armed self-defence forces that have appeared in non-indigenous communities do appear to be genuine expressions of popular desperation, opposed to local officials who do have known links with organized crime. But that is not inconsistent with their also being a reflection of local factionalism. In the case of an *autodefensa* formed in Ostula's municipal seat, Aquila, in 2013, which was promptly disarmed by federal forces and its members imprisoned, the factionalism relates to local conflicts over the distribution of payments by the local mining company. Not only is there a danger that some of those involved in extra-legal paramilitary organizations will themselves turn to crime and extortion if they gain undisputed local control, but the proliferation of armed actors may also complicate the eventual establishment of a more conventional kind of "rule of law" anchored in reformed state institutions.

Another anxiety, voiced in the case of Guerrero, whose PRD governor, formerly affiliated to the PRI, had a long experience of operating as a regional political boss, was that the state government might co-opt armed groups not aligned with the CRAC to suppress resistance to the extension of mining operations by transnational companies. The indigenous CRAC itself supported local teachers and other dissidents in a militant revolt against the governor's authority over a federal educational reform bill, provoking further claims that local self-defence forces were exacerbating violent protest and "ungovernability". In May 2013, the federal government sent the army into Michoacán promising to restore order by renewing the persecution of criminal groups, although the Interior Ministry's insistence that the existence of local *autodefensas* could no longer be justified could be given different interpretations, including anxiety about the capacity of an armed population to resist various kinds of state-sponsored projects.

The processes behind the appearance of groups with paramilitary characteristics in some regions of the country may not always what they appear to be at first sight. Nevertheless, in general terms these developments might be better explained not in terms of a simple "absence of the state" from certain regions, but in terms of the nature of what Goldstein (2012) has termed its "phantom" presence. The mounting violence of recent years can at one level be seen as a consequence of the militarized "war on the cartels" pursued by the PAN government of Felipe Calderón (2006–2012), which cost, at a conservative estimate, nearly 60,000 lives.[7] But I will also argue in what follows that it is the combination of pervasive penetration of the official state apparatus by organized crime and state support for predatory models of capitalist accumulation by "legitimate" economic actors that underlies the current crisis. Like Maldonado Aranda (2012), I see the problem as another unanticipated consequence of the neoliberal transition under the Salinas government: reductions in public spending and state disengagement left rural regions in deepening economic crisis that made illegal economies more important than ever, and the political management of transition rested on improvisations that generated new relations between politicians, business and actors involved in the illegal economy that created a "shadow state" behind the façade of the respectable, institutional apparatus of government (Gledhill 1999).

Although drug trafficking in Mexico has a much longer history, it was during the Salinas period that the Mexican cartels took over trafficking of cocaine to the USA from the Colombians (Campbell 2009; Grillo 2012). Although the past decades have seen an inexorable rise in drug consumption within Mexico itself, it has become increasingly clear that the USA is an important part of the story not simply because of the market it supplies for drugs (and the arms that flow in the opposite direction across the border) but because of the way the Mexican cartels were central to the process by which the US Central Intelligence Agency armed the contra rebels in Nicaragua after Congress blocked federal funding for this purpose, adding to the problems caused by links between senior figures in the Mexican security apparatus and organized crime (Hernández 2012). Trafficking did not represent any significant threat to public security under the old PRI regime (Grayson 2010). Indeed, at the time of Mexico's "dirty war" of the late 1960s and early 1970s against a "communist subversion" that was more of a social justice movement rooted in Christian principles in the case of the guerrilla movements that developed in Guerrero state, a PRI regime whose agents routinely extorted extra-legal payments from poorer citizens not only regulated trafficking by taxing it, but could also call on the assistance of the traffickers in its counter-insurgency operations (Bartra 2000). What changed was that state agents and politicians began to profit more directly from criminal activities, turning what had always been a corrupt system of power into an increasingly "delinquent" one, protecting and nurturing the growth of the illegal economy built on drugs.[8] As a result, the passing years have produced a parallel process of fragmentation in the "real" (that is, shadow) state and in the cartels themselves. This is driven, on the one hand, by the impunity offered by the protection of politicians and elements of the official security forces, and on the other hand, by the struggles to control *plazas*, the territories in which particular groups control the production, transport or sale of drugs. Calderón's security policy exacerbated the situation by accepting US encouragement to "decapitate" the cartels (unleashing violent struggles between lieutenants of fallen drug lords over succession), but fragmentation of the state and of the cartels has also been amplified by the fact that different groups of criminals have enjoyed the support of different political patrons located at the municipal, state and federal levels of government, and in a way that varies between regions and shifts in time as alliances between criminal groups change. In the next section, I show how these processes have worked themselves out on the Pacific Coast of Michoacán.

Agrarian Conflict, Violence and Impunity on the Michoacán Coast

At the start of July 2009, news of the indigenous community of Santa María Ostula, located in the mestizo-dominated municipality of Aquila, hit the front pages of national newspapers. On 29 June, supported by their communal police force and members of the neighbouring indigenous communities of Coire and Pómaro, a large group of men and women from Ostula managed to recover control of a terrain of more than 700 hectares known as La Canahuancera, usurped, according to the Ostulans, for more than forty years by residents of the nearby coastal village of La Placita, founded by invading mestizo ranchers in the nineteenth century and granted an *ejido* during the presidency of Lázaro Cárdenas.

The conflicts between La Placita and Ostula dated back to problems with the official confirmation and titling of Ostula's communal land rights under the agrarian reform programme in the 1960s, but had now escalated to new levels of violence. A year earlier, the teacher acting as President of Ostula's Commission for the Defence of Communal Property (CDBC), Diego Ramírez Domínguez, had been kidnapped and murdered, while leading an attempt to resolve the boundary problem by peaceful legal means in the Unitary Agrarian Tribunal in neighbouring Colima state. Their patience exhausted, the Ostulans invaded La Canahuancera, but were forced to retire on their first attempt after heavily armed men fired upon a group of *comuneros*[9] that included women and children. The communal police subsequently captured some of these aggressors and they were subjected to "moral condemnation" by an indigenous tribunal, although the Ostulans continued to respect the state's official justice system by handing them over to the public prosecutor.

The invasion of the disputed land was planned by a communal assembly. It was decided to give it a new Nahua, name, Xayakalan, and forty families were sent to establish a new settlement on the recovered terrain. The assembly determined that each of the twenty-one *encargaturas del orden*[10] of the indigenous community should make themselves responsible for the construction of palm and adobe houses for the settler families. Thus, under the protection of the national flag and an image of the Virgin of Guadalupe brought from the communal centre in which the main church, schools, communal assembly place and administrative offices are located, the Ostulans repeated a process that had taken place in 1950, when settlers were sent down from the sierras to found the coastal village of La Ticla. There had not previously been any permanent residents in the area bordering the ocean, but this was a strategic response to the perceived threat of community land being taken over and irrigated by non-indigenous farmers backed by important politicians in Colima (Gledhill 2004, 205).

Responding to what was now a fait accompli, the PRD state government promised to broker a definitive solution to the agrarian problem. The landowners from La Placita would receive an indemnification in return for renouncing their rights. The new settlement would be officially recognized as the twenty-second *encargatura del orden* of Ostula. The state government would also broker the official recognition of Ostula's communal police as a "rural defence force" with the Ministry of Defence (Sedena). It failed to deliver on any of these promises and its refusal even to grant official recognition to Xayakalan as an administrative unit meant that its residents could not be assisted from public funds when a hurricane destroyed houses and crops in June 2011, although aid was sent from Cherán, a longstanding ally of Ostula in the Purépecha highlands.

In February 2010, the Ostula CDBC denounced the kidnap of two key figures in the fight to recover Xayakalan, Javier Robles Martínez, an elected member of the municipal council of Aquila, and the teacher Gerardo Vera Orcino. By mid-year, attacks by figures that the Ostulans called "assassins (*sicarios*) and paramilitaries" had resulted in the deaths of eight more *comuneros*. At this point, Ostula not only began to receive the support of human rights NGOs, but also became the subject of an instruction from the Inter-American Court of Human Rights to the Calderón government to take preventative measures, which produced no action whatsoever. By the end of 2011, the tally reached twenty-eight more people killed and eight "disappeared". October brought the death of Pedro Leyva Dominguez, a young activist who acted as link person between Ostula and the national Movement for Peace with Justice and Dignity (MJPD), founded by the poet Javier Sicilia, whose own son was a victim of narco-violence, to question the effectiveness and human cost of Calderón's public security policies.

This phase of the violence appeared to be linked to attempts to resuscitate negotiations over the judicial status of Xayakalan through the Programme of Attention to Rural Social Conflicts of the Agrarian Reform Ministry. Two months after Pedro Leyva was killed, the head of the unofficial *encargatura* of Xayakalan, Trinidad de la Cruz Crisóforo, was kidnapped by a group of heavily armed hooded men when he tried to return to the community accompanied by MPJD activists. Don Trino had taken refuge in Colima for fifteen days after being publicly beaten and threatened with death inside Ostula by a group of *sicarios*. He was now trying to return to participate in discussions about the posture that the community should adopt in its negotiations with the Ministry. Although all the middle-class activists were eventually released without serious physical harm, some of them had to endure the psychological trauma of listening to the screams of seventy-three-year-old Don Trino as he was slowly tortured to death by his kidnappers.

Perhaps the most revealing elements of this tragic episode are the following: firstly, that the escort of Federal Police that was supposed to protect the elderly indigenous leader and the MJPD activists only accompanied them to the entrance to Xayakalan and then suddenly disappeared, without explanation; and secondly, that on the occasion when threats were originally made against Don Trino, Ostulans had denounced known individuals to the authorities, sometimes by name and surname, sometimes by their nicknames. No action was taken. The "paramilitaries" moved freely in the coastal communities, brandishing weapons and threatening people with complete impunity.

By the end of 2011, according to a report by the journalist Blanche Petrich, published in the national newspaper *La Jornada* on 22 December, this harassment was beginning to undermine the spirit of resistance of the defenders of Xayakalan. The father of Pedro Leyva, Santos, was still alive and elected President of the Community Property Commission in 2011, but he was now old and in poor health. The report failed to mention that his predecessor had "disappeared". A meeting with Michoacán's Public Security Secretariat, also attended by representatives of the federal Interior Ministry, Defence Ministry and Public Attorney's Office of the Twenty-First Military District, brought scant results. After Don Trino's murder, a detachment of marines patrolled Xayakalan for a while, but the main focus of military interventions had been on disarming Ostula's communal police, and violence continued to extend into other strategic areas of the indigenous community. In January 2012, gunmen once again denounced by name by members of the indigenous community killed Crisóforo Sánchez Reyes, in charge of La Ticla's irrigation system. In May the body of Teódolo Santos Girón, shot three times, was placed in the entrance to the La Ticla cemetery. Another schoolteacher, fifty-two years old, Teódolo Santos belonged to the PRD and was regional organizer of the presidential campaign of Andrés Manuel López Obrador and his Movement for National Regeneration, despite the fact that the other leaders of the Xayakalan invasion had adopted the Cherán position of rejection of electoral party politics. Yet he was also an integrative figure because he was sympathetic towards the Zapatistas, combining his militancy in the PRD with service as Ostula's delegate to the pro-EZLN National Indigenous Congress.

After 2009, Ostula therefore presented a picture of mounting violence accompanied by a lack of remedial measures on the part of any level of government. The next question to explore is the identity of the authors of this violence.

Drugs, Mafias and Possible Backstage Interests

The most obvious candidates for being its immediate perpetrators are gunmen from organizations involved in the drug trafficking that has long been an important part of the economy of the coastal and *tierra caliente* zones of Michoacán (Maldonado Aranda 2010). At the start of the twenty-first century, control of the drug trade and municipal administration in the Aquila area was being disputed between the Sinaloa cartel and the Gulf cartel, of which the Zetas, a criminal group founded by former military special forces officers, were at that time the paramilitary arm (Grayson and Logan 2012). In 2010, the Zetas became independent, embarking on a bloody war for control of Michoacán's *plazas* with a local group that they had trained, the Familia Michoacana. In Mexico's drug wars violence is communicative: decapitated and dismembered corpses are used, along with banners placed on bridges, to send messages to the enemy and to the population in general. Yet violence was not the only means by which the Familia Michoacana constructed its power within local society. One of its founders, Nazario Moreno González (nicknamed "the Craziest One"), was not simply adept at acting as a patron to cash-strapped farmers and local schools and churches, and as a benefactor of the poor in general, but created his own local religious cult. After the federal police declared that they had "taken out" Moreno in an operation in 2010,[11] two other founding members created a new organization, Los Caballeros Templarios (Knights Templar), which would eventually drive most of what remained of the original Familia Michoacana out of the state (although a reorganized group continued its drug trafficking, kidnapping and extortion rackets in the State of Mexico).

The Caballeros were bitter enemies of the Zetas, but by 2013 were in conflict with Jalisco state's "New Generation" cartel, which they accused of being behind the *auto-defensas* that are persecuting their people in the *tierra caliente*. Yet in their extensive public propaganda (through narco-banners, the media and YouTube) both La Familia and Los Templarios deny being criminal organizations. They present themselves as "social organizations" that are simply seeking to defend the people of Michoacán from abusive federal police forces (although they "respect" the military) and from other bands that they stigmatize as not only "criminal" but also "terrorist".

Although patronage relations and cults may produce some positive local support for criminal organizations, it seems to have been the extensive human rights violations perpetrated during federal operations in Michoacán under the Calderón government that led a larger number of alienated citizens to accept the Caballeros Templarios as the lesser of two evils, despite the fact that their talk of defending the people of Michoacán was hardly consistent with the increasing importance of generalized extortion in the organization's business model. Local people frequently refer to the Templarios as a "mafia". Operating through a cellular structure dispersed through rural communities, the Templarios have established a parallel power that not only controls a good deal of municipal government but also provides its own services in the administration of justice and resolution of individual personal problems, including conflicts with other members of the community and powerful outsiders. The strategy is bold and brazenly hypocritical: the organization has demanded payments from the local managers of major transnational companies such as Pepsico, attacking their installations when payment was denied, but justifying such actions by accusing the companies of covert collaboration with the federal police, while assuring the public that they have no intention of damaging legitimate businesses that dedicate themselves to their proper task of bringing jobs and prosperity to the people. Cherán's indigenous self-defence force was the first community-based organization to challenge the power of the Templarios, who were running local illegal logging operations as well as extorting local businesses (Turati and Castellanos 2012).

Generalized extortion is only one of the downsides of rule by mafias that are apparent from the comparative literature. As Schneider and Schneider (2003) argued in their analysis of the Palermo Mafia in Sicily, besides their contributions to the reproduction of a "subculture of violence", mafias form dense networks with politicians and bureaucrats who often act as conflictive "pieces" of an internally fragmented state, as well as with bankers and other "respectable" private sector interests, such as real estate developers in the Palermo case. There is strong evidence of links between mining interests and paramilitary violence perpetrated by cartel gunmen in various rural contexts in Mexico and Guatemala. Such violence has the great advantage of easy "deniability" by both the companies and government, since violence is easily explained in terms of the drug trade. This is the direction in which we need to take the analysis in order to make deeper sense of the violence to which Ostula has been subjected since 2009.

The coastal area possesses beautiful beaches and the mountains remain suitable for ecotourism despite the ravages of illegal logging. Ostula's *comuneros* have rejected attempts by the state government to persuade them to turn their beaches over to tourist developers in return for compensation in the form of cattle or other rural development resources. An ambitious state tourism development plan envisages the construction of a major new Pacific highway that would have to be cut directly through the indigenous communal territory of Ostula. This offers another motive for people from La Placita to want to retain control of La Canahuancera, which had previously served as a collection point for marijuana brought down from the sierras for shipment out of the region by sea. But the zone still has important untapped mineral resources, which the Italian-Argentinian company Ternium-Hylsa, operator of the Las Encinas iron ore mine in Aquila, seeks to develop. The company has been in conflict with the indigenous community of Aquila[12] over royalty payments: efforts of *comuneros* to blockade the mine have been repressed by federal police interventions. But Ostula has always rejected proposals for mining in its territory which did not give the indigenous community complete powers of co-management and is also opposed to Ternium-Hylsa's aspirations to construct a new port in the area.

Given these conditions, many of Ostula's *comuneros* see the recent violence perpetrated by persons involved in drug trafficking as having other intellectual authors and other agendas.[13] Consideration of agendas that go beyond the dispute over a single piece of land, albeit land whose value is greatly increased by new projects for developing the economy of the region, could also be the key to understanding the roles of both the state and federal governments in this case, given that both strongly supported the extension of mining and tourism development. But we should also bear in mind the extent to which private interests, criminal and non-criminal, are capable of purchasing the services of state agents for their own ends, and the pervasive existence of "parallel powers" running an illegal economy that has become more extensive than drug trafficking alone. Minerals are one of the other commodities that pass through the illegal circuits of the regional economy, destined for China. What comes to the Michoacán coast from China, through the international port of Lázaro Cárdenas, are the precursor chemicals used in the manufacture of methamphetamines, which are now sold locally as well as exported to other regions.

The historical intransigence of the Ostula community in the face of any threat to the integrity of its communal territory, and its repeated "resistance" to the solutions offered by the official agrarian reform apparatus,[14] reflected the fact that it maintained an indigenous concept of territoriality in which sovereignty over a territory and all its resources defined the identity and integrity of the unique human group that occupied that cosmologically ordered and intimately known and "dwelt in" space, in the manner of the Nahua concept of an *altépetl* (Lockhart 1999; Gledhill 2004). Although the entry of political parties into the life of the community intensified factionalism, the defence of communal territory initially transcended these differences, and when party politics was finally perceived as impeding the struggle, the communal assembly opted for its elimination. This move did not occur immediately after the community aligned with the EZLN in 2006, and Ostula's leaders did not follow the EZLN's radical rejection of engagement with the "bad government" of the official state either. Nevertheless, the foundation of Xayakalan marked a watershed, leading in September 2011, to an assembly decision not to allow the installation of voting stations in the community in the November state elections, and a prohibition against *comuneros* standing as candidates in those elections or encouraging others to participate in voting.

In this, Ostula followed the lead of the Cherán autonomists, whose demands to be allowed to elect officials by "uses and customs" were eventually declared constitutional by the state congress after a legal wrangle. In February 2012, the Michoacán Electoral Institute delivered papers ratifying the election of the twelve members of a new communal council, the K'eris. Despite these advances, the Cherán self-defence forces did not succeed in eliminating violent confrontations with neighbouring communities, and harassment of *comuneros* by paramilitary forces continued, obliging the new authorities to continue to demand action on the part of federal security forces. Cherán's "autonomy" therefore remains dependent on the state in crucial respects. Greater poverty and relative geographical isolation are factors that make Ostula more susceptible to repression and "deniable" violence than Cherán, a town in the centre of the state which has good communications by paved highways with other centres of population and an urbanized centre with 10,000 residents. Yet these are not the only limits on the ability of Ostula to continue to practice the "resistance" so characteristic of its past history. In conclusion I will offer a survey of recent changes that in part reflect the way in which the solidarities have the past have been torn apart by the penetration of criminal organizations into the heart of the indigenous community itself.

Conclusion: The Contemporary Limits of Resistance

In the first place, although the defence of territory had always unified the community in the past, important divisions emerged over how to resolve the problem of La Canahuancera. According to his own testimony, Don Trino, principal promoter of the invasion, managed to assemble a group of *comuneros* to pressure the communal assembly not to wait until the problem was solved by legal means. Another group, headed by a former Commissioner of Common Property, continued to advocate a judicial solution even after the Agrarian Procurator's office found in favour of La Placita. Its members were accused of being fifth columnists, leaking information to "the enemy". Nevertheless, the immediate pretext for the invasion was that outsiders married to women from Ostula had settled on the disputed land without permission of the assembly, adding to the problems posed by two mestizos from La Placita who had long been sowing tamarind and papaya there and were supposedly also involved in drug trafficking.

Drug trafficking is the second element that complicates any simple narrative of "resistance". Some members of the indigenous community had dedicated themselves to producing marijuana since the 1980s, but cocaine production and trafficking was centred on the mestizo settlements. More recently, however, methamphetamine trafficking became the principal business, and many young indigenous people have become consumers of these drugs. Some of the local schoolteachers, both natives of Ostula and people born elsewhere, became drug distributors. They worked for a resident of La Placita who had become a municipal official in Aquila. At least four of them have been assassinated, two belonging to the group that advocated a legal solution to the land dispute. The relationship between members of the community and organized crime was further complicated by the violent struggles to control the local *plaza*, which produced executions for "betrayals" resulting from changing affiliations from one group to another.

In the case of the young men, a further factor was access to arms supplied by the traffickers. Members of the Familia Michoacana took advantage of the interest of some young people in the idea of armed self-defence. Presenting themselves as "Zapatista sympathizers", traffickers offered young indigenous men an escape from the everyday humiliation and racism that they had previously suffered at the hands of mestizos, whose ability to project dominance had always been supported by their possession of automatic weapons. Small groups of young people involved in the defence of Xayakalan were led in the night along mountain trails that took them to hidden training grounds in the mountains. At the same time, gunmen identified by *comuneros* as "Zetas" appeared in the house of one of the Ostula teachers who was a member of the PRI. According to their host, they were "municipal security guards" sent to protect the communal centre, over which his house presented a commanding view.

As a result of these conflicts, many young people "disappeared" without their deaths becoming a matter of public record. As we have seen, armed actors linked to La Placita walked freely even in Xayakalan, sowing fear and menacing the leaders of the autonomy movement, whose members began to suspect everyone of being an informer or traitor. Solidarity disintegrated.

But social change was also a factor in this process. From the start, some of the settlers in Xayakalan had been disliked by other Ostula *comuneros* because they were Evangelicals or Jehovah's Witnesses. At least one had served a prison term. To some degree, Xayakalan served as means of hiving off undesirable individuals and dissident minorities from the heart of a community whose Catholic identity had always been central not only to its "autonomous" religious life (the Ostulans organized their own devotions) but also to its management of secular affairs. Some key aspects of the Catholic ritual that bound dispersed settlements into a coherent "community", such as processions carrying images of the Virgin and Saints between different areas, had to be abandoned as insecurity mounted, further weakening the relations on which solidarity had been built in the past.

As in the past, however, no faction managed to achieve a definitive position of dominance. The teacher who brought the *sicarios* to his house was forced to leave and live in Aquila. Nevertheless, as violence produced a rising number of displaced people, loss of personnel and loss of arms weakened the capacity to mobilize around action that Ostula had displayed in 2009. Many *comuneros*, exhausted by violence and insecurity, became more willing to reach whatever accommodation they could with the powers that be, not least so that they could return to receiving benefits from government social development and anti-poverty programmes. All this is ultimately a consequence of the fact that organized crime occupied the vacuum created by the failure of political parties and the ending of traditional forms of political clientelism. Furthermore, in the sense that there had long been relations between delinquent groups and the "constitutional" political authorities in Aquila, the autonomy that the Ostula assembly tried to reclaim from the state by means of rejecting political parties and electoral politics was undermined by the more fundamental relations that operated in the shadows of "legitimate" institutional power. The parties disappeared, but their real owners remained the backstage actors with mafia connections.

Nevertheless, the resort to self-defence was a response to the fact that no level of government was willing to defend the interests of the indigenous *comuneros*, nor offer them guarantees of economic or physical security. It is difficult to see what more can be done in such situations of impunity, but it seems important not to blame the victims. In this paper, I have tried to put the principal analytical focus on the visible and backstage power relations and economic interests that have shaped the situation, directly and indirectly. Although we can identify other processes that caused the death of some of the Ostula *comuneros*, and the hand of organized crime behind the circulation of arms within the community, violence within the indigenous community reflects the impact of wider forces, and the majority of deaths did result from communal resistance to perceived threats of dispossession. It therefore seems necessary to ask if the inaction of different levels of government in the face of the escalation of violence does not indicate that the definitive expulsion of indigenous communities from this zone, the objective of regional and foreign elites in the nineteenth century, has not once again become the real project of the domestic, foreign and transnational elites that covet its resources today. In this sense, history may be repeating itself, but the outcome may be different the second time around.

Ostula's historical capacity to resist was based on an especially strong and resilient communal organization, and a strong sense of collective identity linked to its regional significance as an indigenous religious centre, which also gave it a corps of organic intellectuals, originally literate in Náhuatl, and organizers of an extraordinary tradition of masses sung in Latin without the support of non-indigenous priests (Gledhill 2004). As I noted earlier, this produced a history in which communal assemblies could rein in the divisive personal ambitions of leaders and organize the defence of communal territory across other lines of factional division. Ostula emerged as a distinctive "community of resistance" under the threat of liberal land privatization and mestizo invasions, which sharpened a sense of ethnic difference, although it also led to the internalization of non-indigenous ideas about racial difference that indigenous people also invoked in making distinctions between their communities in moments of conflict. Ostulans came to see themselves as more successful in keeping the mestizo threat at bay than their neighbours, so that the unconditional defence of communal territory became another unifying aspect of the community's identity. The Zapatista affiliation reinforced that sentiment, although many people in Coire and Pomaro were sceptical about the Ostulans' high-risk strategy of taking back Xayakalan. We can now see that the problem was not simply repression. The delicate balances that made it possible to reproduce a coherent community strategy of action were already under strain at the time the assembly took that fateful decision, which set in train a series of events that further undermined the solidarity and consensus on which successful resistance depends.

Postscript

On 13 February 2014, the Ostula assembly resolved to re-establish its communal police force, disarmed by federal forces in 2010, under the command of Semei Verdía, one of a group of young men who had left the region in fear of their lives four years earlier, and had now returned under arms, supported by the recently reconstituted self-defence force of Aquila, and those of the neighbouring mestizo municipalities of Coalcomán and Chinicuila. Two hours later this force occupied La Placita, although the Knights Templar group based there had already pulled out weeks before. The transformation of the situation on the coast reflected months of advances by what were now coordinated mestizo self-defence forces throughout the *tierra caliente* zone of Michoacán. Commercial farmers and cattlemen were now providing financial support to some of the *autodefensas*, and federal security forces had received orders not to impede their advance, so the achievement of power by a faction that had lost a previous round of contention in Ostula was the product of a major shift in the wider balance of forces. The longer term implications of Ostula's dependence on the support of non-indigenous allies remain uncertain at the time of writing, as does the future role of the federal government. It was, after all, the same government that disbanded the original *autodefensa* in Aquila and imprisoned its members, apparently acting on this, as on previous occasions, at the behest of the Ternium mining company, which continues to have a strong strategic interest in expanding its operations into Ostula's territory.

Acknowledgements

I gratefully acknowledge the generous support of the Leverhulme Trust and also want to acknowledge the valuable contribution to data collection made by a Mexican research assistant who must remain anonymous for reasons of personal security, but emphasize that I alone am responsible for the arguments and analysis that the paper offers. I originally carried out fieldwork in Ostula, complemented by archival research, over two years in 2002–2003. Leverhulme funding enabled me to collect updated ethnographic data in 2011–2012, including new interviews with local actors.

Notes

[1] An example from outside Michoacán of which I have some direct knowledge is the conflict between the Canadian Blackfire mining corporation and the inhabitants of Chicomuselo, Chiapas, a non-indigenous municipality close to the Guatemala border in which the leader of the campaign against the mine was assassinated. There has been violent repression of protest movements against casino and up-market tourism projects that displace fishermen and farmers along the length of Mexico's Pacific Coast. Similar concerns motivated recent protests in Oaxaca state against a wind-farm project funded by Spanish capital.

[2] The Cristero rebellion was prompted by the government's closing of Catholic churches, a move that also prompted peaceful forms of "resistance" among middle-class groups in urban areas, although it was the extensive participation of rural villagers that turned the rebellion into a major problem for the post-revolutionary state.

[3]   To give two spectacular examples from 2012, Federal Police, often presented as the solution to the problem of the regular co-optation of municipal and state police by organized crime, attacked a vehicle carrying agents of the US Drug Enforcement Agency accompanied by an officer of the Mexican Marines, and two bands of their own officers engaged in a shootout in the domestic terminal of Mexico City airport.

[4]   Indigenous communal land could not be privatized directly, although it was possible to advance towards privatization by transforming an indigenous communal property regime into an *ejido* and some indigenous communities already held their lands under the *ejido* or private co-property forms of tenure rather than as communal property.

[5]   The COCOPA draft was based on the agreements reached between the EZLN and the previous PRI government headed by Ernesto Zedillo in San Andrés Larráinzar in 1996. The agreements remained unfulfilled by Zedillo and the two succeeding PAN administrations, but the new PRI government that won power in the 2012 elections promised to revisit the matter, appointing Jaime Martínez Veloz, a member of the old COCOPA, to head a new Commission for Dialogue with the Indigenous Peoples, focusing on ensuring equality of access of all citizens, indigenous and non-indigenous, to "justice, education, health care and infrastructure". The EZLN was invited to participate in this new process, but this gesture appeared more propagandistic than substantive, since it was clear that "too radical" autonomy demands remained off the table and that there was ample scope for playing off one set of indigenous interlocutors against another.

[6]   The Spanish colonial regime was based on a system of indirect rule. The original reference to *usos y costumbres* in New Spain relates to the approval of self-government and use of indigenous customary law in the "Republic of Indians". Contemporary uses and customs government is based on selection of community officials through consensus in communal assemblies and the revival of institutions such as councils of elders that were part of the "traditional" governance structures of indigenous communities, although some of these alternative forms of local government are, on closer inspection, invented traditions, or reflect the resignification of forms of organization that previously regulated religious life for secular purposes.

[7]   A figure of 57,449 deaths is widely accepted as a minimum by the Mexican press. There are innumerable methodological deficiencies in the way the Mexican government distinguishes homicides relating to the actions of organized crime and the security forces from other kinds of homicides, and many independent organizations place the death toll considerably higher than this figure. Another problem in accounting the costs of Mexico's public security policies is the lack of government efforts to measure internal displacement of population, though analyses have been made on the basis of official figures published by INEGI, the National Institute of Statistics and Geography. For further details and discussion, see Molloy (2013) and Internal Displacement Monitoring Centre (2012).

[8]   I have borrowed the concept of "delinquent states" in the title of this paper from Brazilian social historian Gaio (2006). The concept emphasizes the role of the state in fostering the development of organized crime, a perspective also advocated in the Mexican case by Campbell (2009).

[9]   Literally commoners: members of the indigenous community sharing in its collective property.

[10]   This is an officially recognized administrative sub-division of a municipality.

[11]   No body was recovered. Revered as a saint in his home community, there were persistent, and as it turned out well founded, rumours that he was not actually dead.

[12]   The original indigenous community of Aquila was extinguished in the nineteenth-century drive to end corporate property, but reconstituted under the post-revolutionary agrarian reform laws in 1981.

[13] Although people from the indigenous communities have been directly involved in marijuana cultivation, the main actors involved in the trafficking of cocaine and methamphetamines are mestizos located in La Placita and Aquila. As we will see in the final section of the paper, more members of the Ostula community have been drawn into involvement in drug trafficking as well as consumption, sometimes through personal or political patronage ties, but the controlling figures remain outside the indigenous community.

[14] In 2006, this included refusal to enter into the official Programme for Certification of Communal Land Rights, another artefact of the neoliberal counter-agrarian reform.

References

Abu-Lughod, Lila. 1990. "The Romance of Resistance: Tracing Transformations of Power Through Bedouin Women." *American Ethnologist* 17 (1): 41–55.

Bartra, Armando. 2000. *Guerrero Bronco: Campesinos, Ciudadanos y Guerrilleros en la Costa Grande*. Mexico City: Ediciones Era.

Boyer, Christopher Robert. 2003. *Becoming Campesinos: Politics, Identity, and Agrarian Struggle in Postrevolutionary Michoacán, 1920–1935*. Stanford, CA: Stanford University Press.

Butler, Matthew. 2004. *Popular Piety and Political Identity in Mexico's Cristero Rebellion: Michoacán, 1927–29*. Oxford: Oxford University Press.

Campbell, Howard. 2009. *Drug War Zone: Frontline Dispatches from the Streets of El Paso and Juarez*. Austin, TX: University of Texas Press.

Cochet, Hubert. 1991. *Alambradas en la Sierra: Un Sistema Agrario en Mexico*. Zamora: El Colegio de Michoacán.

Crehan, Kate. 2002. *Gramsci, Culture and Anthropology*. Berkeley, CA: University of California Press.

Díaz Polanco, Héctor. 1997. *La Rebelión Zapatista y la Autonomía*. Mexico City: Siglo XXI.

Estrada Saavedra, Marco. 2005. "The 'Armed Community in Rebellion': Neo-Zapatismo in the Tojolab'al Cañadas, Chiapas (1988–96)." *The Journal of Peasant Studies* 32 (3–4): 528–554.

Fletcher, Robert. 2001. "What Are We Fighting for? Rethinking Resistance in a Pewenche Community in Chile." *The Journal of Peasant Studies* 28 (3): 37–66.

Gaio, André Moysés. 2006. "O Estado Delinqüente: Uma Nova Modalidade de Crime?" *Cadernos de Ciências Humanas—Especiaria* 9 (15): 137–157.

Gledhill, John. 1999. "Official Masks and Shadow Powers: Towards an Anthropology of the Dark Side of the State." *Urban Anthropology and Studies of Cultural Systems and World Economic Development* 28 (3–4): 199–251.

Gledhill, John. 2004. *Cultura y Desafío en Ostula: Cuatro Siglos de Autonomía Indígena en la Costa-sierra Nahua de Michoacán*. Zamora: El Colegio de Michoacán AC.

Gledhill, John. 2012. "A Case for Rethinking Resistance." In *New Approaches to Resistance in Brazil and Mexico*, edited by John Gledhill and Patience A. Schell, 1–20. Durham, NC: Duke University Press.

Goldstein, Daniel M. 2012. *Outlawed: Between Security and Rights in a Bolivian City*. Durham, NC: Duke University Press.

Grayson, George W. 2010. *La Familia Drug Cartel: Implications for US-Mexican Security*. Carlisle Barracks, PA: Army War College Strategic Studies Institute.

Grayson, George W., and Samuel Logan. 2012. *The Executioner's Men: Los Zetas, Rogue Soldiers, Criminal Entrepreneurs, and the Shadow State They Created, Trends in Organized Crime*. New Brunswick: Transaction.

Grillo, Ioan. 2012. *El Narco: The Bloody Rise of Mexican Drug Cartels*. London: Bloomsbury Press.

Hale, Charles R. 2006. *Más que un Indio: Racial Ambivalence and Neoliberal Multiculturalism in Guatemala*. Santa Fe, NM: School for American Research Press.

Hernández, Anabel. 2012. *Los Señores del Narco*. Mexico City: Grijalbo.

Internal Displacement Monitoring Centre. 2012. *Internal Displacement in the Americas.* Norwegian Refugee Council. Accessed November 24, 2013. http://www.internal-displacement.org/publications/global-overview-2012-americas.pdf

Jasso Martínez, Ivy Jacarnda. 2010. "Las Demandas de las Organizaciones Purépechas y el Movimiento Indígena en Michoacán." *Liminar. Estudios Sociales y Humanísticos* 8 (1): 64–79.

Jones, Delmos J. 1995. "Anthropology and the Oppressed: A Reflection on 'Native' Anthropology." *NAPA Bulletin* 16 (1): 58–70.

Leyva Solano, Xochitl, and Gabriel Ascencio Franco. 2002. *Lacandonia al Filo Del Agua.* Mexico City: Fondo de la Cultura Económica.

Leyva Solano, Xochitl, and Araceli Burguete Cal y Mayor, eds. 2007. *La Remunicipalización de Chiapas: Lo Político y la Política en Tiempos de Contrainsurgencia.* Mexico City: Miguel Ángel Porrua.

Lockhart, James. 1999. *Los Nahuas Después de la Conquista: Historia Social y Cultural de los Indios del México Central, del Siglo XVI al XVIII.* Mexico City: Fondo de la Cultura Económica.

Maldonado Aranda, Salvador. 2010. *Los Márgenes del Estado Mexicano: Territorios Ilegales, Desarrollo y Violencia en Michoacán.* Zamora: El Colegio de Michoacán.

Maldonado Aranda, Salvador. 2012. "Drogas, Violencia y Militarización en el México Rural: El Caso de Michoacán." *Revista Mexicana de Sociología* 74 (1): 5–39.

Meyer, Jean A. 1976. *The Cristero Rebellion: The Mexican People between Church and State, 1926–1929.* Cambridge: Cambridge University Press.

Molloy, Molly. 2013. *Mexico's National Crime Statistics Show No Significant Decline in Homicides and Disappearances.* James A. Baker III Institute for Public Policy. Accessed October 24, 2013. http://blog.chron.com/bakerblog/2013/10/is-drug-related-violence-in-mexico-on-the-decline/

Norget, Kristin. 2010. "A Cacophony of Autochthony: Representing Indigeneity in Oaxacan Popular Mobilization." *The Journal of Latin American and Caribbean Anthropology* 15 (1): 116–143.

Ortner, Sherry B. 1995. "Resistance and the Problem of Ethnographic Refusal." *Comparative Studies in Society and History* 37 (1): 173–193.

Overmyer-Velázquez, Rebecca. 2010. *Folkloric Poverty: Neoliberal Multiculturalism in Mexico.* University Park, PA: Penn State Press.

Pérez Ramírez, Tatiana. 2009. "Memoria Histórica de la Insurrección Cívica Purépecha en 1988." *Política y Cultura* 31: 113–138.

Sánchez Díaz, Gerardo. 1979. *El Suroeste de Michoacán. Estructura Económico-Social, 1821–1851.* Morelia: Universidad Michoacana de San Nicolás de Hidalgo.

Sánchez Díaz, Gerardo. 2001. *La Costa de Michoacán: Economía y Sociedad en el Siglo XVI.* Morelia: Universidad Michoacana y Morevallado Editores.

Schneider, Jane C., and Peter T. Schneider. 2003. *Reversible Destiny: Mafia, Antimafia, and the Struggle for Palermo.* Berkeley, CA: University of California Press.

Speed, Shannon, and Jane Fishburne Collier. 2000. "Limiting Indigenous Autonomy in Chiapas, Mexico: The State Government's Use of Human Rights." *Human Rights Quarterly* 22 (4): 877–905.

Starn, Orin. 1999. *Nightwatch: The Making of a Movement in the Peruvian Andes, Latin America Otherwise.* Durham, NC: Duke University Press.

Turati, Marcela, and Franciso Castellanos. 2012. "Rebelión Contra la Mafia Michoacana." *Proceso* 1864: 30–34.

Too Soon for Post-Feminism: The Ongoing Life of Patriarchy in Neoliberal America

Sherry B. Ortner

In this paper, I seek to bring "patriarchy" back into focus in ways that make sense to a twenty-first century American audience. In the first part of the paper, I discuss the ways in which "feminism" has fallen, or is being pushed, off the contemporary political agenda, leaving a political vacuum with respect to, among other things, patriarchy as a system of power. In the second part of the paper, I use a number of films as texts to show how patriarchy in this sense persists quite vigorously and often brutally in contemporary society, not only as a thing in itself, but also as a form of power that intersects with, and organizes, major institutions of twentieth- and twenty-first-century capitalism: the industrial production site, the military, and the corporation. Finally, I reflect on the films not only as cultural texts, but also as political interventions that at least partially counter the post-feminist tendencies discussed in the first part of the paper.

Feminism can be seen as one of the great resistance movements of the twentieth century. It was tremendously successful, both in the sense of achieving many of its goals and in the sense of attaining a virtually global reach. Now, however, feminism appears to be in a state of crisis. Young women are said to be "post-feminist", while those who identify as feminists are under attack as handmaidens of neocolonialism and neoliberalism.

But patriarchy is still with us—"us", for purposes of this paper, being the USA in the early twenty-first century—in many spheres of life. I emphasize the issue of patriarchy as a particular way of focusing feminist theory and politics. Most people think of feminism as being about "women", and of course that is true, but it is only part of the story. In addition, many people think of feminism as being about "gender", about the cultural division of the world into male and female persons, and—here linking up with queer theory—about other forms of gendered identities (Ortner and Whitehead 1981; Butler 1990). Of course that is true too, but again it is only part of the story. For both "women" and "gender" exist, at least in the modern world, only as elements of a larger formation of power called patriarchy, and that will be the focus of this paper.

Again this paper is confined to patriarchal formations in the USA in the twentieth and twenty-first centuries. While arguably patriarchy is a global, or near-global, phenomenon, its significance in other parts of the world is the subject of intense debate, as will be discussed briefly later in this paper.

Patriarchy in the USA today is more fragmented than it once was, less monolithic and homogeneous, as a result of a century or so, on and off, of feminist activism. Yet it continues to play an often invisible, but highly damaging, role in contemporary social life. The main point of this paper, then, is to try to bring patriarchy back into focus in ways that will make sense to, and perhaps have a galvanizing effect on, a twenty-first century audience. In the first part of the paper, I will discuss an expanded version of the idea of post-feminism. In the second part of the paper, I will try to show how patriarchy persists quite vigorously in contemporary society, not only as a thing in itself, but also as a form of power that organizes and shapes major institutions of twenty-first century capitalism: the industrial production site, the military, and the corporation. The intertwining of patriarchy with other forms of power and dominance is the other key point of the paper. I see this intertwining as a kind of macro-version of Kimberlé Crenshaw's very productive concept of "intersectionality" ([1991] 2007), in which various forms of power cross-cut, cross-fertilize, and amplify one another.

Varieties of Post-Feminism

Starting in the late 1980s, feminist scholars began identifying a condition they called "post-feminism" (Rosenfelt and Stacey 1987; Traube 1994; Tasker and Negra 2007; McRobbie 2009; for summary, see Ortner 2013, Ch. 6). Originally it was meant to describe a new consciousness among younger generations of women. The argument was that younger women today have both incorporated the fruits of the earlier ("second wave") feminist movement and rejected the idea of, or the necessity for, continuing to pursue feminist goals. Put more strongly, younger women are said to view that earlier movement as embodying and advocating a style of femininity/femaleness with which they do not want to be associated: "[P]ostfeminism signals more than a simple evolutionary process whereby aspects of feminism have been incorporated into popular culture ... It also simultaneously involves an 'othering' of feminism ... , its construction as extreme, difficult, and unpleasurable" (Tasker and Negra 2007, 4). Although we have little solid data, ethnographic or otherwise, on what "young women today" are actually thinking, and although we do not even know which "young women today" are in question, in terms of class, race, age, etc., two things seem fairly clear: that even if younger women have not completely rejected feminism, they are extremely ambivalent about it (see Aronson 2007; Ortner 2013);[1] and that most younger women find the label itself extremely problematic. For one small example of the latter point, in a recent interview with the American Idol (talent show) winner Kelly Clarkson (b. 1982), Clarkson was asked whether she viewed herself as a feminist. "No", she replied, "I wouldn't say feminist—that's too strong. I think when people hear *feminist*, it's like, 'Get out of my way, I don't need anyone'" (*Time*, 11 November 2013, 60).

But here let me expand the scope of the idea of "post-feminism". At the same time that younger generations of women are said to be distancing themselves from feminist ideals, or simply from the feminist label, there are challenges coming from other directions as well. The first of these stems from long-standing tensions between "Western feminism" and scholars of gender in other parts of the world, going back at least to Chandra Talpade Mohanty's path-breaking essay, "Under Western Eyes: Feminist Scholarship and Colonial Discourse" (1984). The issues here, to condense severely, include the idea that Western feminism is excessively focused on female autonomy, which is not necessarily seen as a desirable goal by women/feminists in the global south; and that Western feminism is excessively focused on challenging "patriarchy", when other issues, such as poverty, have greater priority for many women/feminists in the global south (see, e.g., Abu-Lughod 2002, 2013).

These concerns have played a major role in shaping several influential recent ethnographic studies (Ong 2003; Abu-Lughod 2005; Mahmood 2005). These studies prominently critique "feminism" in some form as seeking to impose anti-patriarchalism, as well as Western and/or middle class and/or "liberal" values of personal autonomy, on non-Western women and communities. These critiques may well be quite justified in their specific contexts, and in any event the issues behind the post-colonial critique of feminism are intellectually, ethically, and politically very complex. Space forbids engaging with them substantively here; what I point to with these examples is not the substance of their arguments, but their *effect*: another kind of post-feminism.[2]

Finally, and most recently, we have Nancy Fraser's attack on feminism as having become "a handmaiden of neoliberal capitalism" (2013). Fraser provides an interesting capsule summary of second wave feminism as promising "two different possible futures", one in which "gender emancipation went hand in hand with participatory democracy and social solidarity", and the other in which "it promised a new form of liberalism, able to grant women as well as men the goods of individual autonomy, increased choice, and meritocratic advancement" (p. 2 of printout). Now, however, "feminism's ambivalence has been resolved in favour of (neo)liberal individualism" (p. 3 of printout). The poster child for this shift seems to be corporate executive and billionaire Sheryl Sandberg whose best-selling book *Lean In: Women, Work, and the Will to Lead* (2013) focuses on what women need to do to get ahead in the corporate world. I agree with Fraser that both tendencies were present in second wave feminism, although unlike Fraser, I think they are both still actively in play. But again, this is not the place to engage substantively with these issues. Rather I introduce Fraser's argument as one more version of, and contributor to, the broader post-feminist climate.

Looking at these diverse, partially converging, and apparently intensifying aspects of what amounts to not only a post-feminist condition but also a post-feminist movement, one wonders whether the idea, and/or the label, of "feminism" is so fatally tainted by now that it could not or should not be revived. Feminism seems to have become what Erving Goffman once famously called a "spoiled identity", which many are evidently eager to reject.[3] And yet the original *raison d'etre* of the feminist movement, the gender inequalities produced and reproduced within a particular formation of power called "patriarchy", lives on. Indeed I argue that it is patriarchy and not feminism that, *pace* Fraser, thrives under neoliberal capitalism. This brings us to the rest of this paper.

Patriarchy as a System of Power

One of the successes of the earlier feminist movement was to put the idea of male dominance and/or patriarchal power on the table, and to argue that gender inequality worked in much the same way as racial inequality: one group (people of color, or women) was considered in some way to be essentially and fundamentally inferior, and thus open to control and domination, or discrimination and exclusion, by the other group (white people, or men). The original feminist political project then was to work towards a state of gender equality in which neither sex was considered superior/inferior, and in which neither sex had the right to dominate or discriminate against the other. But the American feminist movement has gone through many changes since that time, under the impact of challenges from minority, queer, and (as just discussed) third world women. One way to summarize these changes is to say that the issue of male dominance or patriarchy has become on the one hand more muted, and on the other hand more complicated, more intertwined with other forms of inequality like race, class, and sexuality. This intertwining, which Crenshaw ([1991] 2007) called "intersectionality", is a critical characteristic of all contemporary forms of inequality and it will be central to the present paper as well.[4]

I begin with a few definitions and clarifications. First, I have so far been using the term "patriarchy" very loosely, as an umbrella term to cover the whole range of ideas subsumed within phrases like "male dominance", "male superiority", "sexism", and so forth. Technically, patriarchy is only one form of male dominance, lodged in the figure of the father, and often enveloped in an ideology of protection and benevolence as well as domination and control. But the other terms have their own problems, and I choose "patriarchy" as having the particular virtue of evoking the idea of a social and political formation, rather than the image of a cave man with a club.

Second, while issues of patriarchy may seem irrelevant or of secondary importance to some groups, sectors, and classes of women, for a wide variety of reasons, I will argue later in this paper that the global macro-structure, the overarching system of states, corporations, and military organizations, remains a massive patriarchal system, and has to be addressed as such. That is, many women may feel that they experience little patriarchal oppression in their personal lives; many other women may feel that a patriarchal family and kinship system offers more benefits than costs in the modern world; in both cases—and others—there may be a sense that the important political struggles lie elsewhere. My point, however, will be that that "elsewhere" is itself organized on complex patriarchal as well as political–economic principles that need to be identified and challenged.

At this point, then, I need to focus down on the classic definition of the term, which literally means the rule of the father. Within this definition, patriarchy can be seen as having a particular structure, a particular organization of relations of power that involves not only men over women, but also men over other men. Furthermore, while one can think about patriarchy in pure form—and many all-male institutions approximate that form—in general it is always intertwined with other structures of power: colonialism, capitalism, imperialism, racism, and so forth.

I begin by sketching out a model of patriarchy assembled from a variety of scholarly and popular representations, everything from Freudian theory and feminist theory to ethnography, myth, and movies. I do not try to provide a systematic genealogy of the concept here, as it would take us much too far afield. I simply seek to expose a model or structure that is common to all the representations. In the present section, I will present the basic architecture of the model. In a later section, I will look at three films to consider a variety of elaborations, extensions, and nuances of the basic model, as it plays out in different contexts.

Although patriarchy is a system of social power, it is also a system of cultural categories and personal identities. As a system of cultural categories, it is grounded in a conceptual division of the world into two (and only two) kinds of gendered persons, "women" and "men", defined as both different and unequal. "Women" and "men" are shown in quotes, highlighting the culturally constructed, and normatively imposed, nature of these categories (Ortner and Whitehead 1981). Furthermore, the categories, which are defined as fundamentally and essentially heterosexual, function as both classifiers and identities. It is through the play of life by real people within patriarchal social formations that those categories/identities are reproduced.

Patriarchy as a formation is very old, but probably not (as Freud would have it [1950]) primordial. While pre-state societies probably had varying forms and degrees of male dominance, from virtually egalitarian to highly unequal (Ortner 1996), patriarchy as defined here—minimally as organized around the power of a father-like figure—probably emerges as part of the origins of the state in prehistory (Ortner 1996). If one were going back to nineteenth-century theory on the subject, the relevant theorist would be Engels ([1942] 1972) as much as Freud, although both of them are quite far from contemporary understandings.

Most contemporary societies are not patriarchal from top to bottom, if they ever were. Most are more complex, with multiple arrangements of gendered power, as a result of both the fragmenting forces of modernity and the recurrent cycles of feminist politics. But one does not have to look far to find very clear-cut examples of patriarchal structures of power at work *within* virtually every society in the world today, as it remains a formidable way of organizing not only gender relations, but also other major forms of power and domination.

Patriarchy is a "structure" in the technical sense; it is a set of relations between relations.[5] It is organized around three dyads and their many kinds of interaction: (1) the relationship between a patriarchal figure of some sort and other men; (2) the many homosocial but heterosexual relationships among the men themselves; and (3) the relationships between men and women. In the most classic form of the patriarchal structure, there is a leader who both rewards and punishes the men; there is a body of men who compete among themselves for status and power within the group and in the eyes of the leader; and there are relationships and non-relationships with women, who are either excluded from the group, or included on condition of being subordinated and controlled.

The ethos of different patriarchal structures can vary a great deal. A Buddhist monastery is a patriarchal structure in all the ways just described, but it is (meant to be) productive of peace and spirituality. An elite all-male college is a patriarchal structure, but the emphasis is on the production of a kind of genteel upper class masculinity. In many cases, however, patriarchal organization is mobilized in the service of producing a kind of aggressive masculinity, capitalizing on and intensifying the competitiveness endemic to the male group in these formations. In such cases, the exclusion of women tends to be more absolute, and the boundaries between "men" and "women", "masculinity" and "femininity", tend to be more heavily patrolled. Any breach of these boundaries, like the entry of women into all-male occupations, or into the military, tends to provoke very strong reactions.

The question of breaching social boundaries will be central to several of the film interpretations to follow, and needs a few words here. The issue was very powerfully theorized by Mary Douglas, whose book *Purity and Danger* came out in 1966 but remains relevant and useful to this day. Building on an earlier work by Arnold van Gennep (1960), Douglas argued that the breaching of social boundaries creates "pollution", a state or condition in which the integrity of the group has been weakened or degraded. The underlying model here is the body, which is vulnerable to both the entry of potentially dangerous matter from the outside (food, poison, etc.), and the loss of vital matter from the inside (blood, semen, etc.). From this perspective, the borders of certain kinds of strongly bounded groups, and strongly fortified identities, are similarly fraught with danger; violation of those boundaries will tend to provoke strong, and sometimes, violent reactions. The relevance of this will be clear shortly.

Brief Detour: Films as Multi-Purpose Texts

In the next few sections, I will be using films as texts that tell us something real about patriarchy in the contemporary USA. Two of the films are documentaries, and one is a feature film based on a true story. I will be using the films primarily as ethnographic and/or cultural texts, that is, as in one way or another displaying the patriarchal dynamics just described. This requires some explanation, although I will have to be very brief.

I have recently completed a study of the world of American independent film, devoted to making films that stands outside of the Hollywood mainstream (Ortner

2013). As I discuss at length in the book, independent film people see themselves as trying to tell the truth about the world today, as opposed to (stereotypical) Hollywood, which is invested in fantasy and illusion for the sake of "entertainment". The world of independent film includes both features (fiction) and documentary, although even with features there is a commitment to an ethic and aesthetic of realism. As several observers have remarked, there is a kind of documentary impulse throughout much of independent film, across the feature/documentary divide.

As in much of film studies, one could approach these films by, in a broad sense, deconstructing them—taking them apart for their ideological biases, for their modes of subjectivation of viewers, and so forth. Even documentaries, which claim to be factual, have been the subject of this kind of deconstructive work; in fact they make especially inviting targets for ideology critique. In response to this, however, there is a very interesting literature in film studies about the truth and reality claims of documentaries: On the one hand, scholars agree that documentaries are constructed and manipulated like all (filmic) texts; on the other hand, scholars also agree that documentaries must be understood as pursuing a truth-telling agenda in ways that are different from other kinds of film, and must be interpreted at least in part from that point of view (Nichols 1991; Williams 1998).

Following this latter line of thinking, then, I will treat the films as critical realist accounts of the world we live in. This approach has a number of different components. First, I treat some of the films as "ethnographic", as describing some social and cultural reality (in this case patriarchy), represented at least in part from the point of view of those who inhabit that reality. Second, I treat one of the films as a cultural text, that is, a text not explicitly about patriarchy, but revealing it upon interpretation.

At the same time, all films must be seen as interventions in the public culture, that is, as representations within a space of other representations, aligning with some and contesting others (Appadurai and Breckenridge 1988). Thus I treat the films not only as realist accounts, but also as critical realist accounts, taking a position vis-à-vis both the object being described and the other representations with which they are in conversation. A dimension of this critical stance applies specifically to political films, mostly but not entirely documentaries: the films are meant to provoke action, either in the sense of getting people politically activated, or in the sense of having some kind of impact on policy, or both (Nichols 1991; Gaines 1999).

All of these functions of film, and especially of the kinds of realist films characteristic of American independent cinema, will be visible at one point or another in the discussions that follow. I will sometimes treat the films as descriptive ethnography, sometimes as texts requiring interpretation, and eventually as political interventions in American public culture on the subject of patriarchy today.

Patriarchy in Neoliberal America

I turn now to three films in order to make a number of points. I want to show first that, unfortunately, patriarchy is alive and well in the USA today and still doing a lot of damage. Second, I will use the films to look at variations in the basic model, and to bring out more clearly the variety of harms a patriarchal order inflicts, not only on women, but also on many men, and on persons who do not neatly fit the gender categories. Finally, I want to show how the model or structure plays out both in itself and in parasitic ("intersectional") relationships with other forms of power in an advanced capitalist society: the class structure, the military, and the predatory neoliberal economy.[6]

North Country (Caro 2005)

North Country is a fictionalized account of a true story (Bingham and Gansler 2002) about a woman, called Josie Aimes in the film, who leaves a physically abusive husband and takes a job in the iron mines of Minnesota. The year is 1989, with still only a handful of women working in the mines. The male miners are misogynist in the extreme, but when Josie (Charlize Theron) complains about this to her higher ups, they try to shut her down. After endless and violent harassment, she finally quits, but hires a lawyer and brings a class action suit against the mine owners. The suit succeeds, and establishes one among several legal precedents for all subsequent sexual harassments suits in the USA.

The film is recognizably "feminist" in the classic sense, telling a story of a woman's struggle against discrimination, not as some autonomous neoliberal agent, but on behalf of the working women in general. Again I will return to the overt politics of this and the other films in the conclusions. Here I want to use the film as an ethnographic text, providing a virtual textbook illustration of a well-developed patriarchal order. I said above that a basic patriarchal structure has three intersecting components: the relationship of the patriarchal figure to the group, defined as a group of heterosexual men; the organization of relations among the men, bonded but also competitive among themselves; and the exclusion of women or their inclusion only under male control. Let us then start with the patriarchal figures, the "fathers".

The film is full of fathers, literal and metaphoric, and indeed has a hierarchy of fathers, all of whom are problematic vis-à-vis Josie. After being beaten by her husband, Josie returns to her parents' house. Her own father (Richard Jenkins) looks at her bruised face, seemingly with concern, but then says, "So … Did he catch you with another man?" We understand immediately that the father, who is a miner himself, is with the men. Next, after being both harassed and threatened by the men in the mine, Josie complains to her immediate boss, who gives her no sympathy and tells her she must learn to take it. This is the second father who sides with the men and will not help. Finally, after further and more severe harassment, Josie plucks up her courage and decides to call on the owner of the mine, who had led her to believe she could come to him with her problems. But when she gets there, he is surrounded by men, including her boss, and is told that she must either learn to get along or quit. The mine owner is of course the father of fathers, the boss of the boss; further both the owner and the boss are the bosses of her own father, and all of them have power over Josie.

Now let us look at the group of men, in this case the miners. They appear in the extreme form of the homosocial/heterosexual male group: highly misogynistic, solidary among themselves, and hostile to Josie and the handful of other women miners. They harass the women at work in the most extreme ways short of raping them. There is also a meeting at which they curse the women with vile language, yell with rage, stamp their feet, and altogether seem like a mob about to lose control. Here I want to make two different points.

First, the forms of harassment at work fit Douglas's model of pollution sketched briefly above. There is a virtually visible boundary around the male group and its territory; the women have breached the boundary, and the men respond by mobilizing the material signs of pollution: faeces are smeared on the walls of the women's locker room; someone masturbates on an article of clothing in one of the women's lockers when she is not there, leaving a pool of semen; a woman is locked into a portable toilet, which is rocked back and forth as she screams for help, and then finally turned over, covering her with shit.[7]

But the second point to be made about the men's behavior is historical. As noted above, patriarchal male groups, although always to some degree misogynistic, are not always and necessarily violent. In this case, however, two forms of pressure have been put on the whole arrangement, as both a patriarchal and a capitalist structure. In terms of the patriarchy, we learn at the beginning of the film that the first woman had taken a job in the iron mines in 1975, clearly an effect of the feminist movement of that era. The film is set in 1989, and we understand that Josie is only the most recent in a line of intrusions by women into this male territory, threatening the men in terms of their masculine identities. But the 1989 date is also relevant for the men as workers. The 80s are the time in which the American industrial economy is beginning to collapse, with the closing of factories and other industrial facilities (such as mines) becoming a regular occurrence (as summarized in Ortner 2013, 17, with references). The men then are doubly threatened, as both men and workers; they close ranks and react in ways predicted by Douglas's model.

And finally, what about the women? Within the family we see Josie's mother (Sissy Spacek) as a traditional wife, accepting of the husband's authority. She initially does nothing to contradict or undermine the father's hostile treatment of Josie, and in the early part of the film actively supports the idea that Josie should try to patch things up with the abusive husband. At the mine, as already discussed, we see women excluded from the male group of miners. Those who are "inside" are clearly irritants to the men, and have adopted various adaptive strategies so as not to rock the boat and to avoid retribution. From the women's point of view, Josie is a problem, and they do not support her. But this being the late twentieth century, we also have a third type of woman in the form of Josie, the woman who rocks the boat and threatens to undermine the structure.

In the end, the women miners and the mother come around (as does the father, but that is a different part of the story); Josie becomes part of a legal "class"; the class action suit is successful; and a piece of feminist history is made. But my point here is not to follow the narrative of the film or the real-world history. Rather I have been using the film to show a patriarchal structure at work in a major sector of contemporary American society, both in relatively pure form and as it is intertwined with capitalist relations of power. We saw this intertwining on the dimension of the "fathers", where there is a kind of slippage between Josie's father of kinship, the boss at the mine, and the owner of the capitalist enterprise, all of whom say and do virtually the same thing vis-à-vis Josie, up and down the line. And we saw this slippage at the level of the group of miners, who are threatened as both men and workers, or in other words in terms of both their masculine identities and their material livelihoods, without a clear distinction between the two.

The Invisible War (Dick 2012)

The Invisible War is an award-winning documentary film by Kirby Dick on the subject of rape in the military. In the film, Dick provides both statistical data and the personal testimony of victims to show that the rape of women soldiers in the military is extremely widespread. According to a statistic provided in the film, over 20% of women veterans have been sexually assaulted while on active duty. (The figure for men is a little over 1%; more on male-on-male rape later in this paper.) Some of the more psychologically inclined commentators in the film tend to emphasize that the rapists are "predators", and no doubt some are; one title panel tells us that "15% of incoming recruits attempted or committed rape before entering the military—twice the percentage of the equivalent civilian population". But Dick keeps his eye on the big picture: the patriarchal structure of the military (though he never uses the terms "patriarchal" or "structure"), the ways in which it fosters this behavior, and the fact that the military seems either unwilling or unable to clean it up. Here again I want to show the workings of patriarchy as we see it in the film, within the very particular context of the armed forces.

Let us look first at the "fathers". Once again the film is full of fathers, layer upon layer of patriarchal authority, from lower ranking to higher-ranking officers, what is called in the military "the chain of command". Military commanders at all levels have what one commentator in the film called "an unbelievable amount of power". Their authority over their unit is virtually absolute, and there is almost no way to go outside, around, or over them. Specifically with respect to sexual assault, they can decide whether to believe the victim and take the complaint seriously enough to forward it for investigation or not; in the vast majority of cases, they do not. They either cast doubt on the woman's story, or they tell her it is her own fault, and either way she is urged or even commanded to get over it and get back in line. In some cases, the officers actually turn around and bring legal charges against the women. Many women in the film said the only thing worse than the rape was the commanding officers telling them it was their own fault, refusing to report the rape, and covering up the story. Thus as in *North Country*, we see that patriarchy is not simply the violence of individual men against individual women. On the dimension of the "fathers", here the military officers, it is a hierarchy of power and authority in which superior officers support lower level officers, and all of them support the men.

Now let us look at the relations among the men. In the model I am forwarding here, patriarchy is not just about the authority of the patriarch(s) but about the solidarity of the homosocial/heterosexual group of men. The solidarity of the military unit is an ultimate ideal and value; the men often describe themselves as a "band of brothers" who must be able to depend on one another without question. In 1979, the entrance requirements for women and men in the military were equalized and, except for being banned from combat, women began to enter on the same footing as men (Wikipedia, "Women in Combat"). The date is significant, once again suggesting an effect of the feminist movement of that period. The entry of women into the military appears to have had an effect similar to what we have seen in *North Country*: it violated an invisible boundary and destabilized a central feature of the patriarchal order, the solidarity of the male group. The rapes in turn appear in this context as at once punishments for this act, attempts to expel the intruders, and/or attempts to forcefully establish that if the women are to be "inside the boundary", they must be dominated and controlled. The Douglasian logic, in which the problem is violation of social boundaries, still holds.

Assuming this is correct, one may ask why the retaliation takes the form of rape, rather than the kinds of things we saw in *North Country*. I would suggest that this relates to the specific ethos of the military, which is—unlike the ethos of, say, an iron mine—explicitly an ethos of violence and domination. We see some of this in the film, including an extremely violent recruitment ad for the Marines, and some footage of brutal basic training. Even here, however, we may perhaps see a more specific aspect of the pollution logic at work. After all, rapes are not merely violent assaults on the victim's person, but specifically involve (violently) penetrating the bodily boundary.

The interpretation in terms of boundary violation may also help us think about the relatively high incidence of male–male rape in the military. As noted earlier, male–male rape in the military is also very common; although the film is mainly focused on the women, it also brings this out very clearly. According to one account, men actually make up a larger percentage of sexual assault victims than women—53% to 47% (*The Washington Times*, 20 May 2013). In addition, because of the gender imbalance in the military, the absolute number of men who are sexually assaulted is higher than the number of women. The *proportion* of women raped is much higher than the proportion of men (20% vs. 1%), but it is nonetheless clear that male-on-male rapes represent a significant part of the story.

The issues here are complex in relation to standard American assumptions about heterosexuality and homosexuality. As there does not seem to be any data on the sexual orientations of victims and perpetrators, we can only discuss this question hypothetically. For example, if it is assumed that the victims are homosexual, then the interpretation would be similar to that concerning the rape of women: that they are being punished for intruding in, and polluting, the homosocial/heterosexual group. And in fact they are actually more polluting to the male group than the women, as they have not only violated the social boundaries of the group, but have also challenged the gender binary that is at the basis of the group's identity.

According to one commentator in the film, however, most of the perpetrators and victims are at least nominally heterosexual. In this case, then, we must resort to the more straightforward account of the kinds of relationships involved in any band of brothers: the endless competitive jockeying for status, power, and authority that goes on in tandem with the claims of, and often subjective experience of, solidarity. As one (female) marine officer says in the film, "This is not an issue of sexual orientation, this is simply a matter of power and violence." In other words, the male–male rapes make sense simply as extreme versions of the direct domination of one man over another, regardless of sexual orientation, that is a standard part of the male group within a patriarchal order. Although such domination does not normally take the form of rape in ordinary life, the ethos of violence that is endemic to the army (or prisons) both feeds, and feeds on, the more basic state of endless competition for relative power and status within the male group.

And finally, what about the women? By definition, and in keeping with the basic patriarchal model, women were entirely excluded from the military, except in supporting roles, until recently. Once women began entering the military, it is clear that they have tried to keep their heads down, fit in, and not rock the boat. Along these lines, some of the more depressing parts of an already depressing film are segments involving the women who have headed up something called the Sexual Assault Prevention and Response Office (SAPRO), which was created in response to Congressional pressure to do something about the endless series of sex scandals in the military, the rape epidemic being only the most recent.

SAPRO seems at first to be a step forward, potentially offering the rape victims an alternative to the dead end (or worse) of reporting to their own commanding officers. It turns out, however, that this is not part of its mandate, and that it has no power whatsoever to make the military do anything at all; it can only "strongly suggest". Instead it puts all the emphasis (and, as one commentator wryly remarked, most of its budget) on the "prevention" part of its mandate, for example by producing posters and other kinds of publicity advising women to take precautions so they do not leave themselves open to rape. One ad they produced emphasizes the importance for women of always walking with a buddy after dark, thereby both blaming the victim and normalizing rape in one fell swoop.

This programme has been headed by women since its inception. The first director, a Dr. Kaye Whitley, PhD, talks on screen about the posters and the prevention campaign, but is unable to answer any other questions at all, and comes across as both ignorant and not quite in touch with reality. She is later replaced by a military officer, Major General Mary Kay Hertog, who praises Whitley and says she intends to carry on her work. The effectiveness of the work of this unit may be judged by the fact that, among other things, the head of the Air Force wing of this programme was himself arrested on charges of sexual assault (*Huffington Post*, 16 May 2013).

But the film having been made in 2012, there are several progressive women in the story who in fact are trying to bring about changes. We meet a Captain Anu Bhagwati (ret.), who is the director of the Service Women's Action Network of the US Marine Corps, who clearly takes this very seriously and is trying to make something happen.

We also meet Susan Burke, a lawyer and the daughter of a military family, who brought together several of the victims in a lawsuit against the military. The case failed but Burke plans to continue working on this problem.[8]

The military appears as an almost pure patriarchal structure, a system for the production of violent masculinity, supported by a hierarchy of patriarchal authority, and deployed against any enemy within or without. A military entity has no inherent mission and can be put in the service of any group, nation, or cause. The mission of the American military is to defend the American nation, and the American nation's interests, but that of course brings us back to the connection with capitalism; for the American "nation's interests" are to a great degree the interests of capital, and that brings us to our final film.

Enron: The Smartest Guys in the Room (Gibney 2005)

With this film we leave the grime of the iron mines and the physical violence of the military and enter the world of money and ideas. No locker room will be smeared with faeces, and nobody will be raped. Yet we will see once again the basic outlines of a patriarchal structure, and a different kind of brutality that it can produce.

Enron: The Smartest Guys in the Room is based on a book by the same name by two senior writers for *Fortune* magazine, Bethany McLean and Peter Elkind (2004). It is the story of the rise and fall of the Enron Corporation, a company that dealt in gas and electric power, which was at one time the seventh largest corporation in America. It is specifically the story of a corporation that was organized as much as possible to pursue profit at all costs in an ideally deregulated, free-market neoliberal economy. But the company systematically engaged in accounting and other business practices that ranged from merely questionable to highly unethical to completely illegal, all designed to make the company appear to be in a better financial condition than it was. The point of all this was to keep the price of the stock constantly rising, since most of the wealth of the executives was in Enron stock options. But as various reporters (like McLean) began probing into Enron's finances, the investment banks eventually became less willing to prop the company up with loans, the market analysts eventually became less willing to promote the stock, and the whole thing collapsed.

The culture of the corporation was completely dog-eat-dog, both internally and with respect to their customers and clients. As one trader said on screen, "If I was going to see my boss about my compensation, and I knew that if I stepped on somebody's throat along the way my compensation would be doubled, of course I would do it." Those who did well within the company were richly rewarded with large bonuses, and many individuals became enormously wealthy in the process. At the same time, something like 20,000 employees, who had been encouraged (or in some cases forced) to put all their pension funds in Enron stock, lost not only their jobs and their medical insurance but also all of their retirement savings when the company went broke.

Now let us look at the question of Enron and patriarchy. The story here will be different from those in the films discussed earlier. This is not primarily a story about how women were marginalized or harassed (although they were). In fact women play a relatively small (although ultimately very important) role in the story and I will discuss them first. As usual in a patriarchal structure, there were relatively few women inside the boundaries, except those in supporting roles. Almost all of those who made it to higher levels seem to have slept with their bosses or colleagues, which in general did no harm to the male party's reputation but undermined the credibility of the female party. The most successful of the women executives, one Rebecca Mark, seems to have been as aggressive as many of the men, and was several times listed as "one of *Fortune*'s 50 most powerful women in business" (McLean and Elkind 2004, 253). Mark made a lot of deals, and made a lot of money, but she nonetheless kept running afoul of one or another of the top men, and was not only eventually fired but also blamed by some for the bankrupting of Enron.

The heroines of the story are once again the boat rockers, an executive of one of the dirtiest of the subsidiaries, and an accountant by trade, called Sherron Watkins, who blew the whistle on some key illegal practices (Swartz and Watkins 2004), and the *Wall Street Journal* reporter, Bethany McLean, who wrote one of the earliest critical pieces, declaring Enron stock to be overvalued in relation to the actual worth of the company, and thus opening the company to scrutiny.

Now let us look at the "fathers". The founder, Chairman, and Chief Executive Officer (CEO) of the corporation was a rather affable man called Ken Lay. The President and Chief Operating Officer (COO), and also by all accounts the villain of the piece, was a brilliant and ruthless man called Jeff Skilling. These and others at the top were important not only as a patriarchal hierarchy of fathers/bosses/officers who kept the women and the lesser men down, but also in establishing what can only be described as the violent ethos of the corporation. Lay preached the religion of the neoliberal free market, unencumbered by any human considerations other than the brainpower to make it work and the millions to be made from it. Skilling shared this vision, but conjoined it with a culture of extreme machismo. Among other things he periodically took some favoured male executives and friends of the corporation on dangerous, long-distance, overland motorcycle trips. In the world of Jeff Skilling, to be a successful Enron executive or trader you needed to have both a brilliant mind and (as one executive was said to have) "balls of steel" (McLean and Elkind 2004, 46). Skilling himself said he liked to hire "guys with spikes" (McLean and Elkind 2004, 55).

This brings us to the traders. When Skilling came aboard, Enron was a relatively staid company that owned natural gas production facilities and pipelines, and transacted the movement of physical gas from Point A to Point B. Skilling's "big idea" (and he very much believed in the "big idea") was to turn Enron into something like a financial market in gas products, in which value was determined not by actual supply and demand in real time, but by gambling on supply and demand under future, and thus not fully knowable, conditions. With this transformation, Enron became something like a stock exchange in gas and other forms of energy, and as a result hired large numbers of traders to engage in the trading of the "stock". The trading operation in turn became the biggest and most profitable part of Enron, and the traders ultimately came to wield a great deal of collective power. As the authors say, "They were like a powerful high school clique that terrorizes even the principal." And as one executive says, "They didn't appear menacing ... but they were a mob" (McLean and Elkind 2004, 213). Towards the end of the book, Skilling says, "The traders have taken over. These guys have gotten so powerful that I can't control them any more." (McLean and Elkind 2004, 335)

With the traders then we meet once again the virtually all-male, homosocial/heterosexual group, here with an ethos of both great solidarity and tremendous, cutthroat competition. Their immediate leader was a former army tank captain by the name of Greg Whalley, described by one of the traders as a "screaming stud" (McLean and Elkind 2004, 214). Here is one account of life among the Enron traders:

> [One trader said,] "We were very competitive, and we just didn't feel that we could fail a lot." An executive named Bill Butler used to stalk the floor with an eight-foot-long black bullwhip, jokingly threatening traders who didn't seem to be spending enough time on the phone. Their esprit was such that the traders took great pleasure in outsmarting other parts of Enron, and they didn't show much mercy for one another, either. "If you showed any weakness, the antibodies would attack," says a former trader. "Life at Enron," says another, "was the purest form of balls-out guerrilla warfare". (McLean and Elkind 2004, 217)

As we can see from all the language and stories thus far, we are already well into the jungle—that is to say, the culture of the workplace—in which patriarchy and capitalism are deeply feeding off one another at Enron. Now let us look at how this works out when Enron does business with its customers in the outside world. Here the traders will appear less like the military band of brothers on the home front, threatened by the intrusion of polluting others, and more like the military in action, a group of men whipped up by their leaders and turned loose on the enemy with orders to take no prisoners. This is what happened most famously when Enron entered the electricity market of the State of California.

Enron had been involved, through lobbying, in promoting the deregulation of gas and electricity in California. Eventually the state was partially but not totally deregulated, leaving a situation where the rules were extremely complicated and unclear. It became a particular point of pleasure for the Enron traders to game the system and to make in the process an enormous amount of profit for the company and themselves. As part of subsequent investigations, audio tapes of conversations between traders about the California situation were recovered, and this is where we come back to the synergy between the patriarchal and capitalist mentalities in play. One of the traders' "games" (their term) called Ricochet involved exporting power out of the state when the price was low and then bringing it back when demand rose and prices soared. In one conversation we hear one of the traders say, "So we fuckin' export like a motherfucker." Another says, "Gettin' rich?" and the first says, "Tryin' to." Another strategy involved asking local power stations to go offline "for maintenance" in the middle of the shortage, again pushing the prices up. We actually hear two conversations in which a trader speaks to a man at a local plant asking him to go offline for a while, and the man readily agrees to do it. In yet another conversation, someone in California tells a trader in Houston that there is a fire under a major power line, causing further disruption. The trader is heard to say, "Burn, baby, burn! That's a beautiful thing!"

Even when there was no sexual language, there seemed to be a rape-like quality to the whole thing, a kind of violent and gleeful ravishing of a helpless victim. Nor was I the only one who heard it this way. At one point in this segment of the film, journalist Bethany McLean says, "The Enron traders never step back and say, 'Is it in our long term interest if we totally rape California like this?'" And then we hear the following conversation. The first trader says, "All that money you guys stole from those poor grandmothers in California". And the second trader says, "Now she wants her fucking money back for all the power you've charged her up her ass".

As with the other two films, the playing out of the patriarchal structure is clear, as are the ways in which the wielding of corporate economic power intersects and is infused with the sexuality and aggression of patriarchal relations. Now it is time to pull this all together.

Conclusions

I began this paper with a discussion of several forms of post-feminism, including the ambivalence of younger women about identifying with the feminist label; the negative representations of feminism in some important recent monographs coming from a broadly defined post-colonial perspective; and most recently the charge that feminism has become complicit with neoliberal capitalism. I presented these points not to discuss them substantively—impossible in the present paper—but simply to draw attention to the multiple, and seemingly proliferating, vectors of "post-feminism".

Insofar as feminism has survived as a scholarly and/or political project, it is almost entirely concerned with women and/or gender. What has largely disappeared is a concern with patriarchal power, a concern that was so central to early feminist work. Yet in the course of watching a large number of American independent films, as part of a different research project, I was struck by the degree to which patriarchy is still virtually everywhere. The first point of this paper, then, was to try to make patriarchy visible (again) and to show that it is something we cannot afford to dismiss or ignore. While it can appear in a relatively benign form (though always grounded in an assumption of male superiority and female inferiority), it is often the basis of aggression and violence. Using some of the films as ethnographic and/or cultural texts, I presented three examples of patriarchy in action: the extreme harassment of women in an industrial workplace; the rape of both women and men in the US military; and the ruthless internal competition and predatory business practices of a corporation. In all cases, I showed not only how patriarchy works as a specific arrangement of power relations in its own right, but also how it is deeply enmeshed with other systems of power in this advanced capitalist society. We could clearly see in the examples how the different forms of domination blurred into one another, or fed off one another, each intensifying the effects of the other.

One subtext, or in some cases the explicit text, of some of the post-feminist literature, is a growing sense that other political agendas have become more urgent.

Neoliberal capitalism, environmental degradation, American militarism, and more have begun to capture intellectual and political attention on an ever-growing scale. I share a sense of the tremendous urgency of these issues, which I have written about at length elsewhere (Ortner 2013). My concern, however, is that the momentum of the new movements may completely push a feminist agenda off the table. There is a way in which feminism and anti-neoliberal capitalism (or anti-US militarism, or pro-environmentalism—name your issue) are being set up in some contexts as either-or propositions. But my examples in this paper have shown not only, as I said earlier, that patriarchy is alive and well in neoliberal America, but also that it is inextricably and aggressively intertwined with so much else that is bad in the contemporary world.

As a final point, however, we must return to the films, not as texts for our ethnographic or interpretive use, but as political interventions in American public culture. *North Country* and *The Invisible War* explicitly challenge patriarchal violence and injustice, and the anti-patriarchal subtext of *Enron* is very close to the surface as well. The films may be seen then as implicitly talking back to the post-feminist tendencies I emphasized in the earlier part of this paper. Made in a period when feminism in its classic form seems to be over, and made by men as well as women, they are perhaps harbingers of a new anti-patriarchal politics, for which we do not yet have a name.

Acknowledgements

Deepest thanks as always to those special friends and colleagues who shared with me their sharp critical insights and their wisdom, and (tried to) save me from my worst mistakes: Jessica Cattelino, Gwendolyn Kelly, Abigail Stewart, and Timothy D. Taylor. I am grateful as well to Laura Ahearn, who shared some of her unpublished work with me, and who has always been a valued interlocutor. Thanks too to issue editor Dimitrios Theodossopoulos, issue mate Jacqueline Urla, and the two anonymous journal readers for their very helpful comments. Finally thanks to audiences at the University of California, Riverside (Anthropology), and at the University of California, Los Angeles (Sociology), who pushed me very hard in their respective Q&As.

Notes

[1]   In an earlier work (Ortner 2006), I discussed the factor of ambivalence in resistance movements. The ambivalence we see in post-feminism is thus not new, but where it was recessive at the height of second wave feminism, it is apparently dominant today.

[2]   Another aspect of post-feminism in anthropology can be seen in the declining number of journal articles on subjects related to women and gender. I had a discussion of this point in an earlier draft but had to cut it for reasons of space. The discussion was based on Laura Ahearn's article on keywords in *American Ethnologist* (2014).

[3]   But see a very important project coming out of the University of Michigan that has attempted to rethink the feminist agenda in a global perspective, in response to the post-colonial critique: Lal et al. (2010) and Stewart et al. (2011). I regret not having the space to discuss this work in this paper.

[4]   An earlier version of this insistence on the intertwining of gender and other forms of inequality came from the work of so-called Marxist-feminists in the 1970s, who emphasized the linkages between gender and class under capitalism. See especially Eisenstein (1979).

[5]   The only recent work to explore the question of patriarchy as a "structure" in some sense is Pierre Bourdieu's *Masculine Domination* (2001). But Bourdieu spends a great deal of time on the question of "symbolic domination", that is, of the degree to which women internalize patriarchy as habitus, rather than on patriarchy as a system of social power, which is the primary focus of the present paper.

[6]   In Crenshaw's original discussion of intersectionality, race was a central component. In the three films that follow, however, racial difference is held constant (that is, everyone is white), thereby highlighting the patriarchy factor. Thanks to Abigail Stewart for emphasizing this point.

[7]   One of the elements of the film that I do not have time/space to discuss is that the events in the film are set during the Anita Hill sexual harassment hearings, and we see Hill on television in the background in several scenes. One detail of Hill's allegations, which for some reason always stuck in my mind as strange, was that Clarence Thomas left a can of Coke on Hill's desk with a pubic hair on top. Thinking about it in the context of the present discussion, it makes sense as another material sign of pollution.

[8]   Another female boat-rocker, not in the film, is Senator Kirsten Gillibrand who, according to a *New Yorker* article, was inspired by the film to develop legislation to address the epidemic of rape in the military (Osnos 2013). The legislation failed but Gillibrand has continued to press the issue.

References

Abu-Lughod, Lila. 2002. "Do Muslim Women Really Need Saving? Anthropological Reflections on Cultural Relativism and its Others." *American Anthropologist* 104 (3): 783–790.

Abu-Lughod, Lila. 2005. *Dramas of Nationhood: The Politics of Television in Egypt*. Chicago, IL: University of Chicago Press.

Abu-Lughod, Lila. 2013. *Do Muslim Women Need Saving?* Cambridge, MA: Harvard University Press.

Ahearn, Laura M. 2014. "Detecting Research Patterns and Paratextual Features in *AE* word counts, keywords, and titles." *American Ethnologist* 41 (1): 17–30.

Appadurai, Arjun, and Carol Breckenridge. 1988. "Why Public Culture?" *Public Culture* 1 (1, Fall): 5–9.

Aronson, Pamela. 2007. "Feminists or 'Postfeminists'? Young Women's Attitudes toward Feminism and Gender Relations." In *Feminist Frontiers*, edited by V. Taylor, N. Whittier, and L. J. Rupp, 7th ed., 519–531. Boston, MA: McGraw Hill.

Bingham, Clara and Laura Leedy Gansler. 2002. *Class Action: The Story of Lois Jensen and the Landmark Case that Changed Sexual Harassment Law*. New York: Doubleday.

Bourdieu, Pierre. 2001. *Masculine Domination*. Translated by Richard Nice. Stanford, CA: Stanford University Press.

Butler, Judith. 1990. *Gender Trouble: Feminism and the Subversion of Identity*. New York: Routledge.

Caro, Niki, dir. 2005. *North Country*. Produced by Nick Wechsler.

Crenshaw, Kimberlé. [1991]2007. "Mapping the Margins: Intersectionality, Identity Politics, and Violence against Women of Color." In *Feminist Frontiers*, edited by V. Taylor, N. Whittier, and L. J. Rupp, 7th ed., 431–440. Boston, MA: McGraw Hill.

Dick, Kirby, dir. 2012. *The Invisible War*. Produced by Tanner King Barklow and Amy Ziering.

Douglas, Mary. 1966. *Purity and Danger: An Analysis of Concepts of Pollution and Taboo*. London: Routledge and Kegan Paul.

Eisenstein, Zillah R., ed. 1979. *Capitalist Patriarchy and the Case for Socialist Feminism*. New York: Monthly Review Press.

Engels, Friedrich. [1942]1972. *The Origin of the Family, Private Property, and the State*, edited by Eleanor Leacock. New York: International Publishers.

Fraser, Nancy. 2013. "How Feminism Became Capitalism's Handmaiden—and How to Reclaim it." *The Guardian*, Sunday October 13. Accessed March 17, 2014. http://www.theguardian.com/commentisfree

Freud, Sigmund. 1950. *Totem and Taboo: Some Points of Agreement between the Mental Lives of Savages and Neurotics*. Translated by James Strachey. New York: W.W. Norton and Company.

Gaines, Jane M. 1999. "Political Mimesis." In *Collecting Visible Evidence*, edited by J. M. Gaines and M. Renov, 84–103. Minneapolis, MN: University of Minnesota Press.

van Gennep, Arnold. 1960. *Rites of Passage*. Translated by M. B. Vizedom and G. L. Caffee. Chicago, IL: University of Chicago Press.

Gibney, Alex, dir. 2005. *Enron: The Smartest Guys in the Room*. Produced by Alison Ellwood, Alex Gibney, Jason Kliot, and Susan Motamed.

Lal, Jayati, Kristin McGuire, Abigail J. Stewart, Magdalena Zaborowska, and Justine M. Pas. 2010. "Recasting Global Feminisms: Toward a Comparative Historical Approach to Women's Activism and Feminist Scholarship." *Feminist Studies* 36 (1, Spring): 13–39.

Mahmood, Saba. 2005. *Politics of Piety: The Islamic Revival and the Feminist Subject*. Princeton, NJ: Princeton University Press.

McLean, Bethany, and Peter Elkind. 2004. *Enron: The Smartest Guys in the Room*. New York: Portfolio (Penguin).

McRobbie, Angela. 2009. *The Aftermath of Feminism: Gender, Culture, and Social Change*. London: Sage.

Mohanty, Chandra Talpade. 1984. "Under Western Eyes: Feminist Scholarship and Colonial Discourses." *Boundary 2* 12(no. 3)/13(no. 1) (spring/fall): 338–358.

Nichols, Bill. 1991. *Representing Reality: Issues and Concepts in Documentary*. Bloomington, IN: University of Indiana Press.

Ong, Aihwa. 2003. *Buddha is Hiding: Refugees, Citizenship, The New America*. Berkeley, CA: University of California Press.

Ortner, Sherry B. 1996. "The Virgin and the State." In *Making Gender: The Politics and Erotics of Culture*, edited by S. B. Ortner, 43–58. Boston, MA: Beacon Press.

Ortner, Sherry B. 2006. "Resistance and the Problem of Ethnographic Refusal." In *Anthropology and Social Theory: Culture, Power, and the Acting Subject*, edited by S. B. Ortner, 42–62. Durham, NC: Duke University Press.

Ortner, Sherry B. 2013. *Not Hollywood: Independent Film at the Twilight of the American Dream*. Durham, NC: Duke University Press.

Ortner, Sherry B., and Harriet Whitehead. 1981. "Introduction: Accounting for Sexual Meanings." In *Sexual Meanings: The Cultural Construction of Gender and Sexuality*, edited by S. B. Ortner and H. Whitehead, 1–27. Cambridge, England: Cambridge University Press.

Osnos, Evan. 2013. "Strong Vanilla: The Relentless Rise of Kirsten Gillibrand." *The New Yorker*, December 16: 40–46.

Rosenfelt, Deborah, and Judith Stacey. 1987. "Second Thoughts on the Second Wave." *Feminist Studies* 13 (2): 341–361.

Sandberg, Sheryl with Nell Scovell. 2013. *Lean In: Women, Work, and the Will to Lead*. New York: Knopf.

Stewart, Abigail J., Jayati Lal, and Kristin McGuire. 2011. "Expanding the Archives of Global Feminisms: Narratives of Feminism and Activism." *Signs: Journal of Women in Culture and Society* 36 (4): 889–914.

Swartz, Mimi with Sherron Watkins. 2004. *Power Failure: The Inside Story of the Collapse of Enron*. New York: Currency (Doubleday).

Tasker, Yvonne, and Diane Negra, eds. 2007. *Interrogating Post-Feminism: Gender and the Politics of Popular Culture*. Durham, NC: Duke University Press.

Traube, Elizabeth. 1994. "Family Matters: Postfeminist Constructions of a Contested Site." In *Visualizing Theory: Selected Essays from Visual Anthropology Review*, edited by L. Taylor, 301–321. New York and London: Routledge.

Williams, Linda. 1998. "Mirrors without Memories: Truth, History, and *The Thin Blue Line*." In *Documenting the Documentary: Close Readings of Documentary Film and Video*, edited by B. K. Grant and J. Sloniowski, 379–396. Detroit, MI: Wayne State University Press.

Index

abnormality, resistance as 2, 5–6, 13
Abu-Lughod, Lila 19–20, 39, 94
academic structures, activist research within 31–2
accountability: and academic writing 21, 31; and anti-austerity indignation 74, 76–7, 86
activist anthropology 29–30
activist research 3, 25–6, 30–1, 33
activists: as audience for research 22–3; boundaries of communities 30; and CMP 63; as partners in research 26; policing of 27; refusing research 28
agency: ends and means in 50; structure and infrastructure in 38, 52–3; subaltern 9–10, 61
agonistic ethos 77
'alaqat 47
alter-globalization 30
ambiguities 13, 19, 21, 65, 74–5
ambivalence: in anti-austerity discourse 74, 78, 86, 88; in resistance movements 132n1
American Anthropological Association (AAA) 43, 50
analogic thinking 85
anonymity 19, 27
anti-austerity indignation: as inspiration 5; narratives in 75–7; and nationalism 82–6; officialization of 81; political impact of 80–1, 87
anti-capitalism 63
anti-hegemonic discourse 10, 75, 82, 86–8
anti-hegemonic mobilization 68
antisistema 26–7
anti-terrorism 22
apathy 1
Aquila 95, 102, 104–6, 108–10, 112, 113n12
Arab Spring, as inspiration 5
Arab world, social scientists' presumptions about 44
archives, nontraditional 26
austerity see anti-austerity indignation
authority, anthropology's deference to 52

autodefensas 101–2, 107, 112; see also self-defense forces, local
autonomy: for indigenous communities 100–1, 109; personal 118; Zapatista practice of 99–100

baltagiyya 44–5
Barcelona 6, 26–7
Basque language movement 21–3
Berlusconi, Silvio 59
Bhagwati, Anu 127
Birmingham School tradition 19
blame-oriented discourse 77–8
blaming 78, 82, 101, 127
body, breaching boundaries of 121
Border Patrol (Israel) 66
Bourdieu, Pierre: on masculine domination 133n5; on practical reason 47
Bread Riots 50
British National Party 71n11
Burke, Susan 128
Butler, Bill 130

Cairo, poor women of 47
Calderón, Felipe 102–3, 105, 107
California, Enron in 130–1
Caminando preguntamos 33
Cárdenas, Cuautémoc 100
Cárdenas Batel, Lázaro 100–1
Cárdenas del Río, Lázaro 100, 104
carnivalesque caricatures 84, 85
causality, pre-existing ideas of 7, 10, 74–5, 86–8
CDBC (Commission for the Defense of Communal Property) 104–5
chain of command 125
character assassination 78
Cherán 101, 105–7, 109
Chiapas 96–7, 99, 101, 112n1
Chicomuselo 112n1
Clarkson, Kelly 118
CMP (Contemporary Metropolitan Protest) 58–65, 69–70

Coalcomán 95, 112
cocaine 103, 109, 114n13
COCOPA (Commission of Concord and
  Pacification) 99–100, 113n5
Coire 95, 104, 111
Colima state 104–5
Colombia 101
communal police 101, 104, 106, 112
communal territory 108, 111
communicative channels 38–9, 46–9, 51
Community-based Research 23
community engagement 23, 32
community resistance 96, 111
connections 47
consensus-based decision-making 28–9
conspiracy theories 7
Constituent Imagination 24
contentious politics 3, 94
contingency, in historical events 50–1
co-optation 8, 23
Copenhagen Climate Summit 34n10
corruption 47, 59–60
coup, battle over meaning of 52
CRAC (Coordinadora Regional de Autoridades
  Comunitarias) 101–2
Crenshaw, Kimberlé 117, 119, 133n6
crisis, never-resolving 51
Cristiada rebellion 96–7, 112n2
crypto-colonialism 87, 89n7
Cultural Anthropology 50, 71n1
cultural critique 17–18, 29–30
cyberspace 46, 70

decision-making, indeterminacy in 34n10
decisive moments 50–1
de-contextualization, selective 6
defiance, choreography and orchestration of
  64
de la Cruz Crisóforo, Trinidad (Don Trino)
  105–6, 109
delinquent states 113n8
depoliticization of resistance 94
dialogic action 49–50
difference, culturalist model of 52
direct action, ethnographic study of 28–9
dispossession, resistance to 97
dissent: ethnography of 22; marginalizing 61,
  68
documentary film 121–2
do-it-yourself ethic 27–8, 31
domination: awareness of order of 9–10;
  complicity with 87; intersection of forms of
  131; symbolic 133n5
Don Trino *see* de la Cruz Crisóforo, Trinidad
Douglas, Mary 121, 124, 126
drug cartels 101–3, 106
drug trafficking 101, 103, 106, 108–9, 114n13

East India Company 39, 51
Egypt: clerical regime in 60; communication
  channels in 48–9; ethnography and activism
  in 44–5; January 25th Revolution in 39–45,
  48, 50, 52, 59; neoliberalism in 42–3;
  resistance and infrastructure in 38–9, 47
ejidos 97–8, 104, 113n4
electoral politics: and anti-austerity indignation
  81–2, 86–7; indigenous communities and 101,
  106, 108–9; and indirect resistance 75; and
  protest 70
Elkind, Peter 128–9
emotions, visible expression of 6
empowerment debt 43
encargaturas del orden 104
energy projects, resistance to 96
engaged scholarly projects 32–3; *see also*
  academic structures, activist research within
Engaging Contradictions 25
Engels, Friedrich 120
Enron: The Smartest Guys in the Room 128–32
essentialist stereotypes 6
ETA (Euskadi ta Askatasuna) 21–2
ethnographers, relationship with communities
  of study 31
ethnographic methods: in film 122–3; outside
  the university 24–5; police use of 27; state and
  corporate use of 32
ethnographic thickness 17, 20–1, 24
ethnography of resistance: in the academy 31–2;
  and activism 23–4; intellectual influences on
  17–18; new approaches in 33; personal
  trajectories in 29–30; reflexivity in 22; refusal
  to be subject of 28
ethno-nationalism 75
ethno-religious divisions 63–5; *see also* religious
  identity
EU (European Union), Greek attitudes to 59, 82,
  86, 89n4
everyday life: in conditions of revolt 52;
  impossible and unimaginable in 11, 51;
  resistance in 9, 11–12, 17, 19–20, 75
exoticizing resistance 1–5, 12–13, 94
EZLN (Zapatista Army of National Liberation)
  96–100, 106, 108, 111, 113n5

Facebook Revolution 48
factionalism 102, 108
false consciousness 1, 7–9, 12, 94
false equivalences 68–9
Familia Michoacana 106–7, 110
fascism 80–2
fathers, in patriarchy 119–20, 123–5, 129
feminism: contemporary attacks on 116–19,
  131; poststructural 39; and women in labor
  force 124; and women in the military 126
feminist anthropology 18–19

feminist ethnography 21, 28
films, independent 121–2, 131–2
financial crisis, local discontent with 76, 80, 86
financial markets 51, 129
Foucault, Michel: and knowledge 10; on power 19–21, 61, 94
Fox, Vicente 99–100
Fraser, Nancy 118–19
free radio movement 28
Freud, Sigmund 120

gada' 44–5
Gandhi, Mohandas 64
Garzón, Balthasar 21–2
geek networks 49
gender, as cultural category 120, 123
gender inequality 19, 29, 119
Germany, Greek discourse about 83–5
Gillibrand, Kirsten 133n8
Gody, Leonel 101
Goffman, Erving 119
Golden Dawn 80, 83, 91
Good Government Councils 99
Graeber, David 67
Gramsci, Antonio: in anthropology 19; and hegemony 8–10, 61, 94
Greece: anti-austerity discourse in 74, 76–80, 82, 85–8; anti-austerity protest in 10, 40, 58–9, 75; discussions of the powerful in 78, 83–5; nationalist attitudes in 82–3, 87–8; words for indignation in 88–9n1
Guatemala 107
Guerrero state 95, 101–3
Gulf cartel 106
GUPCO (Gulf of Suez Petroleum Company) 41–2

Hanson, Ole 67
hegemonic narratives 74–5, 87
hegemony, dialectical relationship with resistance 1, 9–10, 12–13, 94
Hertog, Mary Kay 127
hidden transcript: analysis of 9; and autonomy of subaltern spaces 5, 75; hegemonic narratives in 87; and indirect resistance 10
Hill, Anita 133n7
historical events: academic work during 43–4, 53; temporality of 50
history: nationalist conceptualization of 87; recurring patterns in 85, 87
hiyla 43
Hollywood 121–2
Huldai, Ron 65–7
hurly-burly 52

idealization: inspiration within 5; as pathologizing 2

illegal economies 103, 108
images, sanitized and idealized 4
imaginaries, nontraditional 26
imagination, emancipatory 86
IMF (International Monetary Fund) 43, 82–3, 86
incompetence, faked 61, 64
Independent Greeks 80
Indian Rebellion of 1857 39, 51, 54n9
indignants: as subject positions 76–7; use of term 88–9n1; see also anti-austerity indignation
indirect resistance: anti-austerity indignation as 78, 86–7; and hegemonic ideas 74–5, 82, 88; Scott on 8–10, 12
inequality: exposing mechanisms of 29; limits of resistance to 11; naturalization of existing 4
infrastructure, as public good 46–7
insecurity 27, 83, 110
intentionality 19–20
Inter-American Court of Human Rights 105
International Labor Organization Convention 169 97
Internet 48–9
interpretative vacuum 86
intersectionality 116–17, 119, 123, 133n6
interviews, rejection of 26, 29
The Invisible War 125–8, 132
Iraq 53, 64
IRB (institutional review boards) 31–2
irony 75, 77, 84
irrationality: dissent treated as 7, 78, 86; subaltern accused of 94
Israel: anti-austerity protests in 59–60; delegitimization of protest in 6, 60–1, 66–7; occupation of West Bank and Gaza 64, 66
Italy 59, 83

Jadaliyya (website) 40, 44, 46
Jalisco state 95, 107
Juris, Jeff 25

K'eris 109
Knights Templar see Los Caballeros Templarios
knowledge: mobilization 24–5, 33; politics of 21; production 25, 29–30, 33

labelling resistance 4
Laboratory for Transformative Practice in Anthropology 32–3
labor movements, demise of 69–70
La Canahuancera 104, 108–9
Lagarde, Christine 83
land reform 62, 94, 96–8, 100
language activism 21–3
Lapid, Yair 60
La Placita 95, 104, 108–10, 112, 114n13

La Ticla 104, 106
Latin America: neoliberal development model in 94; urban protest in 64
Law, John 51–2
Lay, Ken 129
laziness, orchestrated 19, 61
Leaf, Dafni 66
Leyva, Santos 105–6
Leyva Dominguez, Pedro 105
liminality 2, 4–6
liquid fear 67
local traditions 61
López Obrador, Andrés Manuel 106
Los Caballeros Templarios 106–7, 112

mafias 97, 107; see also organized crime
Maine, Henry 39, 51–2
male–male rape 125–7
managerial techniques, corporate 23
Mantena, Karuna 39–40, 51–2
Mao Zedong 64
marginalized populations, ethnography of 22
marijuana 108–9
Mark, Rebecca 129
Martínez Veloz, Jaime 113n5
martyr images 45
Marx, Karl 46–7
Marxist-feminists 133n4
McLean, Bethany 128–31
MEChA (Chican@ Student Movement of Aztlán) 24
media, activist channels of 27–8
men, homosocial/heterosexual groups of 126–7, 130
Merkel, Angela 83–4; caricature of 84
mestizos 95, 98, 109–10, 114n13
metaphors 47–8, 75–7, 85
methamphetamines 108–9, 114n13
Mexican indigenous communities: outsiders' understandings of 94; politics of 96; racism against 95; state inaction to violence against 111; state relationship with 97–100
Mexican Revolution of 1910 95, 98
Mexico: community resistance in 96–7, 101–2; constitutional reforms in 97–8; dirty war in 103; drug wars in 106–7; federal indigenous law in 99; Spanish colonial rule in 113n6
Michoacán state: communal councils in 109; and drug trade 108; elites and indigenous communities in 95; indigenous movement in 100–1, 112; organized crime in 101–2, 106–7; Ostula community in 94; self-defense forces in 102
Middle East, resistance in 39
migrants: Greek discourse on 77, 82–3, 86, 89n4; securitization of 68
militant ethnography 24–5, 32

military: in Egypt 39, 46; gender relations in 117, 125–8; in Mexico 106–7
mining: in Mexico 94–6, 108; and paramilitary forces 107
miscommunication, deliberate 61
Mizrahim-Israelis 64
MJPD (Movement for Peace with Justice and Dignity) 105
mnimónio 79–81
mobile phones 47–9
moral panic 68
Moreno González, Nazario 106
Morocco 58–9
Morsi, Mohamed 38–40, 43, 46, 49–50
Mubarak, Gamal 42
Mubarak, Hosni 40–5, 47–9
municipal wardens 66
Muslim Brotherhood 38–9, 42, 45–6, 49–50

Nahua community 11, 93, 100–1, 104, 108
nationalism: in anti-hegemonic discourse 10, 87–8; defensive 74–5, 77, 82
'native' concepts 40, 46–7
neocolonialism 116
neoliberalism: activists succumbing to 23; corporate behavior under 128–9; as de-legitimizing 9; feminism seen as 116, 118, 131; in Mexico 97–8, 103; and patriarchy 123, 132; resistance to 42–3, 60, 75, 80
neoliberal multiculturalism 97–8
nepotism 47, 59
networks, anthropological description of 47
New Democracy 80
'New Generation' cartel 107
Nicaragua 103
noise 51
non-compliance: passive 64; passive-aggressive 61
North Country 123, 125–6, 132
numbers, the cold language of 78

Oaxaca state 100–1, 112n1
Occupy Movement, Wikipedia on 71n2
Oficinas de Okupación 28
okupas 26–9, 31
Orabi Rebellion 50
organized crime: deaths due to 113n7; and indigenous communities 109–11; in Mexican state apparatus 97, 102, 113n3; presenting as social movement 97, 107
orientalization 74, 86
Ortner, Sherry 20–1, 62, 93
Ostula: conflict with La Placita 104–6, 109–10; drug trafficking in 114n13; internal politics of 96, 108–11; rejection of development projects in 107–8; resistance as way of life in 11, 94; self-defense forces in 95–6, 101–2, 110–12

OWS (Occupy Wall Street): beginnings of 60; as 'noise' 51

Palermo Mafia in Sicily 107
PAN (National Action Party) 97, 99, 102, 113
paraethnography 46
paramilitaries 101–2, 105
participant observation 26, 31–2
participation, virtual 70
Participatory Action Research 23
PASOK 80–1
pathologizing resistance 1, 5–7, 12–13, 94
Patras 76, 78–84, 89n3
patriarchy: and corporate power 128–31; cultural categories of 120; feminism's focus on 118; in film narrative 122–5; in the military 125–6; as power structure 117, 119–21, 133n5
patronage 47, 61, 101, 107
Pearl Roundabout 65
peasant resistance 34n1, 63–4, 69–70
Peña Nieto, Enrique 99
Peru 102
political-party interests see electoral politics
pollution, and social boundaries 121, 124, 126
Pómaro 95, 104, 111
populism 68–9, 75, 82
Portugal 58–9, 71
positivist paradigm 24
post-feminism 116–19, 131, 132n1
power: complicity, collaboration and hybridization with 62; dichotomy with resistance 5, 8, 19, 39; and intersectionality 117; patriarchal 119, 131; resistance as diagnostic of 38–9, 42; signification of 53; workings of 3, 7, 20
power relations, inescapability of 94
power structures: adaptation to 4, 62; challenges to 19; creative responses to 75
practical reason 10, 47
PRD (Party of the Democratic Revolution) 100–2, 104, 106
PRI (Institutional Revolutionary Party) 97–103, 110
privileging of the social 52
Program of Attention to Rural Social Conflicts 105
protest: emergent modalities of 18; master tropes of 74; public 63, 70, 81, 87; repression of 68–9; see also CMP; urban protest
public anthropology 23, 32
public space, taking over 64–6, 68
Puerta del Sol square 65
Purépecha community 93, 100–1, 105

racial difference, non-indigenous ideas about 111
racial inequality 119

racism, polite 82–3
Ramírez Domínguez, Diego 104
rape: as metaphor for corporate trading 131; in the military 125–7, 131, 133n8
the reasonable 6
rebel cities 64
reflexivity 17–18, 21–3, 28
Reinventing Anthropology 18
religious cults 97, 106–7
religious identity: in Egypt 64; in indigenous communities 110–11
remunicipalization 99–100
representational agency 52–3
representations, politics of 28
research: engaged 17, 31–3; non-traditional distribution of 25; power relations in 23, 25
resistance: anthropological interest in 1–3, 12, 18–21; co-option of language of 65, 68, 70, 71n11; covert and overt 5, 61–2, 64; culture of 11, 96; de-exoticization of 1–2, 88; de-pathologization of 1; as innovative interpretation 7; local meaningfulness of 12–13, 93; new indices of 53; quotidian see everyday forms of resistance; reasons for fading of 7–8; theoretical concept of 62, 69–70; thick description of 20, 24, 28; as way of life 11
resistance studies 3, 62, 78, 93–4
resistance theory 69
resisting subjects, as uncivilized 3–5
revolt, and social theory 39–40, 50–3
revolution: battle over meaning of 53; resistance as substitute for 69
rhetoric 75, 85, 88
Robles Martínez, Javier 105
"The Romance of Resistance" 19, 39
rondas campesinas 102
Rothschild Avenue 65–6
Ruiz, Ulises 100

Sabea, Hanan 39, 50–2
Said, Khaled 40
Salinas de Gortari, Carlos 97–100, 103
Sánchez Reyes, Crisóforo 106
Sandberg, Sheryl 118
Santos Girón, Teódolo 106
SAPRO (Sexual Assault Prevention and Response Office) 127
Sawaris, Nabil 49
SCAF (Supreme Command of the Armed Forces) 44, 54n7
Schäuble, Wolfgang 84; caricature of 84
scholarly productivity 32
Scott, James: and CMP 62–3; power/subaltern binary in 5, 8–10; on resistance 1, 19, 60–1, 71n8, 75; Weapons of the Weak 17, 78
Seattle 64, 67

securitization 46, 58, 67–8
security culture 27
self-defense forces, local 96, 101
self-government, indigenous 99–100
self-interrogation 11
self-management 28
semen 121, 124
sense-making practices 7, 78
sexual assault 125, 127; see also rape
shara'iya 45
signifiers, empty 68
Sinaloa cartel 106
Skilling, Jeff 129–30
social action: attempted halt of 48; motivation
    of 44–5; transforming context of 52
social boundaries: breaching 121, 126;
    transcending 98
social convention 48
social-democratic values 63, 69
social infrastructure, of communicative
    channels 38–9, 46, 48–9
sociality 47, 49, 87
social justice 11, 24, 60
social media 58, 63, 81
social movements: epistemic work on 30;
    scholarly work on 23–4
social sciences, morally-engaged turn in 23
social services, as mechanisms of control 68
social structure, dynamic model of 51
space, symbolic load of 64–5
Spain: anti-austerity movement in 26, 28, 40, 59;
    indignados in 81
spoiled identity 119
spokespeople, movement rejection of 28
spontaneity 81, 89n3
squatters 6, 26–8
state: phantom presence of 102–3; private
    interests' infiltration of 108
subalterns: covert resistance by 64, 71n6;
    relationship with domination 4, 8–10, 61–2
subaltern spaces: as autonomous 5, 75, 88, 94;
    thick descriptions of 20–1
subjectification, rejection of 28
subject positions, in anti-austerity indignation
    76–7
subversion, tacit 61
suffering, in Greek moral imagination 77
surprise, in anti-austerity indignation 76
symbols, violent attacks on 45
Syntagma Square 65
SYRIZA 80–1, 83

Tahrir Square 40–2, 44, 49, 65
Taksim Square 4, 40
Tamarod: battle over meaning of 53; and Egypt's
    social infrastructure 39, 46, 49–50
Tel Aviv, 2011 protests in 6, 58–9, 64–7, 70

Ternium-Hylsa 108, 112
territoriality, indigenous conceptions of 94,
    108
theodicy, secular 77
thick description 17, 20–1, 23, 26, 29–30
Thomas, Clarence 133n7
tierra caliente zones 106–7, 112
tourism, in Mexico 94, 96, 108, 112
traders 128–31
trickery 43
Tunisia 58–9

Ultras 42
unemployment, structural 49
United States: assumptions about sexuality in
    126; in defensive nationalist discourse 77;
    drug trafficking to 103; military in 128;
    patriarchy in 117, 121; repression of protest
    in 67
University Square, Bucharest 65
urban protest 2, 12–13, 64–5, 71n9; see also
    CMP
'uses and customs' 100–1, 109

Vera Orcino, Gerardo 105
Verdía, Semei 112
violence: as communicative 106; ethos of 126–7,
    131; and pathologization 6; political 22;
    structural 11; symbolic constitution of 45

Wall Street 65
wasta 47
Watkins, Sherron 129
weapons of the weak: scholarly interest in 61–2;
    trickery as 43
welfare state 59–60, 68–9
Western feminism 118
Western hegemony 81, 85, 87
Whalley, Greg 130
Wittgenstein, Ludwig 52
women: adaptations to patriarchy 124, 133n5;
    control of bodies of 45; in corporate culture
    128–9; exclusion of 121, 123; in the military
    125–7

Xayakalan 104–6, 108, 110–11
xenophobia 10, 74, 82, 87

Yesh Atid 60
youth, knowledge base of 49
YouTube, cartel propaganda on 97, 107

Zalman, Sally 45
Zapatistas see EZLN
Zedillo, Ernesto 113n5
Zetas 106–7, 110
Zuccotti Park 60, 65, 67

For Product Safety Concerns and Information please contact our EU representative GPSR@taylorandfrancis.com Taylor & Francis Verlag GmbH, Kaufingerstraße 24, 80331 München, Germany

Batch number: 08158490

Printed by Printforce, the Netherlands